Ballet in the Cold War

Ballet in the Cold War

A Soviet-American Exchange

ANNE SEARCY

OXFORD
UNIVERSITY PRESS

OXFORD
UNIVERSITY PRESS

Oxford University Press is a department of the University of Oxford. It furthers
the University's objective of excellence in research, scholarship, and education
by publishing worldwide. Oxford is a registered trade mark of Oxford University
Press in the UK and certain other countries.

Published in the United States of America by Oxford University Press
198 Madison Avenue, New York, NY 10016, United States of America.

© Oxford University Press 2020

All rights reserved. No part of this publication may be reproduced, stored in
a retrieval system, or transmitted, in any form or by any means, without the
prior permission in writing of Oxford University Press, or as expressly permitted
by law, by license, or under terms agreed with the appropriate reproduction
rights organization. Inquiries concerning reproduction outside the scope of the
above should be sent to the Rights Department, Oxford University Press, at the
address above.

You must not circulate this work in any other form
and you must impose this same condition on any acquirer.

Library of Congress Cataloging-in-Publication Data
Names: Searcy, Anne, author.
Title: Ballet in the Cold War : a Soviet-American exchange / Anne Searcy.
Description: New York, NY : Oxford University Press, [2020] |
Includes bibliographical references and index.
Identifiers: LCCN 2020008342 (print) | LCCN 2020008343 (ebook) |
ISBN 9780190945107 (hardback) | ISBN 9780190945121 (epub)
Subjects: LCSH: Ballet—Political aspects—United States. |
Ballet—Political aspects—Soviet Union. |
United States—Relations—Soviet Union. | Soviet Union—
Relations—United States. | Cold War.
Classification: LCC GV1588.45 .S43 2019 (print) |
LCC GV1588.45 (ebook) | DDC 792.8—dc23
LC record available at https://lccn.loc.gov/2020008342
LC ebook record available at https://lccn.loc.gov/2020008343

1 3 5 7 9 8 6 4 2

Printed by Integrated Books International, United States of America

Publication of this book is supported in part by the AMS 75 PAYS Endowment of the
American Musicological Society, supported in part by the National Endowment for the
Humanities and the Andrew W. Mellon Foundation.

For Frederick

Contents

Acknowledgments ix
Note on Transliteration and Translation xi

Introduction 1

1. A Cold War Welcome: The Bolshoi Ballet's 1959 Tour of the United States 17

2. Bringing an American Report Card to Russia: American Ballet Theatre's 1960 Tour of the Soviet Union 45

3. A Question of Taste: The Bolshoi Ballet's 1962 Tour of the United States 71

4. "Ballet Is a Flower": New York City Ballet's 1962 Tour of the Soviet Union 97

Epilogue: Exchange in the Twenty-first Century 129

Note on Abbreviations 133
Notes 135
Index 175

Acknowledgments

I am enormously grateful to the many people who have helped me as I researched, wrote, and revised this book, first of all to the artists and audience members who allowed me to interview them for this project: Marina Kondratieva, Michael Colgrass, and Judith P. Zinsser.

The book would not have been possible without my time as a fellow at the Center for Ballet and the Arts at New York University, generously also sponsored by the Jordan Center for the Advanced Study of Russia. I am grateful to the institution itself and to the support there from Jennifer Homans, Andrea Salvatore, Nancy Sherman, Amanda Vaill, and the other fellows. In addition, I conducted the research for this project with help from a Richard F. French prize from the Harvard Music Department, an Abby and George O'Neill Graduate Research Travel Grant from the Davis Center for Russian and Eurasian Studies, and an Alvin H. Johnson AMS 50 Dissertation Fellowship from the American Musicological Society.

I am enormously grateful to my editor, Norm Hirschy, for his encouragement, belief, and insightful recommendations on how to shape the book, as well as his ability to answer dozens of emails seemingly before I had hit send.

Many archivists helped me in locating sources for this project, including Dmitri Viktorovich Neustroev and Irina Nikolayevna Kalugina at the Russian State Archive for Literature and Art and Vera Ekechukwu and Geoffrey Stark at the University of Arkansas Libraries, as well as the archivists at the Museum of the Bolshoi Theater, the Russian State Archive of Socio-Political History, the State Archive of the Russian Federation, the Houghton Library, and the New York Public Library for the Performing Arts. I am also grateful to Robert Greskovic and Wenshuo Zhang for allowing me access to their personal archival collections. I thank the Jerome Robbins Rights Trust for allowing me to access the Jerome Robbins papers, and the George Balanchine Trust for granting me permission to use images of his choreography in this book.

As I prepared for my research, I received advice and logistical support from Robyn Angley, Stephanie Plant, Hugh Truslow, Jill Johnson, and the Higher School of Economics in Moscow. I also am thankful for the many years of support from librarians including Liza Vick, Kerry Masteller, Andrew

Wilson, Nancy Zavac, Amy Strickland, and Joy Doan. I received invaluable assistance as well over the years from Nancy Shafman, Eva Kim, Karen Rynne, Kaye Denny, Charles Stillman, and Dianne Gross. My colleagues at the Frost School of Music, including Marysol Quevedo, Melvin Butler, Brent Swanson, and David Ake, have also encouraged me in my research. I am also grateful for the support of my colleagues at the University of Washington.

I am profoundly thankful for the many years of support, encouragement, and mentoring from both of my advisors, Carol Oja and Anne Shreffler. I am also deeply grateful to Kevin Bartig, who was always willing to look at chapters and provide encouragement as I made my way into the field. I am also thankful to Danielle Fosler-Lussier for her insights on Cold War music and politics. In addition, many colleagues, mentors, and friends have given feedback on my drafts over the years, including Julie Buckler, Katie Callam, Elizabeth Titrington Craft, Hayley Fenn, Joseph Fort, John Gabriel, Joshua Gailey, Aaron Hatley, Monica Hershberger, Hannah Lewis, Emily MacGregor, Lucille Mok, Matthew Mugmon, William O'Hara, Samuel Parler, Frederick Reece, Caitlin Schmid, James Steichen, Michael Uy, and Micah Wittmer. Olga Panteleeva gave invaluable help in checking some of my translations.

I am profoundly grateful for my friend Nora Nussbaum, who has been unflagging in her support, always just a phone call, email, or train ride away. It is truly impossible to thank my parents enough. Margaret Searcy and William Searcy have loved and encouraged me all my life. I also want to thank my family, Christopher Searcy, Michelle Afkhami, Elizabeth Afkhami Searcy, Kathryn Afkhami Searcy, Anna Reece, and Graham Reece. Without them, none of this would be possible. Last, and most of all, I thank Frederick Reece. He has been with me through every draft. He has listened to all my worries and celebrated all my good fortune. I dedicate this book to him.

Note on Transliteration and Translation

I have used the Library of Congress transliteration system for Russian in bibliographic citations. In the text itself, I have suppressed all soft signs and changed -ii to -y and -aia to -aya at the ends of family names. I have also made exceptions in the cases of figures who are well known in the United States under alternate transliterations, relying on the spelling of their names in English-language programs from 1959 and 1962. For example, I use Tchaikovsky instead of Chaikovsky and Maximova instead of Maksimova.

Unless otherwise noted, all translations are my own.

Ballet in the Cold War

Introduction

Madison Square Garden, New York City, May 1959

A slender woman charges diagonally across the stage. As she reaches the center, she leaps to the side, arms flung out in front, feet pointed behind her. An audience of thirteen thousand people, some sitting so far away that the woman looks like nothing but a tiny dot, gasp as she flings herself into the unknown. There is a moment of anxiety as she hangs suspended. Then her muscular partner catches her in his outstretched arms, and the viewers erupt into screams and cheers.

The young woman and her partner are Soviet citizens, Raisa Struchkova and Alexander Lapauri, and they are as astonished by the thunderous applause as the viewers are with their performance. The hall is filled with Americans, and yet it is the most appreciative public that the two dancers have encountered. The audience members in turn are mesmerized. They have waited in the cold and the rain and paid a hefty sum to see this famous company. They are stunned, both with their good fortune and with the strangeness of watching their Cold War enemies dancing a waltz. In the orchestra pit are dozens of American musicians, playing light music by Moritz Moszkowski under the baton of a Soviet conductor. They can only understand some of what he says, but somehow the notes spin out as light and bouncy as ever, propelling the dancers into greater and greater feats of virtuosity.[1]

This scene of international encounter is one moment of the Cold War ballet exchange, a series of tours that sent elite Soviet companies around the United States and American ones around the Soviet Union. Struchkova and Lapauri were just two out of hundreds of participants in the exchange, which began in 1959 and lasted until the end of the Cold War. Throughout this process, American and Soviet citizens came together in surprising ways, to perform with one another, to view each other's ballets, and to solve the logistical tangle that is international touring.

But the tours were not organized merely to be pleasant. They were supposed to change the world. They were set up to end the Cold War, either by encouraging détente through artistic collaboration or by persuading the audience to adopt a new ideology. Of course, the ballet exchange was not the only method by which these aims were to be achieved; there were missiles and talks, armies and exhibitions, sporting matches and industrial plans, and countless other events and strategies. Nevertheless, the ballet tours were genuinely meant to make their mark on this diplomatic, economic, and military chessboard. They were as much of a daring leap as a ballerina's flying fish dive.

That jump into the unknown remains, to a degree, unexplained. In what way and through what processes the ballet tours impacted the Cold War is still open to debate. For a long time, scholars credited most of the agency in the Soviet-American cultural exchange to the countries sending out performers, reading cultural diplomacy primarily as a way in which nations represented themselves to the world. Indeed, the exchange was an important way for the United States and Soviet Union to depict themselves on an international stage. Thus studying cultural diplomacy presentations can provide vital insights into the ways in which political and artistic leaders wanted their countries to be viewed around the globe.[2]

Nevertheless, cultural exchange is an inherently two-way process, and its encounters are shaped as much by audiences as by performers. As the viewers in Madison Square Garden watched Struchkova leap across the stage, they compared her performance to their previous experiences with ballet. They judged the relationship between her movement and the orchestra's music by their knowledge of American dance. They understood the ballerina's relationship both to her partner and to themselves in light of what they had read about the dancers in American newspapers. In other words, the American audience did not see these performances in a vacuum. They saw Soviet ballet through the prism of their own cultural expectations. The opposite was equally true; Soviet audiences interpreted and judged American ballet according to the artistic standards they already possessed, not according to Western frameworks of meaning. This book is about these moments of encounter, the ones that ended in frustrated misunderstanding as much as those that created new cultural ties.

The Development and Practice of Soviet-American Cultural Exchange

The growth of official American and Soviet cultural diplomacy began slowly and haphazardly in the years just before World War II.[3] Beginning in the 1920s but intensifying especially in the 1950s, the Soviet Union sent musicians, dancers, actors, and literary and art exhibitions on tours abroad in order to win allies among the intelligentsia of other countries. The Soviet government sent its artists to socialist and non-socialist countries, encompassing all six inhabited continents, though they spent the most money and person-hours on cultural diplomacy tours in Western Europe. In the year 1959, for example, the Soviet government sent artists on many dozens of tours to locations around the world, including ballet dancers from the Kirov to Latin America, a puppet theater to Italy, and an exhibition of children's art to Norway.[4]

During the late 1950s and early 1960s, cultural diplomacy in the Soviet Union was controlled by a number of interrelated and competing bodies, including the State Committee for Cultural Ties (GKKS) and the Union of Soviet Societies of Friendship (SSOD).[5] The most important to the day-to-day running of the ballet exchange and thus to this study, however, were the Ministry of Culture and its subsidiary organization, Goskontsert (an abbreviation of State Concert Agency). The latter organization was founded in 1956 to arrange performing arts tours of all kinds, both within the Soviet Union and in exchanges with countries around the world.[6]

The United States began its first formal cultural diplomacy program during World War II. Throughout this period, most American cultural diplomacy was sent to South America as part of the "Good Neighbor" policy to influence or control the other governments in the Western Hemisphere.[7] Briefly following World War II, the United States focused its cultural diplomacy efforts on Japan and Germany in order to reshape local cultures in the wake of fascism.[8] By the early 1950s, however, the success of the Soviet cultural diplomacy programs began to make some American State Department personnel nervous. Eventually, the US government established the cultural presentations program to combat the Soviet program and its messages about the United States.[9] As part of this same transition, American cultural projects in West Germany were modified so that they advocated for anti-communism rather than de-Nazification.[10]

Officials at the State Department ran the cultural presentations program in logistical terms, but they refused on ideological grounds to allow a state body to make any artistic decisions. In order to solve this problem, the State Department delegated these judgments to the American National Theatre and Academy (ANTA), which formed expert panels to choose performers for the cultural presentations program.[11] Like its Soviet counterpart, US cultural diplomacy supported various performing arts tours, including those by symphony orchestras, dance companies, solo singers, choirs, and jazz bands.[12]

From the end of World War II up through the early 1950s, the relationship between the governments of the United States and the Soviet Union was so antagonistic that direct cultural exchange between the two countries was practically nonexistent. Stalin's death in 1953, however, paved the way for gradual détente.[13] Over the course of the mid-1950s, scattered artistic tours bridged the Soviet-American gap, and in 1958 the United States and the Soviet Union signed the Lacy-Zarubin agreement, which provided for a reciprocal exchange of artists, media objects, scientists, and students between the two superpowers.[14]

Ballet was only one dance style among many used for cultural diplomacy in the Cold War. On the American side, the State Department relied heavily on modern dance as well. Indeed, the ANTA dance panel tended to feel that modern dance was unambiguously American in a way that ballet was not and thus could represent the United States well on an international stage. The panel often favored the companies led by Martha Graham and José Limón. Nor was ballet the only style of dance on the Soviet side. The USSR often toured its State Folk Dance troupes, the Moiseyev and the Beryozka, and the Moiseyev was the first Soviet dance company to visit the United States.[15] Nevertheless, within the Soviet-American exchange, ballet took on a special significance. The art form was always a cornerstone of Soviet cultural diplomacy, and in the United States it was associated very strongly with Russia and, increasingly, with elevated cultural prestige. In the early exchanges with the USSR, the ANTA panel often picked ballet companies both because they wanted to match Soviet achievement company for company and because Goskontsert was more enthusiastic about approving ballet than other types of dance.[16]

The justifications for the Soviet-American cultural exchange varied wildly, not just between the two countries but also within them, and historical accounts of the programs have taken up these competing narratives.

For some, the exchange seems a type of sublimated military encounter, like the Olympics.[17] For others, it was a cultural avenue for fostering détente.[18] For still others, the exchanges' primary goals were logistical, to enable the Soviet Union to earn valuable foreign currency or allow the United States to draw the Soviet Union into the capitalist economic order.[19] Perhaps the most popular explanation for the exchange in the United States at the time was the assertion that it enabled free American culture to undermine the Soviet government's credibility with its intelligentsia.[20]

Whatever the goal, the key to the exchange, as enshrined in the Lacy-Zarubin agreement, was reciprocity. Though each side hoped to gain some type of advantage through the arrangement, aiming for reciprocity prevented the other country from using cultural diplomacy to leap ahead. As musicologist Danielle Fosler-Lussier has pointed out, however, the messy process of conducting the exchange constantly got in the way of this ideal.[21] Cultural life in the two superpowers was organized so differently and understood so differently that there was no way for the tours to mirror one another as the paper agreements claimed they would. The Ministry of Culture and Goskontsert, both state bodies, ran the Soviet side of the cultural exchange, while the American government delegated decisions to a variety of private entities, from company directors to impresarios. ANTA, which controlled some of these decisions for the State Department, operated as a semi-private, semi-public group. Their goals and methods never fully aligned with the State Department's, and American impresarios were even further outside the control of the American government.[22]

While a number of private impresarios played a role in the exchange, by far the most important to ballet was Sol Hurok. Hurok was a Russian American immigrant who had moved to the United States in 1906. He began organizing American tours for Russian artists, including Feodor Chaliapin and Anna Pavlova, as early as the 1920s. Hurok also arranged for many Russian ballet companies to tour the United States and was at least partly responsible for ballet's growing popularity with American audiences during the mid-twentieth century. Throughout his career he advocated vigorously for Soviet-American exchange, beginning decades before the Lacy-Zarubin agreement was signed. Once the agreement was in place, Hurok arranged the bulk of the Soviet cultural diplomacy tours in the United States, including all of the tours by the Bolshoi.[23]

Hurok's interventions into cultural diplomacy repeatedly undermined reciprocity in the Soviet-American exchange. The impresario often conducted his own private negotiations with the Soviet Ministry of Culture and the Bolshoi Theater before any official negotiations with the US government took place, and to some degree the State Department was then locked into the decisions that Hurok had made.[24] Partially as a result of this and partially for other reasons, American tours in the Soviet Union lost money while Soviet tours in the United States made money.[25] American audiences were happy to pay Hurok's high prices for Bolshoi tickets, and while Hurok paid the Soviet performers, they were expected to turn over a large portion of their salaries to the government when they arrived back in the USSR.[26] Meanwhile, American dancers kept their salaries. American tour costs were paid with funds provided in part by the State Department, with some small help from Goskontsert and the ballet companies themselves.[27] Combined with differences in the size of the halls, performing schedules, and exchange rates, this meant that the American government consistently had to subsidize American performers to go to the Soviet Union, while the Soviet government made money on their exchange with the United States. Moreover, the Soviets placed stringent restrictions on which cities American artists could visit.[28]

As a result, in addition to gaining a substantial amount of money, the Soviet government was able to arrange long and expansive tours for its ballet companies in the United States, while American dance companies were confined to a limited schedule in the same four or five cities—almost always including Moscow and Leningrad (now again St. Petersburg). Soviet ballet tours in the United States were hampered only by Hurok's ability to find stages large enough to fit the company's productions. In 1962, the Bolshoi stopped in New York, Los Angeles, Cleveland, San Francisco, Washington, Detroit, Philadelphia, Chicago, and Boston.[29] On multiple occasions, American officials tried to convince Hurok to follow the principle of reciprocity in his arrangements with Soviet groups.[30] Such efforts, however, remained unsuccessful, because while Soviet officials and some American ones treated Hurok's organization as a mirror to Goskontsert, they had radically different operating procedures and agendas.

Cross-Cultural Reception as Transliteration

The issue of reciprocity was not simply a diplomatic or logistical problem, however. It also proved to be a difficult ideal on an aesthetic level. Soviet-American cultural diplomacy was organized around the belief that dance and music could be exchanged between the two countries without creating cultural friction. Indeed, music and dance were considered very useful because they were believed to be universal languages that would require no translation. As dance historian Clare Croft and others have argued, the Cold War–era belief in classical music and ballet's universality was tied to the notion that such elite, white upper-class art forms were free from ideology and unaffected by social circumstances. Diplomats and artists imagined that audiences all over the world would understand classical music and theatrical Western dance without any need for interpretation.[31] This aesthetic backdrop assumed there could be a type of reciprocal, unencumbered artistic interaction between audience and artist in the same way that the Lacy-Zarubin agreement assumed there would be a transparent, equal logistical exchange.

As such, the underlying assumptions of the exchange mirrored attitudes about communist and capitalist ideology at the heart of the Cold War. The US government believed that capitalist ideology and culture should spread without check throughout the world, and the Soviet government believed similar things about communist ideology and culture. To each superpower, the other's influence was an unnatural barrier to the dissemination of their chosen political and economic models.[32] Without this barrier, ideologues believed, communism or capitalism could spread everywhere. Accepting any need for translation or interpretation, like accepting a need to modify ideology, would be an admittance that this culture was not universal.

Of course, ballet and music are not universal languages. As reception theorists and historians have shown, meaning in music and dance is not produced solely by an author, whose intentions are easily and uniformly read by all audiences. Rather, different audiences create different meanings from a single work. Reception historians have demonstrated this fact primarily by showing changing interpretations of a work of art over time.[33] Cultural diplomacy invites, or rather demands, that we look at a different jump: not in time but in place.[34] Doing so allows us to acknowledge the importance of the audience in creating a work of art while imagining what happens when the audience's interpretative strategies have not been developed to suit it.[35] During the Cold War exchanges, American and Soviet ballet viewers did not understand what they were watching as the choreographers, composers, or dancers intended, because the interpretive strategies they had at their disposal had been developed for a different type of repertory.

In the case of cultural diplomacy, the reception process can be modeled through an analogy to transliteration. Transliteration is the practice of rewriting words from one script into another, for example converting

English's Latin alphabet into Russian's Cyrillic. Unlike translation, which focuses on conveying the information contained within a set of words to its audience, transliteration only conveys the sounds, the sensory impressions, of the language. As no two scripts are perfectly alike, strange gaps and misunderstandings can arise as the sounds of one language are displayed through the letters of another. Moving from English to Russian, for example, the soft "g" in George Balanchine is transliterated as "дж" (or dzh to transliterate it back to English), separating out the letter's dull attack from its buzzing finale.

Similarly, in the Cold War exchange, the sensory impressions produced by a particular ballet were maintained from one country to another. But those sensory impressions—seeing a dancer raise her arm or hearing a trumpet ring out—were experienced through the prism of the host country's cultural expectations. The effects of this shift can be quite profound. Since a ballet's meaning is produced in collaboration with its audience, new viewers can produce very new interpretations.

The metaphor of transliteration is not meant to imply that all the ways in which audiences experience ballet are logocentric. Sometimes exchange viewers found new political, philosophical, or narrative meanings in a ballet, but sometimes they simply related to the sensory experience in a different way. Audiences are prompted by their cultural expectations to focus their attention in particular ways. They also compare the sensory experiences of a new work to their sensory experiences of ballet in the past. This in turn can open up new horizons for seeing and hearing. For example, when the New York City Ballet performed in the Soviet Union in 1962, audiences were less likely to use the strategy of structural listening favored by American critics and so were more likely to notice elements of Balanchine's choreography other than his attention to musical form.

The Soviet-American ballet exchange is a particularly rich area for examining this type of cross-cultural interaction because the two schools of American and Soviet ballet were so close and yet so far apart. Many American ballet companies had been founded by Russian émigrés fleeing World War I and the communist revolution. Between 1917 and 1959, the two systems had been driven apart by isolation and ideology, but they still shared a great deal of common practice. Ballet critics and audiences from one side of the divide could therefore easily imagine themselves to be experts in a universal art form. At the same time, the two schools were far enough apart, particularly in their strategies of interpretation, that they saw and experienced substantially different things in each other's ballets.

Even today, the differences between American and Soviet ballet are often summarized in starkly binary terms: in the United States, choreographers made abstract ballets, while in the Soviet Union, they made narrative works. Such binaries, however, mask deep similarities between ballets in the two countries. In the Soviet Union up through the 1950s, the officially accepted genre of ballet had been the *drambalet,* which merged dramatic theater with dance, often bringing to life classic literature in a style of movement that bore a close relationship to silent film. In the late 1950s and early 1960s, an overhaul of Soviet politics in the wake of Stalin's death ushered in new aesthetics across the arts. Many younger choreographers began to promote a new style of dance known as *choreographic symphonism.* In choreographic symphonic ballets, dance was still narrative, but it took many structural cues from the musical score. Such artists developed choreographic motifs like musical leitmotifs and used counterpoint between different parts of an ensemble.[36]

During the 1930s and 1940s, many American choreographers created short ballets similar to the Soviet drambalety, works such as *Rodeo, Billy the Kid, Fall River Legend,* and *Fancy Free* that featured folkloric settings and nationalist references. They were short ballets choreographed in naturalistic pantomime and driven by explorations of the characters' psychological development. By the mid-twentieth century, however, much like in the Soviet Union, ballet in the United States underwent a profound shift. George Balanchine, the most prominent American choreographer of the era, based his ballets closely on musical works and abandoned realistic narrative. Balanchine's ballets responded to minute musical details in their scores, from texture and melody to instrumentation and form.[37]

These similarities between American and Soviet dance make the binary narratives constructed during the Cold War all the more interesting and all the more revealing of the ways in which political and aesthetic arguments can be intertwined. In these binary narratives, the differences between American and Soviet ballet are usually pinned down to the differences between Balanchine's authorial intentions and the Soviet state's authorial intentions. Instead, as this book demonstrates, the main differences between Soviet and American ballet can actually be located in the interpretive strategies used by Soviet and American critics and audiences. In other words, the distinctions between Soviet and American ballet lie less in how the dancers move and more in how the viewers watch and listen. Thus the rhetorical battles between the two schools were sharpened during the Cold War, as critical accounts of the exchange tours drew firm lines of opposition.

In both the United States and the Soviet Union, music played a central role in the shift of ballet aesthetics during the mid-twentieth century. Musical analysis and discussion thus played a central part in any serious debate between American and Soviet dance. While most Soviet critics argued that dance should express something meaningful found in music, American critics usually believed that dance should illustrate musical forms. Critical battles in the exchanges therefore often hinged on assertions that the other side did not really understand music. The Soviet-American ballet exchange can thus illuminate important differences in the roles that music played in the Soviet Union and the United States. Moreover, given the centrality of the exchange to the development of ballet culture worldwide, it can illuminate the meaning that music has for ballet audiences around the world today.

There are some difficulties involved in reconstructing the reception of the Soviet-American exchange tours, related to the limits of the source material. Most important, it is supremely easy to access the interpretations of critics and supremely difficult to access the interpretations of anyone else. This is no small problem for reception history, as the critic's need to write about an artwork creates a certain framework and set of interpretation strategies of its own. The views of critics cannot be taken as synonymous with the views of the audience at large. Moreover, in the Soviet Union, reviewers had to publish in state-owned journals and were therefore subject to ideological pressure and even censorship.[38] In an attempt to combat this one-sided view of reception, I have interviewed an audience member at the Bolshoi's American performances in 1959. I have also tried to pay close attention to any reports about audience reactions: booing, applause, screams, ticket purchasing, fan letters, and comments.

But neither is this a reason to throw out the critics' accounts wholesale. Critics play an important role in shaping broad audience opinions, particularly in relation to cultural diplomacy tours, in which a much larger body of people read about a visiting company than can purchase tickets or make a trip to the theater. As Fosler-Lussier has recently articulated, the reception of a cultural diplomacy performance is central to its impact. Fosler-Lussier draws on Daniel Boorstin's theory of the pseudo-event to explain how cultural diplomacy can affect widespread popular opinion. Boorstin defined the pseudo-event as a production, meeting, or other event staged, not for its actual in-the-moment purpose, but rather with the intent of being reported through mass media to a wider audience. Fosler-Lussier argues that in operating as a pseudo-event, the American cultural exchange program gave foreign audiences some agency to draw their own conclusions about the United States, while at the same time providing those audiences with positive events to ensure that the conclusions would be favorable. In this way, cultural exchange performances were a more effective means of shifting global opinion than outright propaganda, because propaganda often made audiences feel manipulated.[39]

Within this model for understanding cultural diplomacy, local reception plays an important and largely underexplored role. If the cultural diplomatic event's greatest advantage was that it allowed local audiences to come to their own conclusions, then this could also be the program's greatest flaw. Any conclusions about the United States or Soviet Union were filtered through local media and therefore through local aesthetics. In many instances, ballets were interpreted in ways that their creators and performers had not anticipated, sometimes in ways that were at odds with the foreign policy goals of the touring nation. Soviet critics discussed American ballet only using the rhetoric and vocabulary that they already had to discuss their own ballets. Similarly, American critics and audiences engaged with Soviet ballet on American terms. The American critics transliterated Soviet ballet, but they never translated it. They observed and interpreted the sensory experience of that ballet through their own terms, but they never tried to understand how the Soviet performers saw and heard it.

Perhaps, then, the safest option for these tours was for companies to perform ballets that were already international standards or that resembled ballets on the other side of the Iron Curtain. Often during the Cold War cultural exchange tours, audiences lavished the greatest praise on those productions that closely resembled popular local repertoires. Even in these instances, however, critics drew those repertories into their own system of aesthetics and politics. For example, excerpts from *Swan Lake* were performed by both American and Soviet companies on cultural diplomacy tours, but the ballet was valued in the two countries for different reasons.

Examining reception in a more nuanced way can help scholars and politicians understand how cultural diplomacy impacts international opinion. This study thus takes part in ongoing discussions about the effects of culture, or so-called soft power, on global politics. In a 1990 book *Bound to Lead,* political scientist Joseph Nye divided global power into "soft" (cultural, diplomatic) and "hard" (military, economic), advocating that more attention should be paid to soft power methods of impacting international relations. However, Nye never fully explained how culture could exert power in the world, instead relying on an index of "attractiveness" to describe how much foreign populations admire or despise American cultural products. This single variable "attractiveness" belies the complex relationships between a work of art and its audiences.[40] For example, even though American audiences in 1962 loved the Soviet work *Ballet School,* that fact did not necessarily convince them to love the Soviet Union. Instead, many appreciated the ballet precisely because it gave them the buoyant impression that the United States was winning the cultural Cold War. While it was attractive to American audiences, it did not advance the Soviet government's geopolitical goals.

Chapter Overview

The following chapters present in detail four tours from the early Soviet-American ballet exchange, by the Bolshoi Ballet in 1959, American Ballet Theatre in 1960, and both the Bolshoi and New York City Ballet in 1962. This was the era of first contact between Soviet and American ballet, and, moreover, this was the only period in which the Americans almost matched the Soviets tour for tour. The greater Soviet-American cultural exchange continued after 1963, but by the latter part of that decade, the American State Department had moved toward using fewer ballet companies.[41] The close focus on these four tours does come at the expense of covering two additional tours that were part of the exchange during these early years: by the Kirov Ballet in 1961 and by the Joffrey Ballet in 1963. The chapters are arranged in pairs, instances in which the companies were exchanged either directly or almost directly.

Chapter 1 discusses the Bolshoi Theater's first tour of the United States in 1959. The company was greeted by a frenzy of excitement from American reporters and audiences. While the popular response was rapturous, however, the critics were more cautious about their visitors. Reception of the company was divided in two. The critics praised the dancers, particularly the Soviet ballerinas, while they disparaged the choreography and music. In doing so, they separated out what they believed was an apolitical style of performance from deeply politicized choreography. This split was highly gendered and allowed critics and audiences to sympathize personally with the performers while condemning the ostensibly more political works themselves. Critics in the United States labeled these ballets as conservative, a complaint that would permeate American reviews of Soviet dance throughout the Cold War.

Chapter 2 turns to American Ballet Theatre's (ABT) often-overlooked 1960 tour of the Soviet Union. The tour took place under highly fraught circumstances. Ballet was considered a uniquely Russian art form in both the United States and the Soviet Union. Some members of the State Department advisory panel felt that sending any ballet troupe to the Soviet Union left the Americans too open to ridicule or censure. At many points in the spring and summer of 1960, both the Soviet and American governments threatened to withdraw support from the tour. In dealing with these political concerns, ABT director Lucia Chase developed a strategy for presenting her company and the United States as the leader of an international, elite art form. Through repertoire and casting choices, she balanced the troupe's profile, showing it as both an international company and a patriotic American organization. Moreover, the company's American works bore striking similarities to Soviet ballets and were therefore praised by Russian critics for displaying common aesthetic and political values. Much to the surprise of everyone involved—including Chase herself—the strategy and the tour were successful.

Chapter 3 explores the Bolshoi Ballet's 1962 tour of the United States, which took place during the Cuban Missile Crisis. In the wake of the crisis, President Kennedy and his family staged numerous public meetings with the Bolshoi dancers to soothe the mounting political tensions. In the critical reception of the Bolshoi, however, a less conciliatory strain emerged, as American reviewers wrapped their understanding of the Bolshoi's performances in domestic aesthetics related to class. The word "taste" appeared frequently in reviews of the Soviet company on both the Bolshoi's productions of Russian classics such as *Swan Lake* and its new offering, *Spartacus*. The American critics understood the Soviet works through the lens of taste, a framework related to domestic struggles about the positioning of ballet in an aesthetic and class hierarchy. These concerns were in turn related to a desire to foster the United States' status as an emerging ideological empire.

The New York City Ballet's 1962 tour of the Soviet Union has received far more scholarly attention in the United States than any other ballet exchange tour. It was a dramatic event: the first time that Russian American choreographer George Balanchine returned home following his emigration in 1924. The tour also took place, like its counterpart, during the Cuban Missile Crisis. Previous scholarly accounts have claimed the Soviet reviews of New York City Ballet were heavily censored, and that, as a result, the tour undermined the authority of the Soviet government with the intelligentsia. Chapter 4 re-examines this tour, using transliteration as a way of modeling the Soviet response to Balanchine. This re-examination shows that Soviet cultural authorities were not at all hostile to the choreographer or his company. The Soviet critics mostly accepted Balanchine's ballets, but they reframed his accomplishments within the debates about drambalet and choreographic symphonism. According to Balanchine's Soviet critics, his works were successful precisely because they reaffirmed the value of the Russian systems of training, artistry, and meaning.

The Epilogue addresses how these issues have played out in the last few years, focusing on the figures of David Hallberg and Alexei Ratmansky, two artists who have worked in both the American and Russian ballet worlds. Through a brief examination of their careers, the Epilogue shows how deeply the rhetorical strategies that were worked out during the Cold War continue to dominate discussions of ballet in the United States and Russia, despite the many obvious overlaps of personnel and repertoire in today's globalized ballet culture.

Throughout, the book dwells on moments of transliteration and misinterpretation, for the potential of the exchange to create new meanings and new experiences in ballet. Audiences and critics interpreted the works onstage in complex ways that could create paradoxical effects on public opinion. While the tours' diplomatic successes could promote friendly relations between the two superpowers, in the end performers and audiences on both sides refused to engage deeply with each other's aesthetic philosophies.

Such misinterpretations have as much bearing on our current grasp of twentieth-century ballet as the works themselves. These misunderstandings, some accidental and some willful, have shaped the ways in which Americans view Russian ballet and the ways in which Russians view American ballet. The transliterations of the cultural Cold War have never been undone, and each version, the Soviet version of American ballet and the American image of Soviet ballet, remains a powerful and strange cultural object in its own right.

During the Cold War, the ballet exchange attracted intense political and artistic fascination, hope, and fear. Its practice altered the course of dance in both the United States and the Soviet Union. It was also a centerpiece of Soviet-American exchange writ large, perhaps more important and more heavily publicized than any other art form. As such, this book illuminates both the history of twentieth-century ballet and the development of Soviet-American relations.

1
A Cold War Welcome

The Bolshoi Ballet's 1959 Tour of the United States

When the Bolshoi Ballet made its first tour of the United States in 1959, the American reaction was tremendous. Fans lined up overnight for tickets, newspapers gushed over the troupe's every appearance, and audiences screamed and cried at the performances. At the company's final curtain call at New York's Metropolitan Opera House, the applause lasted half an hour. Outside, a police cordon was established to keep the street clear of fans who crowded the sidewalks to see the dancers in person. Similar enthusiasm met the troupe over and over again as it made its way around the United States.[1]

But the applause alone tells only half the story. American reception of the Soviet company was firmly divided. Ballet fans, critics, and politicians welcomed the Bolshoi dancers with open arms, praising them in extravagant terms. The company's ballerinas, in particular, were objects of endless fascination in the American press, many treated as though they were Hollywood stars. But while the Soviet performers were welcomed in the United States, the ballets they presented were not. American critics glorified Soviet dancers while at the same time disparaging the works they danced. The very reviews that waxed rhapsodic about ballerina Galina Ulanova in *Romeo and Juliet* tore apart Leonid Lavrovsky's choreography for the same ballet.

By dismissing the Soviet repertoire while celebrating the Soviet dancers, American critics drew on the Western philosophical tradition of mind-body dualism. In ballet reception, this manifested itself in a separation of choreography, which was understood as intellectual and masculine, from performance, thought to be corporeal and feminine. Using this gender binary allowed reviewers to criticize Soviet politics via their repertoire while continuing to express their enjoyment at the company's appearances via the performers.

The specific criticisms heaped on the Bolshoi's repertoire drew on American tropes about the backwardness of the Soviet Union. At its heart, Cold War ideological competition was a fight for a historical narrative, a

Ballet in the Cold War. Anne Searcy, Oxford University Press (2020). © Oxford University Press.
DOI: 10.1093/oso/9780190945107.001.0001

contest over what style of government—communist or capitalist—was the next appropriate stage in global development. Americans often claimed that the Soviet state was a remnant of the nineteenth-century Russian autocracy, rather than a radical twentieth-century form of government. For American dance critics, this translated into a belief that Soviet ballet was also old-fashioned. Review after review complained that the Soviet company was stuck in the past.

The insistence on this type of reception is all the more noticeable when comparing American reviews of the Bolshoi's two full-length Soviet works on the 1959 tour: *Romeo and Juliet* and *Stone Flower*. The two ballets were brought to symbolize two distinct periods of Soviet dance: *Romeo and Juliet* for the socialist realist drambalet of the 1930s and 1940s and *Stone Flower* for Thaw-era choreographic symphonism. To their Soviet performers, the two works had highly distinct ways of conveying meaning to the audience. But American reviewers had trouble seeing the difference. As American critics and audiences transliterated the ballets, they had no interpretive strategies to parse the distinctions between the two works' styles of movement, storytelling, and musical construction. Instead, American reviewers simply understood both ballets as narrative, Soviet works and therefore as aesthetically conservative.

To this day, Americans continue to see the Bolshoi as old-fashioned and to separate its performers from its repertoire. Critics and historians in the United States still assert that the Bolshoi's dancers are virtuosic but that their repertoire is conservative, propagandistic, and even vulgar.[2] The reasons for this reception lie not so much in the works that the Bolshoi performs, but in the ways that Americans have been trained to see them, ways that grew directly out of the Cold War. In order to change how Americans view the Bolshoi and experience its ballets, then, it is necessary to return to the story of this first encounter and to unpick its misunderstandings.

The Bolshoi Is Coming!

Founded in 1776 by Prince Pëtr Urusov and Michael Maddox, the Bolshoi Ballet had a long and illustrious history under Russia's imperial government, second in prestige only to the Mariinsky Theater in St. Petersburg. The Bolshoi gained new significance following the Russian Revolution and the relocation of the national government to Moscow. As Leningrad was held under increasing suspicion for its imperial and Western ties, Moscow grew in power, and the Bolshoi became a prominent symbol of state authority.[3] Visiting dignitaries were customarily taken to see the ballet, and portions of the company toured internationally under the sponsorship of the Soviet government. Khrushchev complained that he had accompanied so many foreign ambassadors to the Bolshoi that his dreams were haunted by a mixture of tutus and tanks.[4] As one of the Soviet Union's premiere cultural exports, the Bolshoi was a natural choice for the Soviet-American exchange. Just one year after the Lacy-Zarubin agreement was signed, the Bolshoi made its way to the United States for the first time in its nearly two-hundred-year history.

Americans awaited the company's arrival with breathless eagerness. Newspapers and magazines across the country, from the *New York Times* to *Dance News,* from the *San Francisco Chronicle* to *Women's Wear Daily,* ran seemingly endless articles describing the company, its dancers, and its repertoire. On April 13, 1959, a picture of the Bolshoi graced the cover of *Newsweek* over the title "Direct from Moscow—Russia's Best."[5] Coverage included descriptions of the dancers' daily regimens, the charity events that would take place at the performances, and hints of the tense negotiations around each decision of location and scheduling.[6]

On the Sunday before the company began performances at the Metropolitan Opera House, *New York Times* critic John Martin ran an article jokingly titled "Dance: Please! Messrs. Hurok, Khrushchev, Bolshoi, What Are You Doing to Us?," in which he claimed that:

> The coming visit of the Bolshoi Ballet from Moscow (is there anybody alive who does not know that it opens at the Met on Thursday?) has caused more strife and dissension in this country than anything since the War Between the States. [...] Politics? Anti-communism? Send the Reds back where they came from? Nonsense; it is just that everybody wants tickets. [...] People not only want to see it, but they will commit arson, perjury, mayhem and murder to do so.[7]

Martin's complaints, though exaggerated, were understandable. Tickets almost completely sold out to Hurok's pre-subscribers, a cadre of devoted dance fans who were given the opportunity to make advance purchases. Of those who were not on the list, thousands stood in line for over five hours through intermittent rain to purchase tickets.[8] Balletomanes hoping for standing room began showing up at the box office thirty-nine hours in advance.[9]

Excitement about the Bolshoi's tour was not uniform. The Daughters of the American Revolution passed a resolution condemning cultural exchange with communist-bloc countries. Their language and timing suggested that they intended to target the Bolshoi tour.[10] Such protests, however, were ineffective. Demand for tickets was so high that Hurok tacked on a secondary New York engagement for the company at Madison Square Garden.[11]

An advance group from the Bolshoi, including lead ballerina Galina Ulanova and conductor Yuri Faier, touched down in New York on April 8, 1959. Faier arrived early to work with the American musicians who would accompany the troupe throughout the tour. Ulanova came to warm up the American press. Three days later, on April 12, the main part of the company arrived, together making up a contingent of 102 Soviet dancers and twenty-two support staff.[12] The opening days of rehearsal in the United States were somewhat rocky. During the week leading up to the premiere, many dancers complained that the stage floor at the old Metropolitan Opera House was pitted. Though stagehands rushed to fix the problem, the theater never quite met the expectations of the Soviet visitors.[13] Choreographer and artistic director Leonid Lavrovsky described the stage in a letter to his wife as "excellent and comfortable, but dirty to the point of indecency."[14]

Lavrovsky felt that the entire city was dirty, a "silver-gray with terrible buildings and boring streets."[15] The other members of the Soviet delegation tended to agree with him, but, despite widespread ambivalence about New York itself, the Bolshoi dancers immensely enjoyed visiting the United States. According to Marina Kondratieva, "We were very interested in the stores because at that time there was nothing [like that in the USSR], absolutely nothing. The 1950s was a very hard time. . . . And of course, for us it was interesting just to go and not to buy anything. Just to look and see what is stylish there . . . For us it was like a museum."[16] In their limited spare time, members of the company were put through their paces with a sight-seeing schedule that included a boat ride around the city and a trip to the zoo, as well as a viewing of *West Side Story* on Broadway.[17] Many of the artists were able to connect with friends or family who had emigrated from Russia following the 1917 Revolution. Yuri Faier, who had believed his brother to be dead for thirty years, was reunited with his sibling during the company's stay in New York.[18]

One problem that persistently beset the tour schedule was the size of American theaters. The Bolshoi stage was immense, eighty-six feet by seventy-seven feet, and the productions performed by the company were designed in commensurately epic proportions. When the company toured, there were few American theaters large enough to host it. Washington, DC, boasted not a single theater that could fit any of the full-length ballets. Soviet officials worried that having the company skip the capital would be seen as an insult to the American government.[19] In the end, Hurok and the Bolshoi directors decided to send a small cast to Washington to perform just one gala program, a mix of short ballets and virtuosic numbers from larger works.[20]

Following the stop in New York and the one-day engagement in Washington, the Bolshoi traveled to Los Angeles for a series of performances at the Shrine Auditorium. The premiere drew out many Hollywood celebrities, including Clark Gable, John Wayne, and Dinah Shore. Members of the Bolshoi company enjoyed life on the west coast much better than in New York; some remarked to local newspapers that Los Angeles was a more beautiful and cleaner city and that they liked the palm trees.[21] Lavrovsky wrote home that Los Angeles reminded him of southern cities in the Soviet Union, but "more grandiose." In Los Angeles there was "lots of green, air, and you feel better. In New York there is no air and it is impossible to breathe."[22] The glamour of southern California aside, life on tour was hard. Long rehearsals took up most of the dancers' day hours, and it was sometimes difficult to communicate with family back home, as many of Lavrovsky's letters attest.[23] The group was accompanied by agents from the KGB, who reported back on the dancers' activities.[24] After the trip to Los Angeles, the company spent a short time in San Francisco, after which they left the United States for an appearance in Canada before heading home to the Soviet Union.[25]

From New York to San Francisco, American audiences were nearly ecstatic about their Soviet visitors. At the company's April 16 premiere at the Metropolitan Opera House, Ulanova was called back onstage for seventeen curtain calls.[26] On the last night at the Met, the audience went wild. Walter Terry labeled the scene "a happy riot."[27] Lavrovsky tried to describe it in a letter to his wife:

> It was not merely success, but something furious. People screamed, cried, tore up their programs and threw them into the air, whistled, which is an expression of very great recognition. They threw flowers here and there.[28]

The mania of the American fans stunned everyone, including the dancers. According to Kondratieva, the troupe had never encountered such an extreme reaction at home.[29] When the company then went on to perform at Madison Square Garden, they garnered 13,700 viewers, the largest ballet audience in American history.[30]

Such a rapturous reception reflected the American culture of Hollywood celebrity. Much as fan magazines tended to fixate on Hollywood starlets, newspapers followed the Bolshoi ballerinas around New York and Los Angeles, reporting on their reactions to the cities' attractions. These articles often focused on Ulanova and her fellow ballerina Maya Plisetskaya, the two most important dancers in the company. Ulanova had grown up in St. Petersburg, Russia, and trained in the Imperial Ballet School just as the revolution was transforming her country. She established her career during the 1930s in Leningrad before moving to the Bolshoi Theater in 1944. In the 1950s, films of her dancing, including her performances of *Giselle* and *Romeo and Juliet*, circulated around the globe, making her one of the most important international stars of ballet.[31] When the Bolshoi came to the United States, American critics expressed a hunger to observe her dancing in person. Many early articles about the tour ran headlines such as "Russian Ballerina to Tour U.S." and "Galina Ulanova: Long-Awaited Visitor Arrives" as though the other one-hundred-and-one dancers were only there to support her.[32] When she finally appeared, the critics were not disappointed. Reviews almost uniformly named her one of the greatest dancers of all time.[33]

American critics were highly interested in Ulanova's age, an admittedly astounding forty-nine during the American tour. Many drew particular attention to the dancer's skill at seeming to morph into the figure of a young girl for her role as Juliet. As Milt Freudenheim described in the *Chicago Daily News*, "Ulanova, by daylight a plain woman of 49, miraculously evoked the youth and beauty of a teen-age Juliet."[34] Terry called her Juliet "girlish . . . impulsive, unsure, questing, and eager."[35] The critics' emphasis on Ulanova's girlishness represented an attempt to depict the dancer according to mid-twentieth-century American models of non-political feminine celebrity, turning her into a type of Soviet "girl next-door," similar to movie stars such as Esther Williams and Doris Day. In some ways Ulanova fit the girl-next-door tropes of American fan culture very well.[36] She was portrayed in Soviet literature as highly self-disciplined and sexually pure. The characters that she played on stage were often chaste heroines clad in wispy white dresses.[37] At the same time, the Soviet ballerina was not personally beautiful or youthful enough to fit the stereotype of the American starlet perfectly, and while her chastity and demure behavior fit the bill well, her political engagement in a communist state certainly did not. One American reporter described her appearance at a press conference, claiming that the dancer

> lacked the glamour traditionally associated with an internationally acclaimed star. She has gray-streaked blonde hair casually combed back, a wide smile revealing a gold canine tooth, a pale complexion with little if any makeup, and dazzling blue eyes. . . . She appears more the housewife than the dancer.[38]

Ulanova's inability or unwillingness to play the part of traditional celebrity continued to puzzle the American press corps throughout the tour. Another reporter wrote that he found her "quite aloof, dry and rather cold."[39]

The American press often contrasted Ulanova with her dark-haired counterpart Maya Plisetskaya, the company's second biggest star. Plisetskaya's relationship to the Soviet state was the polar opposite of Ulanova's. She came from a prominent family of artists, including her uncle, Asaf Messerer, a former dancer who continued to serve the Bolshoi as a coach and repetiteur in the 1950s and 1960s. Plisetskaya's father, a bureaucrat and communist party member, was executed during the Great Purges of the 1930s. Her mother, silent film actress Ra Messerer, was arrested shortly thereafter and sent to the Gulag with her infant son.[40] Plisetskaya's family history made her understandably distrustful of the Communist Party, and the feeling was apparently mutual. From 1953 to 1959, Plisetskaya was prevented from traveling outside of the communist bloc.[41] Leading up to the Bolshoi's tour of London in 1956, the theater directors had assumed that Plisetskaya would play a major role in the expedition.[42] At the last minute, however, her name was removed from the touring roster, ostensibly to keep up the standards of the Bolshoi's performances at home. She was similarly kept away from the 1958 tour to France and Belgium, on equally spurious grounds.[43]

For the American tour in 1959, the decision on whether or not to take Plisetskaya was pushed back until the last possible moment. In February 1959, Hurok met with Georgy Zhukov, from the State Committee on Cultural Ties, to convince him to allow Plisetskaya to tour with the Bolshoi, but Zhukov refused to speak with him on the matter.[44] As late as March 20, 1959, it was still undecided whether or not Plisetskaya would accompany the Bolshoi Theater to the United States.[45] Finally, just a few days before the start of the tour, Plisetskaya's inclusion was approved.[46] Likely, the change in policy was the result of Plisetskaya's recent marriage to composer Rodion Shchedrin, who remained in Moscow during the company's tour, essentially serving as a hostage to guarantee the ballerina's return.[47]

American reporters knew some of the political trouble that Plisetskaya had been facing in the Soviet Union and these rumors were occasionally printed in the American press, particularly by Walter Terry.[48] In general, however, American newspapers preferred to place Plisetskaya in a framework that they knew and understood from Hollywood reporting, portraying her as a femme fatale in the vein of Elizabeth Taylor.[49] While Ulanova was famed for her portrayals of Giselle and Juliet, relatively demure roles, Plisetskaya was renowned for her version of Odette/Odile in *Swan Lake*. On the 1959 tour she also starred as the lead in the bacchanalian *Walpurgis Night* and as the Mistress of the Magic Mountain in *Stone Flower*, where she wore a tight-fitting body suit that was much commented on in the American press. Her unusually flexible upper body and fiery stage presence made her the ideal magical queen. Rumors abounded in the American press that Plisetskaya had a rivalry with Ulanova or that she was romantically involved with a British embassy official.[50] Her reputation was enhanced by the fact that, unlike Ulanova, Plisetskaya was considered a stunning beauty. The *Daily News* labeled her the "Bolshoi bombshell."[51] During her trip, she posed for a photo-spread in *Vogue* magazine (Figure 1.1), which described her as a "long-legged Russian beauty with deep, big eyes."[52] Critic Miles Kastendieck called her "electrifying" and Winthrop Sargeant of the *New Yorker* named her the company's most thrilling dancer.[53]

Prokofiev as Mediator

The American critics' adoration of the Bolshoi dancers contrasted very sharply with their distaste for the company's repertoire, particularly for the troupe's Soviet ballets. American reviewers had difficulty understanding the artistic goals of works such as *Romeo and Juliet* and almost uniformly described the ballet as old-fashioned. This was a disappointment, since *Romeo* was part of the Bolshoi's plan to impress American audiences with a combination of classical works and newer Soviet choreography. The

Figure 1.1 Photo spread of Plisetskaya from *Vogue*, November 1, 1959. Irving Penn, Vogue © Condé Nast

company's repertory for its North American tour included two nineteenth-century ballets, *Swan Lake* and *Giselle,* as well as two Soviet works, *Romeo and Juliet* and *Stone Flower.*[54]

Not only did the Bolshoi combine new and old when touring, but they also had an important mediator in composer Sergei Prokofiev. Both *Romeo and Juliet* and *Stone Flower* had scores by Prokofiev, one of the only composers to have spent equal time in Russia and the West. Prokofiev was born in 1891 in Ukraine, and he was educated at the conservatory in St. Petersburg. In 1918, just after the Russian Revolution, the young composer left for the United

States and remained in the West for over a decade.[55] In 1936, after years of coaxing from Soviet officials, the composer returned to Russia. During the last third of his life, Prokofiev struggled to find his footing in the Soviet Union, where some bureaucrats held the composer in deep suspicion for his ties to the West.[56] Nevertheless, he managed to achieve periods of substantial public success, culminating in the mid-1940s, when he received Stalin prizes for his second Soviet ballet *Cinderella* and his Fifth Symphony.[57] In 1948, a series of denunciations at the Union of Composers shook the Soviet musical world. Prokofiev and other prominent composers were accused of "formalistic distortions and anti-democratic tendencies."[58] During the same period, he developed severe health problems, and the last years of his life were painful, financially difficult, and artistically frustrating.[59]

Despite the relative disapprobation in which he died in 1953, Prokofiev was gradually canonized by the Soviet government over the following few decades. In large part, his rise to posthumous glory was driven by the needs of the state's cultural diplomacy program. Because Prokofiev had spent time in the United States and Europe between 1918 and 1936, Western audiences were familiar with his compositional style. Prokofiev himself had conducted his Suite no. 2 from *Romeo and Juliet* with the Boston Symphony Orchestra in 1938, before the ballet even premiered in its full form.[60] This made Prokofiev and his ballet music ideal for the purposes of the exchange, a kind of midway point between American and Soviet tastes. In 1956, the Bolshoi selected *Romeo and Juliet* for its tour in London. English audiences received the ballet with fervor, an event that affirmed Prokofiev's value to the Soviet government.[61] A year later, in 1957, Prokofiev was posthumously awarded the Lenin Prize for music, the highest honor in the Soviet arts.[62]

When the Bolshoi came to the United States, therefore, Prokofiev's music was advertised as one of the tour's major attractions. Souvenir programs for the Bolshoi's performances featured a full-page biography of Prokofiev that named him "one of the foremost musicians of this century."[63] The biography suggested that his music bridged the gap between Russian classics such as *Swan Lake* and newer Soviet works such as *Romeo and Juliet*, claiming that the composer's "musical language is highly individual as he combines the traditions of Russian classical music with bold and even daring innovations."[64]

Centering Prokofiev in the 1959 tour, however, was more than a simple case of Realpolitik. His works also formed the backbone of the Soviet ballet canon. The composer's *Romeo and Juliet* was considered by most Soviet experts to be one of the pinnacle achievements of twentieth-century ballet. The work was the greatest example of the drambalet, a genre developed in the 1930s and 1940s under Stalin's government. Drambalety were often based on literary classics and attempted to combine massive historical set pieces with psychological drama. The works relied on a new type of pantomime developed during the 1930s through the collaboration of choreographers Vasily Vainonen, Rostislav Zakharov, and Leonid Lavrovsky with actor-dancers such as Ulanova. This new style of silent acting was more realistic and relied less on the audience's presumed knowledge of pantomime vocabulary or musical quotation. Drambalety operated on an immense scale, both in terms of duration and in terms of production. Large, historically accurate sets and well-populated casts not only endowed the ballets with a sense of grandeur and spectacle, they also lent an air of realism to the works, as mandated by socialist realism, the official Soviet aesthetic philosophy and style of the Stalinist period. Drambalet choreographers and librettists also introduced new subject matter to the ballet. Where nineteenth-century choreographers had adapted fairy tales, comedic stories, and swashbuckling adventures, drambalet choreographers adapted classic literary works by authors such as Pushkin, Shakespeare, and Balzac.[65] This shift was part of a general turn in Stalinist culture toward the literary, musical, and theatrical classics of the nineteenth century.[66]

While the drambalet was shaped by the aesthetics of socialist realism, its roots lay further in the past, in the theatrical innovations of Konstantin Stanislavsky and Vladimir Nemirovich-Danchenko. As founding directors of the Moscow Art Theatre (MXAT), Stanislavsky and Nemirovich-Danchenko had revolutionized Russian drama over the first two decades of the twentieth century, attempting to create a strictly realist style that would communicate both the outer and inner truth of a play. In order to accomplish this, Stanislavsky demanded intensive preparatory work and psychological analysis from his actors.[67] Stanislavsky's methods had a wide impact on the theatrical arts of Russia; by the first two decades of the twentieth century, choreographers such as Michel Fokine and Aleksander Gorsky had already begun to adapt the MXAT methods to ballet in works such as *Petrushka* and *Don Quixote*.[68]

During the 1930s and 1940s, the drambalet solidified the ties between MXAT and the ballet. Much as Stanislavsky's actors were called on to find the emotional truth in their parts, dancers were called upon to find the emotional and psychological underpinnings of their characters. Rostislav

Zakharov introduced the Stanislavskian technique of table work to the ballet, requiring dancers to research their characters before learning new choreography.[69] Stanislavsky's methods proved particularly useful to ballet toward the end of the 1930s, when choreographers turned away from creating the type of stock everyman roles found in *Bright Stream* or *Flames of Paris* and toward more complex characters in works such as *Lost Illusions* and *Romeo and Juliet*.[70]

While Soviet choreographers produced drambalety throughout the 1930s, 1940s, and even 1950s, the genre is widely thought to have culminated with Prokofiev and Lavrovsky's *Romeo and Juliet* in 1940.[71] Prokofiev completed the score in the mid-1930s, just following his return to the Soviet Union. His music filled the requirements of the drambalet nearly perfectly. The composer faithfully transcribed the events of the Shakespearean play, including even such minor scenes as Mercutio and Benvolio teasing Juliet's nurse.[72] The work is divided into fifty-two numbers, each very short, unlike the typical nineteenth-century ballet score, which was divided into long scenes and shorter set dances. Each one of the fifty-two numbers in *Romeo and Juliet* corresponds with some change in the dramatic action onstage and is titled by those actions, for instance "The Duke's Order," "Preparations for the Ball," and "Romeo Resolves to Avenge the Death of Mercutio."[73]

Moreover, the music is guided by narrative development. In the Act I, Scene 2 balcony duet, Prokofiev transforms the nineteenth-century *pas de deux* from a rigid formal structure into a flexible work of dramatic theater. In classical nineteenth-century ballet, a pas de deux consisted of four distinct parts: an opening *adagio* for two dancers together, a solo variation for each dancer, and a fast coda for the two dancers again. Over the arc of this four-part structure, tempos increased, culminating in a heart-pounding coda designed to show off the dancers' virtuosity. In the *Romeo and Juliet* balcony pas de deux, Prokofiev abandoned this classical structure in order to follow the emotional arc of Shakespeare's play. The balcony pas de deux does contain three sections of the nineteenth-century pas de deux: an opening, one variation for Romeo, and a final "Love Duet." Unlike in the classical form, however, in which there is a break between each short section for the dancers to bow, all three parts of the balcony pas de deux are played continuously, blending into one dramatic scene. Rather than constantly increasing in tempo, Prokofiev's duet both begins and ends slowly. This structure reflects Shakespeare's text, which climaxes near the middle of the scene as Romeo and

Juliet swear love to one another, and then lessens in tension as the characters make more prosaic arrangements to meet the following day.

In order to narrate the story, Prokofiev relied on a complex system of leitmotifs, short musical ideas associated with specific characters, objects, or concepts. These evolving musical gestures allowed Prokofiev to explore the Shakespearean story in great depth, as they created an auditory path through the ballet, linking different moments of the story and revealing character development through sound. For instance, the opening theme of the "Dance of the Knights" ["Tanets rytsarei"], perhaps the most famous musical selection of *Romeo and Juliet*, is strongly tied in the ballet to the Capulets. When this music first appears, for a dance at the Capulet ball, the melody arpeggiates a minor triad in uneven, dotted rhythms with a heavy string, percussion, and brass orchestration. The sound conveys the heavy power and oppression of the family. The same leitmotif returns in Act II to accompany Mercutio's fatal duel with Tybalt. In this later incarnation, the dotted minor triad serves as an accompaniment for a higher, screeching melody in the violins. In Act III, the same motif plays as Lord and Lady Capulet try to force their daughter to marry Paris. With each new appearance, the theme relates feudal restrictions and violence to the power and prestige that the Capulet family displayed at their ball. Ballet composers had used such techniques long before Prokofiev.[74] Nevertheless, they were particularly suited to the drambalet, since they allowed the audience greater understanding of elaborate literary plots and greater insight into the characters' psyches. Overall, *Romeo and Juliet* bears a much closer resemblance to Prokofiev's through-composed operas, such as *Fiery Angel* and *Betrothal at a Monastery*, than to his Diaghilev-era ballets. Musicologist Simon Morrison has even hypothesized that the earliest version of the libretto may have been drafted for a potential opera, rather than a ballet.[75]

As Morrison has chronicled, Prokofiev was deeply concerned when his new ballet languished in developmental purgatory for many years. While the composer managed to get a partial staging of the ballet in Brno in 1938, the work was not produced in full until 1940, when the directorship of the Kirov Theater assigned the project to Lavrovsky, a drambalet choreographer. Lavrovsky persuaded an unwilling Prokofiev to make certain changes to the score, including some alterations to the orchestration, the addition of a group dance in Act I, and two variations for the main characters, changes that made the work more palatable to the Soviet ballet establishment. Prokofiev protested, but Lavrovsky insisted or made the alterations himself, and the ballet premiered on January 11, 1940, at the Kirov Theater.[76]

Like Prokofiev's music, Lavrovsky's choreography hews very closely to the original play's narrative structure.[77] In many instances the transformation from Shakespearean text to dance could be incredibly slight, a tiny exaggeration of the movement an actor might make onstage. In Shakespeare's play, just before Romeo enters the Capulet ball, he has a strange foreboding feeling about the evening, saying to his friends, "for my mind misgives/some consequence yet hanging in the stars/Shall bitterly begin his fearful date/With this night's revels." He ends this speech by remarking, "But he that hath the steerage of my course,/Direct my suit. On, lusty gentlemen!"[78] In Lavrovsky's version, Romeo is about to exit stage left, going into the ball, when he pauses. The orchestra plays a fragment of the theme that will later appear in the balcony pas de deux, and Romeo turns, steps forward to the audience, and slowly touches his heart, a look of bewilderment on his face. He swings his arm back toward the ball, still looking at the audience, before collecting himself and heading off.

Lavrovsky's choreography was primarily based in the silent, realistic pantomime of the drambalet. Nevertheless, his ballet included numerous sections of more heightened dance, particularly the three pas de deux that form the structural backbone of the ballet. In these three sections, Lavrovsky employed a choreographic leitmotif to symbolize Romeo and Juliet's love for one another. As the two sweep together for the first time in the balcony pas de deux, the dancers arrange themselves standing side-by-side, Juliet performing an arabesque, with their inner arms raised above their heads and their outer arms pointing out to the sides (Figure 1.2b). Rather than supporting her at the waist, as is common in nineteenth-century ballet partnering, Romeo holds Juliet's upraised hand. Though the man still supports the woman, here that support does not imply that the woman is weak. Rather, the symmetry of the arabesque motif emphasizes the equality of their relationship. The motif is distinctly reminiscent of *Worker and Kolkhoz Woman*, the monumental sculpture created by Soviet artist Vera Mukhina for the 1937 Paris World's Fair (Figure 1.2a). In both statue and choreographic leitmotif, the man and woman are positioned parallel to one another, arms reaching upwards and forwards into a new world. Both the wedding and farewell pas de deux of Lavrovsky's *Romeo and Juliet* are saturated with iterations of the symmetrical arabesque motif (Figure 1.2c–d). In all three duets, Lavrovsky also uses a modified version of the motif, with the two dancers' inner arms wrapped

Figure 1.2 Vera Mukhina's *Worker and Kolkhoz Woman* (a), with three screen captures of Mikhail Lavrovsky and Natalia Bessmertnova in *Romeo and Juliet* (b–d). From *Romeo and Juliet* performed by the Bolshoi Ballet, 1976 (Kultur, 2004).

around each other rather than held up high. While the first version shows the revolutionary power of their love, this second hints at the characters' intimacy. Together, they help narrate the unfolding of Romeo and Juliet's relationship over the course of the ballet, tying together with the musical leitmotifs to elaborate and comment on the events of the play.

Lavrovsky also went to great efforts to stage his *Romeo and Juliet* in the style of historical realism that was fundamental to the drambalet. Following Stanislavsky's and Zakharov's practice of tablework, Lavrovsky opened rehearsals for the original production of *Romeo and Juliet* by discussing the ballet's historical setting. The choreographer encouraged his dancers to understand their parts by learning about the Crusades, the importance of family in the Renaissance, and the accumulation of wealth by aristocratic clans.[79]

Lavrovsky claimed that his choreography would also draw from historical dance sources. His realization of "The Dance of the Knights" was supposedly based on a sixteenth-century English dance.[80] Set designer Pëtr Viliams met Lavrovsky's demands, crafting sets and costumes with exquisite period details (Figure 1.3).[81]

Lavrovsky interpreted the setting of *Romeo and Juliet* through the Soviet lens of class struggle and historical teleology. He saw the play as the clash of two "epochs," the Middle Ages and the Renaissance. The earlier era is embodied in the older aristocrats. The production emphasizes their massive wealth and the gender inequality characteristic of their society.[82] In the "Dance of the Knights," the rich women of the Capulet family move so as to show off their elaborate and heavy dresses, and when the men drop pillows as part of the dance, a rank of servants comes onstage to pick them up. The new epoch is represented by the younger aristocrats, including Romeo, Juliet, and Mercutio. In rebelling against their parents, therefore, Romeo and Juliet are fighting against an older, oppressive class system.

Prokofiev shared neither Lavrovsky's historicism nor his Marxism. Just as the composer complained that Lavrovsky added traditional solo variations and group dances to the ballet, thus obscuring its narrative flow, so

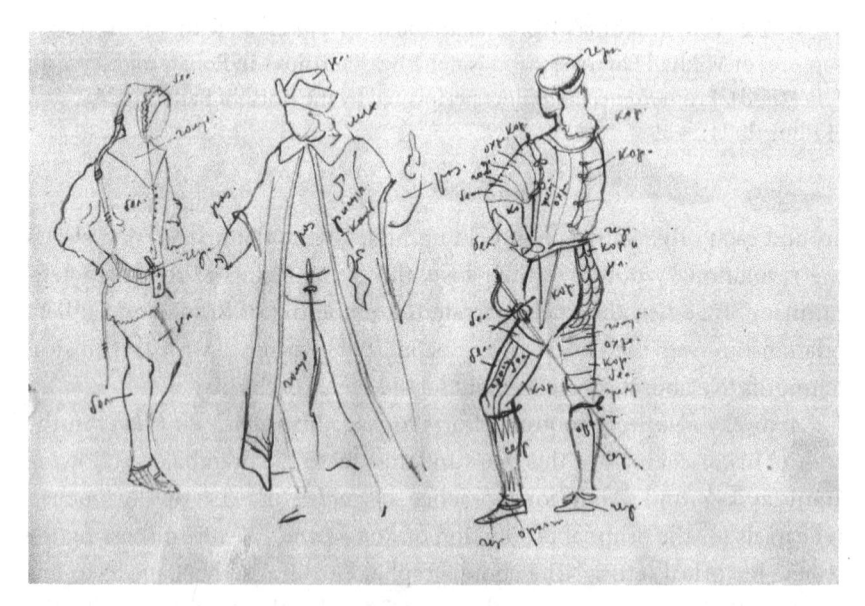

Figure 1.3 Costume sketches for *Romeo and Juliet* by Viliams, RGALI f. 2336 o. 1 d. 81 l. 23.

too did the choreographer discuss the anachronisms of Prokofiev's score, such as including a baroque gavotte at a Renaissance ball.[83] That Prokofiev and Lavrovsky disagreed about the production, however, did not prevent them from creating the premiere example of the dramballet in the Soviet canon, a work that helped propel Lavrovsky into the artistic directorship of the Bolshoi in the mid-1940s. In 1946, when Lavrovsky restaged *Romeo and Juliet* for the Bolshoi, again with Galina Ulanova in the lead role, the work won the Stalin Prize, first class.[84] It is hardly surprising then that, thirteen years later, *Romeo and Juliet* was the crown jewel of the Bolshoi's touring repertory.

Romeo and Juliet in the United States

American audiences in 1959 seemed to react to *Romeo and Juliet* as anticipated: with wild applause. American reviewers, however, criticized the ballet sharply for being old-fashioned. Their belief in the conservative nature of the Bolshoi reflected the fact that, rhetorically, the cultural Cold War was rooted in a disagreement about historical progress. According to the dominant political philosophies in both the Soviet Union and the United States, history was moving along a fixed course toward a better future. Soviet politicians believed, as Marxist theory taught, that the communist revolution had been an inevitable product of historical progression. American politicians, descendants of nineteenth-century liberalism, argued that they supported the appropriate, measured progress of history toward greater individual freedom.[85]

Thus, the clash between the two societies could be seen as a clash between two versions of a teleological narrative of world history. American scholars frequently asserted that the USSR was an example of a country stuck in the past, incapable of developing along the appropriate liberal historical narrative. This argument was articulated in one of its most influential forms by Russian American sociologist Nicholas Timasheff. In his 1946 book, *The Great Retreat*, Timasheff claimed that Stalin's government had abandoned any potentially revolutionary Bolshevik policies in favor of a retreat into nineteenth-century bourgeois values. Timasheff's Great Retreat thesis had an enormous impact on Soviet studies in the United States.[86] While Timasheff's analysis of the period has merits, particularly in pointing out the shocking change of tactics used under the Stalinist government, it also relied on a belief in historical progress. As historian Matthew E. Lenoe has pointed out, Timasheff's *Great Retreat* accepted as a premise "an extremely simple version of modernization theory in which 'backward' societies progress in geometrical fashion toward democracy, market economies, government provision of welfare benefits, and all the other fine characteristics of the 'advanced' Anglo-American states."[87]

Such a belief in historical progress lay at the heart of artistic modernism as well. By the 1950s, American dance, like many other Western art forms, had turned toward abstract formalism, and dance critics were beginning to narrate a history of their genre in which society moved naturally from realist art toward a more abstract aesthetic. Many American critics thus deemed *Romeo and Juliet* conservative because it did not resemble contemporaneous American ballet, particularly those works created by George Balanchine. In an article in the *New York Herald Tribune* entitled "Bourgeois Decor at Bolshoi," Emily Genauer called the sets "inferior . . . old-fashioned, heavy and unimaginative," and remarked that "Their choreography generally conforms more closely to tradition than ours."[88] Walter Terry of the *New York Herald Tribune* claimed that the ballet featured "very hearty and old-fashioned acting and some dancing."[89] Critics in 1959 largely ignored the score to *Romeo and Juliet*, probably because it was already widely known in the United States from the orchestral suites. Those who did mention the score claimed that Lavrovsky had failed to live up to Prokofiev's modernist vision. In the *New York Journal-American*, Miles Kastendieck remarked, "Pantomime and dancing are closely interwoven. . . . The impression remains that [Lavrovsky] has not achieved the contemporaneity Prokofieff expresses."[90]

Some American critics specifically mentioned Balanchine in their discussion of the Bolshoi. Louis Biancolli commented "They have much to teach us in how to stage a 3½-hour ballet without skimping on wardrobe or decor. But they have much to learn from companies like our City Center Ballet [Balanchine's company] in bold experimentation and freedom from stereotype."[91] Tellingly, John Martin of the *New York Times*, the only prominent American critic to defend Lavrovsky, did so by comparing *Romeo and Juliet* to one of Balanchine's works, *Orpheus*. Thus, while Martin could acknowledge the worth of Lavrovsky's choreography, he could only do so from within the confines of modernization theory, by reference to an American choreographer.[92]

Many American critics directly linked artistic conservatism to political conservatism, and used the ballet to connect the Soviet government to the nineteenth-century tsars. Genauer claimed that the old-fashioned nature of the Bolshoi could be explained by the fact that Diaghilev had fled St. Petersburg "in specific protest to the tradition-strangled Imperial ballet in Russia."[93] Thus Genauer not only suggested that ballet in Russia was more conservative than in the West, but she also equated the imperial institutions of the 1900s directly with the Soviet institutions of the 1950s. In a review for the *Sunday News*, John Chapman remarked that the company represented Russian rather than Soviet culture. In this instance, Chapman claimed to approve of the theater's conservatism, remarking "What was good enough for the Czars is good enough for me."[94] Such an approval or thirst for imperial Russian ballet would continue to play out in the American reception of the Kirov Ballet in 1961 and the second Bolshoi tour of the United States in 1962.

Many critics delighted in pointing out the hypocrisy of the fact that the Soviet government, supposedly dedicated to overturning the luxuries of the past, lavished such outrageous amounts of money on a ballet company. In *Women's Wear Daily*, Thomas Dash noted with irony that *Romeo and Juliet* was "a sumptuous production, which only communists can afford."[95] In a more pointed attack, Irving R. Levine wrote:

> In Russia, where food is a problem, clothing is a luxury, housing is a joke and nothing is in large supply except propaganda, the Bolshoi Ballet carries on with an opulence undreamed of by Britain's Royal Ballet, the Paris Opera Ballet, or the New York City Ballet.[96]

Levine went on to describe the Bolshoi Theater itself as a manifestation of this policy, illustrating for his readers the hall's "six red gold tiers and a center box once occupied by Imperial Czars, now by Communist czars."[97] While Levine's political jab is clear, his tone also evinces a slight jealousy about the Bolshoi's ample funding, a jealousy that would often percolate in American commentary on the ballet exchange. Levine's article was primarily political, and most of the theater reviewers were more circumspect. Overall, however, the newspapers suggested that by retaining the imperial trappings of the tsars, the Soviet government demonstrated that it was stuck in the nineteenth century.

Stone Flower in the Soviet Union and the United States

Romeo and Juliet had faced similar accusations about traditionalism and conservatism during the Bolshoi's 1956 tour of London, the first time that the company had ever appeared outside of the Soviet Union.[98] In addition to sharing some ideological concerns with their English counterparts, American reviewers were familiar with the British press, and probably incorporated some of the same terms and language into their own writing on the company, unconsciously or consciously.[99] On the Bolshoi's 1956 tour, however, the pleas for something more "modern" could be taken literally. At Covent Garden, the Bolshoi dancers had performed *Giselle, Swan Lake, Romeo and Juliet,* and *The Fountain of the Bakhchisarai.* Of those four, *Romeo and Juliet* was the most recent, having premiered in 1940.

On the Bolshoi's 1959 tour of the United States, however, they brought a much newer ballet, *Stone Flower,* a work that had premiered only two years previously and that was supposed to represent the forefront of new choreographic methods in the Soviet Union. *Stone Flower* was one of Prokofiev's last compositions. The libretto was based on Soviet writer Pavel Bazhev's 1939 collection of faux-fairy tales set in the Ural Mountains.[100] In the ballet, a young stone carver named Danila aspires to create a malachite vase in the shape of a flower so lifelike that it will embody the real beauty of nature. In his quest, he journeys to the Copper Mountain, where the magical Mistress of the Copper Mountain, after testing his resolve and selflessness, gives him the craft secrets he craves. At the same time, however, the Mistress has fallen in love with Danila and attempts to keep him in the Mountain. Back in the village, Danila's fiancée Katerina fends off the advances of the corrupt foreman Severyan. In the end, after seeing Danila and Katerina's love for each other, the Mistress of the Copper Mountain kills Severyan and allows the young stoneworker to return to his beloved.[101]

Lavrovsky wrote the scenario for *Stone Flower* with Mira Prokofieva during the late 1940s and early 1950s, a period in which composers and other artists were reeling from the 1948 shake-up at the Union of Soviet Composers.[102] The libretto for *Stone Flower* is thus relatively heavy-handed in its socialist message. As described in the story, Danila hopes to harness the stone carving technique to help "the people," though of course it is unclear why the people need flower-shaped vases so very badly. Severyan, the foreman, cruelly whips the villagers and leers at Katerina. The third act is set in a Ural mountain fair, which gives an excuse to present a large number of folk dances.[103]

Broadly speaking, the music to *Stone Flower* resembles Prokofiev's other two Soviet ballets, *Romeo and Juliet* and *Cinderella*. The score is structured narratively, as a string of short dramatic numbers. There are leitmotifs, most prominently the brass fanfare that introduces the Mistress of the Copper Mountain and saturates the rest of the ballet. In some ways, however, the ballet is slightly different. There are more incidental dance numbers than in *Romeo and Juliet*, including a number of waltzes for the stones in the garden of the Mistress of the Copper Mountain and one longer piece, the "Ural Fantasy," which opens the folk festival.[104]

Prokofiev originally wrote the score of *Stone Flower* for a 1954 drambalet production by Lavrovsky. The version performed on the Bolshoi's American tour, however, was a much more successful and innovative staging done in 1957 by choreographer Yuri Grigorovich. Grigorovich began his choreographic career in the early years of the Soviet Thaw, a period of dramatic political change triggered by Stalin's death in 1953. In the subsequent decade, Nikita Khrushchev and his followers pushed to de-Stalinize the Soviet Union. It was this political shift that opened up cultural exchange with the West. During the following decade, as the country moved away from many Stalinist policies, or at least was open to debates about the benefits of such policies, strict adherence to the tenets of socialist realism was also called into question.[105] In ballet, this manifested in increased criticisms of the drambalet. In its place, a young group of artists, including Grigorovich, promoted a new type of dance called choreographic symphonism or symphonic dance.[106] Instead of focusing on ballet's ties to dramatic theater and literature, the choreographic symphonists wanted to turn toward its similarities with music. They did not necessarily argue, however, that dance structures in a particular ballet had to follow the corresponding music exactly in real time. Rather, they advocated that choreographers make use of musical techniques such as motivic development and counterpoint. Choreographic symphonism did not reject narrative subjects for ballets, but instead embraced them as part of the music.[107]

In creating his version of *Stone Flower*, Grigorovich developed many of the artistic techniques that would prove fundamental to choreographic symphonism.[108] Foremost was a new pacing of the ballet. Grigorovich jettisoned almost all the realistic silent acting that had been so central to the drambalet. Instead, the work was danced from beginning to end. Grigorovich delineated the personalities of his main characters by creating a distinctive movement vocabulary for each one. The Mistress of the Copper Mountain, who in the story alternately takes the form of a lizard and a beautiful woman, dances with her elbows jutting out from her body and often bends her wrists to display her splayed-out palms. Like the libretto and music, Grigorovich's choreography reflects Marxist-Leninist ideology and Soviet symbolism. The movement vocabularies for the main characters thus reflect their class identities. Danila flies across the stage with fists and legs outstretched, as though constantly fighting his way through the world. Not only does his martial posing suggest the power of the working classes, but his leaping shows that he is literally uplifted and occupies a higher moral plane than the other characters. In contrast, Severyan's choreography is characterized by downward motion: a ponderous, wide swinging step with an extra stomp on the ground.

In this work, the site of meaning shifted away from the pantomime sections and toward choreographic leitmotifs, which had only played a small role in drambalety. Grigorovich combined, layered, recalled, and developed these much as Prokofiev worked with his musical leitmotifs. Grigorovich would later expand on this technique further in works such as the 1968 *Spartacus*, but already in *Stone Flower* certain choreographic combinations returned over the course of the ballet, linking important events and characters. For instance, Katerina's choreography emerges from the folk dances performed for the celebration of her betrothal to Danila, in which she and her friends hold their arms out to the sides with their palms facing forward. Elsewhere in the ballet, Katerina often returns to a similar pose, keeping her arms in front of her, palms facing upwards, and moving with her feet in parallel rather than turned out. The constant use of this movement endows Katerina with a sense of innocence and moral purity as well as a connection to the peasant class.

Simon Virsaladze, the designer for *Stone Flower* and Grigorovich's lifelong collaborator, rejected the strict realism of the drambalet era. In its stead, Virsaladze crafted a simple set that stood at the back and allowed the rest of the stage to be occupied by the dancers. This stylized backdrop takes the form of a giant piece of malachite, which opens up to reveal more realistic sets at various points in the action, such as Danila's peasant hut, the woods, and the folk festival. The intense green of the malachite dominates the ballet, and while costumes are often realistic, they too make symbolic use of color—jewel tones, particularly green, for the supernatural characters, contrasting reds for the folk festival scene, and white for the main characters and their friends.

From the perspective of the drambalet, one of the most surprising scenes in Grigorovich's *Stone Flower* was the "Ural Rhapsody." Within the plot of the ballet, "Ural Rhapsody" depicts the opening of a fair in the Ural Mountains. Unusually for Prokofiev's Soviet ballet scores, the number is quite long, lasting over eight minutes.[109] On the broad level, the number can be divided into two sections, the first tinged with minor mode and the second half with major. Within each of these sections, Prokofiev contrasts two or three themes. Many of the melodies have a folk-like flair; the two main themes of the rhapsody's second half are taken from folk dances from the Act I betrothal scene, one from the Dance of the Maidens and the other from the Dance of the Bachelors. Prokofiev also plays with contrasting metrical structures in the rhapsody. In the first half of the piece, the meter stresses each quarter note, pushing the dance to a brisk, near-frenetic pace. In the second half of the rhapsody, Prokofiev halves that pulse, instead emphasizing every half note; the surface of the music is noticeably less busy, and the piece develops an almost majestic presence. In both sections, the meter switches multiple times, and Prokofiev builds up to the climax of the eight-minute selection as much through metrical disjuncture as he does through harmonic tension.

In traditional drambalet productions, Soviet critics would have expected this scene to be staged with a realistic pantomime fair. Prokofiev presumably anticipated that the rhapsody would look something like the first scene of Michel Fokine's *Petrushka,* only more rural. Instead, in Grigorovich's production, as Soviet critic Mikhail Gabovich writes, "we see a stunning whirlwind of movement . . . where dance finally absorbs and assimilates pantomime."[110] Groups of dancers weave about the stage in a counterclockwise circular pattern, eventually coming together to dance around a maypole. Grigorovich's choreography follows a similar formal layout to Prokofiev's music, juxtaposing contrasting motifs. Like the music, the main choreographic motifs are drawn from the betrothal scene in Act I. Unlike Prokofiev's music, however, the choreography is not split in two; rather the dance is a long-form juxtaposition of the three main choreographic motifs. The choreography is sometimes layered contrapuntally; certain dance steps continue in the background while other steps are performed in the foreground. Grigorovich takes advantage of Prokofiev's large-scale metrical framework by using steps from the Dance of the Maidens more and more over the course of the piece. In these folk-inspired movements, the performers' long, elegant gait gives the slower metrical pulse a sensation akin to gliding. In the climactic moment of the music, the Dance of the Maidens is synthesized with the running motif until they converge into a unison of the Dance of the Bachelors. Together, this "whirlwind" that could both tell a story and reflect formal musical principles pointed to a new direction for ballet, one that would reign triumphant in the Soviet Union for the next thirty years.[111]

Two years after its premiere in Leningrad, Grigorovich restaged his production of *Stone Flower* at the Bolshoi. The work's Moscow debut took place in March 1959, just weeks before the company began its American tour.[112] Soviet critics were delighted with Grigorovich and Virsaladze's production of *Stone Flower* at the Bolshoi. The review of the ballet for *Muzykalnaia zhizn* signed by Dmitri Shostakovich claimed that the music, dance, and design of the production were combined "as though created by one artistic will."[113] Some reviews of the ballet mentioned that it would be included on the Bolshoi's tour of the United States, and a short column signed by American singer Paul Robeson in *Sovetskii artist* claimed that he was sure the ballet would meet with a positive reception there.[114]

The excitement trickled into American newspapers. In the days leading up to the Bolshoi's arrival in the United States, Grigorovich's *Stone Flower* was hailed in the American press as the Soviet Union's first real foray into modern ballet. As always, such modernist rhetoric was tied to politics. Margaret Lloyd of the *Christian Science Monitor* claimed, "Artistically, *The Stone Flower* is probably the first revolutionary ballet in the history of revolutionary Russia."[115]

In their observations on *Stone Flower*, American critics transliterated the ballet through their experiences with American neoclassical works, particularly those by Balanchine. The reviewers generally seemed to believe that the purportedly "modern" section of the ballet must be the stone dances, since it bore some surface similarities to Balanchine's ballets. This scene comprised a series of dances for the Mistress's anthropomorphized Jewels, played by women in brilliant, skin-tight costumes. While these dances have a place in the story arc of the ballet, as they show Danila first admiring the stone garden and then mastering his powers, the focus is more on movement than on plot. As in many of Balanchine's ballets, ranks of ballerinas move about the stage in abstract patterns and perform modified versions of classical steps. Grigorovich's jewel-women have their hands held up behind their heads with their elbows out, transforming ballet's traditional, soft *port de bras* into something sharp and gem-like. Furthermore, Virsaladze's open, uncluttered set and skin-tight costumes are similar to the modernist New York City Ballet productions, in which dancers perform on a bare stage and wear practice costumes of leotards and tights.[116] In an article from March 22 that anticipated the Bolshoi's arrival, John Martin informed his readers

> The present production [of *Stone Flower*] ... is the first Soviet ballet to go in for "modern" ideas of décor, with Versaladze [sic] as the designer. Undoubtedly influenced by the company's recent contacts with Western Europe, where its productions were generally considered old-fashioned, this revival appears to have been conceived specifically for the American tour.[117]

The American reviewers' focus on the Act I jewel dances indicates how little they understood the Bolshoi's new aesthetic. These dances were rarely singled out for praise by Soviet reviewers. Instead, the Soviet critics focused on the combination of pantomime and dance, the strong connections between classical and folk movement throughout the ballet, the union of music and choreography, and Virsaladze's simple but convincing sets. The American critics, however, trained to view skin-tight costumes and plotless ballet as modern, searched for modernity in those sections of Grigorovich's ballet most similar to what they knew.

Stone Flower thus did not live up to the Americans' expectations for modernism. Most critics accused the production of being a passé imitation of twentieth-century American dance. Kastendieck wrote that the *Stone Flower* showed that "what is new in Russia has become almost routine in New York" and compared the jewel scenes to Radio City Music Hall productions.[118] Martin noted that "its modernity is definitely dated," and Walter Sorell remarked that "Most of its choreographic conceptions strike us as scarcely modern; some of it would be tagged vintage in 1930."[119] This time, even Prokofiev's music did not escape the general criticism. Jay Harrison accused it of being "nothing but a nineteenth century score brought up to date by the inclusion of a wrong note here and there and the observance of some rhythmic amenities said to be modern."[120]

The Choreography-Performer Split

The American critical disdain for Soviet choreography and even for Prokofiev's later Soviet compositions clashed with the ecstatic praise for the company's dancers. Often this clash took place in a single review, as critics excoriated the choreographers for the same dramatic practices that they praised in the dancers' performances. Walter Terry wrote that Ulanova "makes every gesture a poem in dance: her very walk is like a thermometer of emotional changes; her runs are alive with urgency." This was part of the same review in which he called Lavrovsky's production of *Romeo and Juliet* "heavy, ponderous, and, at times, dull."[121] Kastendieck applauded Kondratieva's lyricism and Plisetskaya's virtuosity but complained bitterly that the Bolshoi had substituted such virtuosity for artistic creation.[122]

The critical framework that American reviewers employed during the 1959 tour was based on a gendered understanding of ballet that split the mental act of choreography from the physical act of performance. Western philosophers from Aristotle to Descartes have posited that the mind is separate from the body, and both dance and gender scholars have frequently pointed out that this split has been associated with a gender binary. As Elizabeth Grosz wrote in the introduction to her 1994 work *Volatile Bodies,* "Women are somehow *more* biological, *more* corporeal, and *more* natural than men."[123] In the world of classical ballet, men have traditionally held positions as artistic directors and choreographers, while women have been valued for their beauty as dancers.[124]

When the Bolshoi ballet company performed in the United States, their roles as diplomats brought a newly political set of meanings to the traditionally gendered split between choreographer and dancer. American politics during the Cold War, particularly foreign politics, were also highly gendered. Not only did men occupy almost all important American diplomatic and political positions, but gendered language and concepts enforced a certain code of masculinity on those working in the State Department. In historian Robert D. Dean's words, the American diplomatic elite was an "imperial brotherhood."[125] American dance critics, while not members of that brotherhood, were part of a society that believed foreign policy to be a masculine arena. In reviewing these productions, therefore, these critics often approached the "masculine" parts of the production—the choreography, music, and set design—as political, while they approached the "feminine" side of the production—the performance—as non-political.

Critics and reporters endlessly described the physical presence of the female dancers. Milton Bass jokingly remarked that the Bolshoi dancers refuted American propaganda about how ugly Russian women were, writing, "I don't know about the girls they left behind them, but every one of the Bolshoi dancers has a marvelously slender body and a pixie-like charm that is upsetting."[126] American newspapers published many versions of the same photograph of six Bolshoi ballerinas to announce the company's arrival.[127] In these images, the women are displayed in a long line-up, each with a bouquet of roses; the props and dress highlight their femininity and the pose suggests the dancers' interchangeability and their desire to please their audiences.

Toward the end of the Bolshoi's stay in New York, the distinction between the political, intellectual side of diplomacy and the physical performance of the Bolshoi dancers was made explicit in a remark by Drew Pearson of the *New York Mirror*:

> So far, diplomats have not been able to bridge the gap between the political animosities of the United States and the Soviet Union; nor have [. . .] the heads of states meeting at the summit in 1955. But the lithe beauty of Ulanova's body and face; the suppleness of Susanna Zayugina in the Sabre Dance and the ragged expressive hands of Yuri Faier as he led 70 American musicians and 100 Russian dancers in perfect rhythm—they did what trained diplomats and skilled politicians have not been able to do. They helped the Russian and American people understand each other.[128]

In his remark, Pearson carefully juxtaposes Ulanova's and Zayugina's innate feminine physicality against the masculine heads—literally the minds—of state. In doing so, he exaggerates the irrationality of the performers' power and the strange juxtaposition he sees between politics and dance.

To some degree, the Bolshoi's self-presentation welcomed this treatment. The company performed ballets with virtuosic main roles, drawing attention to the women who performed them. Hurok, anxious for the tour to please American audiences, constantly put the ballerinas in front of the cameras. Furthermore, since audiences were happy and critics pleased with the dancers, it was to a large degree considered a success for the Bolshoi Theater and for the Soviet government. Nevertheless, the American reviews created a twofold understanding of Soviet ballet that has persisted in the scholarly literature and dance criticism up to today. They separated out the choreography and composition of Soviet ballets from their performance, judging the first according to the standards of modernization theory and the second according to the standards of celebrity culture.

The reception of Soviet ballet continues to reverberate in current political discourse. International relations scholar Kimberly Williams, in her monograph *Imagining Russia*, analyzes representations of Russia in American popular culture since the fall of the Soviet Union in 1991. According to Williams, Americans, rejoicing in their Cold War triumph, frequently personify Russia as a victimized woman in need of an American cowboy to rescue her. Williams believes that this gendered representation of Russia has had practical political ramifications, and she posits that it probably developed out of Cold War–era American culture.[129] The Bolshoi's tour of the United States in 1959 and the American reaction to it represents just such an early instance of the discursive patterns that Williams describes.

The simultaneous desire to fetishize the Soviet ballerinas and to relegate them to an apolitical status betrayed a genuine nervousness on the part of Americans about the potential power of dance in the Cold War. Some American writers made jokes about the Bolshoi ballet "conquering" Americans, and others tittered that their loyalties could not so easily be bought, however much they liked the Bolshoi dancers. Inez Robb, for instance, joked that "I have survived my brush with Communist culture unscathed in my devotion to life, liberty and the pursuit of happiness, no less than in my dedication to freedom, democracy and the capitalist system."[130] These comments were rarely posed as anything but punch lines, but the laughter still betrayed their authors' uncertainties. Americans genuinely worried that appreciation for Soviet culture might slide ever so gradually into appreciation for communism. The American critics both loved and feared their Soviet visitors, and they dealt with this fear by turning to the traditional language and ideology of gender dualism, excoriating the mind—the male choreography—but admiring the body—the female performances. In doing so, they could both welcome and disarm the Soviet threat.

2
Bringing an American Report Card to Russia

American Ballet Theatre's 1960 Tour of the Soviet Union

Until September 13, 1960, no American ballet company had ever danced in the Soviet Union. On that day, American Ballet Theatre stepped out onto the stage of the Stanislavsky Theater in Moscow, Russia.[1] As the curtain rose, the Soviet audience was greeted by a familiar sight: ranks of ballerinas in tutus, each one with her feet in fifth position and arms resting in a graceful *port de bras*. As the conductor brought his baton down, the strings played the sparse and sharply accented opening of Pyotr Tchaikovsky's Suite No. 3 for Orchestra, Mvt. IV. The dancers began to move simply through a series of classical ballet positions, led by Chilean-born ballerina Lupe Serrano and Ukrainian American dancer Igor Youskevitch. The ballet was George Balanchine's *Theme and Variations*, and it was followed on the program by a series of American and Russian works that included music by Aaron Copland and Johann Strauss and choreography by Marius Petipa and Agnes de Mille.[2]

Much has been made of the stark difference between American and Soviet ballet during the twentieth century and of the astounding newness of American works when they appeared in Russia in the 1960s. American Ballet Theatre's Soviet tour, however, was not calibrated to shock its audiences. Rather, the programming and cast choices positioned the company as the locus of a global network, with a roster of international ballet stars and a repertoire of Russian, American, and European works, some of which were very familiar to the Soviet audiences. The cast of Ballet Theatre's tour included Native American dancer Maria Tallchief, American immigrants like Youskevitch, and some dancers without American citizenship, such as Danish principal Erik Bruhn. They pirouetted and arabesqued to the steps of choreographers foreign and domestic, modern and classical, to the music of composers including Jacques Offenbach, Frédéric Chopin, and Leonard Bernstein.[3]

Ballet in the Cold War. Anne Searcy, Oxford University Press (2020). © Oxford University Press.
DOI: 10.1093/oso/9780190945107.001.0001.

The international conglomeration that Ballet Theatre presented to its audience was the product of tensions within and without the company. Over a four-year period, from 1956 to 1960, these played out in a struggle between Ballet Theatre director Lucia Chase, the American State Department, and Goskontsert to set up the Soviet exchange tour. Up to a month before Ballet Theatre's opening in Moscow, it seemed more likely than not that the company would never make it to the Soviet Union. When Chase first envisioned the tour in 1956, she dreamed of introducing Soviet audiences to American choreography. But as the long years leading up to Ballet Theatre's premiere eroded confidence in the company and presented diplomatic problems, the venture turned into a goodwill tour designed to please its audience in any way possible. In practice this meant taking on dancers no longer affiliated with the company and rounding out the repertoire with a number of Russian ballets.

At the same time, the company did fulfill its promise to show American ballet to the Soviet Union, performing populist works by Agnes de Mille, Jerome Robbins, and William Dollar: *Rodeo, Fancy Free,* and *The Combat*. Even these pieces, however, turned out to have strong resonances with the Soviet audiences. In their essentializing nationalism, realistic narratives and settings, and emphasis on hyper-masculinity, the American populist ballets bore a close similarity to Soviet works from the same period. It was through these similarities, not through a parade of difference, that Ballet Theatre impressed its hosts with the value of American ballet.

Indeed, throughout the tour, the company embodied two different images: one, a homegrown American ensemble with American repertoire and dancers, and the other, an international body of stars conversant in a variety of classical and contemporary styles. That the company presented such seemingly contradictory profiles turned out not to be a weakness, however, but rather one of its great strengths. The intermingling of dancers from various European and American countries represented the growing collaborations among Western elites. The United States' need to make international alliances during the Cold War, epitomized in the development of NATO, helped foster this sense of international community.[4] Moreover, balancing its American populism and Russian classicism, all wrapped up in a lighthearted package, American Ballet Theatre appealed to the similarities between American and Soviet dance.

Because of its conciliatory rather than confrontational style, Ballet Theatre's Soviet tour has been almost completely overshadowed in the historical record by the New York City Ballet's tour two years later. While the New York City Ballet tour has been discussed in multiple academic articles and is frequently referenced as a major event of the cultural Cold War, Ballet Theatre's earlier tour has only been the subject of a single academic article. When the Ballet Theatre tour is brought up, it is usually treated as a short introduction to New York City Ballet.[5] By reintroducing this tour into the story of the Cold War cultural exchange, this chapter blurs the stark contrasts that are often set up between American and Soviet art. Because Ballet Theatre presented Soviet viewers with works that responded well to Soviet transliterations, their audiences understood and valued their performances. By all accounts, the shows were almost all sold out and viewers applauded enthusiastically. Soviet critics welcomed the company's Russian works and appreciated the chance to see contemporary American ballet. Thus, the tour has been overlooked in the historical record for precisely the same reason that it was so successful: because the company never sought to undermine Soviet ballet but rather strove to present itself as a worthy player on the international stage.

Ballet as American Cultural Diplomacy

American Ballet Theatre's 1960 tour set out to answer a question that had haunted dance in the United States for half a century: could ballet be American? To be sure, there were specific and immediate pressures in 1960 forcing Chase to rearrange her repertory and cast for the Soviet tour. Those pressures, however, reflected a tension that had been at the heart of the company since its founding. In fact, in many ways the 1960 tour was merely the culmination of a decades-long struggle within Ballet Theatre over this very issue.

The foundation for Ballet Theatre was laid in the 1920s and 1930s, an era in which most ballet companies in the United States performed under the moniker "Russian Ballet" or "Ballets Russes." Ballet Theatre was no exception. The troupe's first incarnation was as the Mikhail Mordkin Ballet Company, a group formed by one of Anna Pavlova's former partners to showcase his choreography and provide jobs for his dancing students. In 1939, Mordkin was pushed out of the leadership role and the company was simply renamed Ballet Theatre. After Mordkin's exit, the troupe's most prominent choreographer was Michel Fokine, the Russian émigré who had earlier created *Firebird, Petrushka,* and *Les Sylphides.* In the early days following its transformation into Ballet Theatre, the company toured under the management of Sol Hurok, and the impresario advertised them as "the greatest in Russian Ballet."[6]

At the same time that the company possessed some Russian ballet bona fides, however, it was also an organization based in the United States. Some of Ballet Theatre's managers wanted the company recognized more for its American repertoire, specifically for its ballets by artists born in the United States. During the 1940s, Ballet Theatre produced a number of ballets by American-born artists, commissioning Robbins's *Fancy Free*, de Mille's *Tally-Ho* and *Fall River Legend*, Eugene Loring's *The Great American Goof*, and re-staging de Mille's *Rodeo* and Loring's *Billy the Kid*. In 1946, the side of the management more invested in its Americanness, Lucia Chase and scenic designer Oliver Smith, took control of the company away from Hurok.[7]

Chase's decision to seize power in 1946 reflected her increasingly central role in Ballet Theatre. Chase was born in 1897 to a wealthy Connecticut family. As a child, she had trained as an actress, dancer, and singer. In her early twenties, she moved to New York to pursue a career in theater. At the age of twenty-nine, Chase married a wealthy industrialist, who died only a few years later. Despite the setbacks of the Great Depression, Chase's husband left her and her two sons the handsome fortune of seven million dollars. In the wake of his death, Chase decided to pursue ballet, joining the Mikhail Mordkin company as a founding member. In addition to dancing in the company, Chase also financed Ballet Theatre semi-anonymously through all its various incarnations. She almost single-handedly met the deficit in the company's yearly expenditures, which gradually led to a more and more public administrative role as she aged out of dancing.[8]

During the 1950s, just as Chase openly became the company's director, Ballet Theatre began an international touring schedule, which quickly merged with a public diplomatic function. The group's first tour of Europe, in 1950, was sponsored in part by the US State Department. This trip was successful enough that the State Department began choosing the troupe on a regular basis for cultural diplomacy tours. Such diplomatic, international success also cemented Ballet Theatre's status as a national organization.[9] It was only during this period that the company took the name "American Ballet Theatre," rather than Ballet Theatre, specifically to mark it on the international stage.[10]

Ballet Theatre had been touring on behalf of the US government for six years when members of the State Department began seriously considering the possibility of an exchange with the Soviet Union. Sending an American ballet company to Russia quickly became a major topic of conversation at the ANTA dance advisory panel, a group that included among its members Chase and de Mille.[11] The idea made most of the dance experts nervous. Ballet was defined in the West as an inherently Russian art form, and Soviet ballet was still a vast unknown. To the panel, the idea of the Soviet tour seemed a risky proposition. One member commented, "Bringing a ballet company to Russia is like bringing in a report card."[12]

Chase and her fellow ABT leaders, however, very quickly saw the benefits of the tour for her company. Not only would the organization make a certain amount of money from the exchange, but far more important, it would gain the permanent cachet of being the first American troupe to dance in the USSR. It would cement Ballet Theatre's status as American Ballet Theatre. In late 1956, well before the Lacy-Zarubin agreement was signed, Ballet Theatre's leadership began lobbying for a Soviet tour.[13]

In response, the ANTA panel was divided. Ballet Theatre may have been the most important American ballet company in the 1940s, but over the course of the 1950s, it had lost a certain amount of prestige, funding, and personnel to Balanchine's New York City Ballet. Some of Ballet Theatre's best dancers, including Maria Tallchief, had transferred to Balanchine's company. Nevertheless, early in ANTA panel discussions about the Soviet tour, New York City Ballet leadership indicated that they had no interest in touring the Soviet Union.[14] When Balanchine's company was put out of the running, Ballet Theatre was chosen almost as a default.

From the time Ballet Theatre became the front runner for the Soviet tour, problem after problem beset the company. Chase was particularly faced with difficulties regarding personnel, questions that were intimately tied not only to the quality of the dancing but also to the question of what would make the company seem American.[15] Many dance panel members believed that the company should not perform in Russia without Tallchief, Youskevitch, Alicia Alonso, and Nora Kaye, all important dancers who had worked with Ballet Theatre during its heyday but since moved on to other jobs.[16] Other panel members were concerned about sending any dancer to the Soviet Union without American citizenship, including two of Ballet Theatre's remaining principals, Violette Verdy and Eric Bruhn, who were, respectively, French and Danish. Chase was enraged, stating at a dance panel meeting in October 1957, "If you want to choose a Company, start your own. *This* is the Ballet Theatre."[17]

In 1958, however, an unexpected calamity befell the company, diminishing their chances of securing the Soviet tour. While traveling in Western Europe for the State Department, a truck containing Ballet Theatre's scenery, costumes, and personal effects caught fire and was reduced to cinders. The equipment for twelve ballets was lost.[18] The accident made the Soviet trip even more alluring, as the government's financial support could have helped put the company back on its feet. However, just as Chase desperately needed ANTA's help, the State Department decided to issue a crackdown on the panel's use of the cultural exchange program to finance only a few prominent dance groups. Without the financial help from a State Department–sponsored tour, Chase and Smith were forced to disband the company.[19] During the aftermath of the fire, in the fall of 1958, Jerome Robbins's Ballets U.S.A. became the favored company for a Soviet tour.[20] Chase never gave up, however, and continued to press the ANTA panel at every opportunity. In 1959, following information that the Soviet Ministry of Culture had deemed Robbins's company unsuitable, the panel's opinion swung back in the favor of Ballet Theatre.[21]

Thus it was a somewhat worn-out and diminished company that finally secured the coveted Soviet tour for 1960. Perhaps as a result of the debilitating financial losses and the break in continuity, Chase became more accommodating about recruiting dancers to join Ballet Theatre just for the summer tour. Members of the ANTA panel sent out letters badgering important ballerinas to accept the contract by claiming that participation was a patriotic duty.[22] In her memoirs, Maria Tallchief recounts the unusual pressure she was under:

> It was explained to me that this was a very important tour with political consequences. Ballet Theatre would be breaking barriers, and the State Department was very much involved in working out the logistics. A great deal was at stake. No one wanted to risk the off chance that a major American performing arts institution might have anything less than a triumph in the Soviet Union. So, after talking to government representatives, I felt that as an American I owed it to my country. I gave in.[23]

Even after securing ANTA support, Ballet Theatre continued to face repeated challenges to its status as the selected group. The first came from the home front, when the company opened its two-week spring season at the

Metropolitan Opera House in April 1960. The newly assembled dancers were able to rehearse only briefly before the opening performance.[24]

The season was a disaster. John Martin eviscerated it in the May 15 issue of the *New York Times*, declaring, "If the American Ballet Theatre actually goes to the Soviet Union (which heaven forbid!) to represent the United States... it will be a profound national humiliation."[25] Martin criticized the dancing, particularly on the part of the inadequately rehearsed corps, but focused the bulk of his wrath on Chase for failing to hire an artistic director. The review went on to remark that "to send a drab, hastily thrown-together Gopher Prairie Civic Ballet to a country where the ballet has had 200 years of richly subsidized, carefully administered, deeply dedicated, universally honored achievements, is irresponsible in the extreme."[26] In the conclusion, he called on the ANTA panel to rescind their support of the company.

Martin's review immediately took a heavy toll on Ballet Theatre's domestic business prospects. Letters poured in from American venues, asking if the company was still dancing at its former high standard. Many of Ballet Theatre's business contacts expressed concern that ANTA might withdraw support; they had in part booked the company with the hope that the luster of the Soviet tour would sell tickets. A few canceled, and many more threatened to cancel, their engagements with Ballet Theatre.[27]

Such concern was not unfounded. On April 21 and May 11, the ANTA panel convened meetings at which they discussed the disastrous Met season and debated the possibility of canceling the Soviet tour. In the end, the panel promised to maintain its support but reserved the right to cancel in the event that certain conditions were not met.[28] Ballet Theatre was instructed to recruit Kaye and Tallchief for appearances in Russia, improve the conducting, and secure de Mille's blessing on their performances of *Rodeo*.[29] Three of the demands were followed, but while Kaye considered joining the company and assisted Tallchief in learning some of her parts, in the end she declined to sign the contract to appear in the Soviet Union.[30] Nevertheless, the panel never again threatened to revoke the tour.

At the same time that Martin's review put pressure on Ballet Theatre, the choice of tour impresario turned into an unexpected difficulty. Initially, Sol Hurok had expressed interest in conducting the negotiations, but he quickly backed out of the arrangements.[31] In his place, the State Department was forced to find a new tour manager who had the necessary Russian-language skills and contacts to organize the visit. They chose Anatole Heller, a French impresario who led the Parisian agency Bureau Artistique International.[32]

Heller and his company had worked with ANTA before, organizing tours for the Cleveland Orchestra and the New York Philharmonic.[33] Unfortunately, Heller had also worked with Ballet Theatre in the past and not at all to Chase's liking. Chase complained that Heller had tried to come between her and the dancers, believing that he could run the company better.[34] To make matters worse, following Martin's disastrous *New York Times* review, Chase and the rest of the Ballet Theatre staff were convinced that Heller was circulating the bad press around Europe in an attempt to poison their reception.[35] In his dealings with the Ballet Theatre staff, Heller was at times dismissive. Charles Payne, the troupe's associate director, commented that he thought Heller was impressed by the Russians and "more convinced than ever of the stupidity of Americans and, I would guess, the poor quality of American ballet."[36]

Despite these fears, Heller did turn out to be a competent negotiator, capable of working with the Soviets. This was important, because in addition to the domestic complications that Ballet Theatre faced, they also encountered stiff resistance from Goskontsert. The bureau proved strangely reluctant to sign a contract with Ballet Theatre, despite a binding agreement in which the Soviet Union had promised to host another American tour in 1960. Part of Goskontsert's hesitation was likely due to financial pressure from their government. According to Heller's information, when Ballet Theatre asked for its invitation in spring 1960, Goskontsert had already used up its 1960 budget, as well as a portion of the 1961 budget, on a very successful tour of *My Fair Lady*.[37]

Moreover, Goskontsert operated under a directive to ensure the ideological and artistic quality of the groups touring in the Soviet Union.[38] The Soviet bureaucrats from Goskontsert, according to Heller, felt that European impresarios were passing off inferior attractions on them, and they did not want to be hoodwinked into taking American Ballet Theatre.[39] As time went on, the delay itself became part of the problem in securing Soviet booking. The possibility of arranging for theaters on such short notice in multiple Soviet cities seemed ever slimmer.[40] In the summer of 1960 Heller struggled to pin Goskontsert to a firm contract. He flew to Moscow for negotiations while Ballet Theatre conducted their tour of Western Europe. All the while the tour's September fate hung over their heads. Would they go home, disappointed, or journey on to Moscow? Chase, other Ballet Theatre managers, and even Heller fretted over the uncertainty of the tour's future.[41]

Some progress was made in late June, when Goskontsert agreed to accept Ballet Theatre as long as a specialist from the Soviet Union saw and approved them.[42] During the company's performances in Holland, Alexei Chichinadze, a dancer and choreographer at the Stanislavsky Theater in Moscow, arrived to observe the company. Ballet Theatre's regisseur, Dimitri Romanoff, who spoke Russian, met Chichinadze at the theater and accompanied him to his seats. After the evening's performance, Chichinadze sat down with Romanoff to give his opinions on all the ballets. Chichinadze felt that *Graduation Ball, Les Sylphides, Fancy Free,* and the company's nineteenth-century pas de deux should be taken to Moscow, but that Antony Tudor's *Miss Julie* and Agnes de Mille's *Fall River Legend* should be left out of the Soviet programs. On balance, Chichinadze agreed to recommend the company to Goskontsert.[43]

Following this favorable report in mid-July, the bureaucratic wheels began to turn again, but another month of stalling tried everyone's frayed nerves. Finally, on August 17, Chase received word that the tour negotiations were complete. She sent a telegram to the Ballet Theatre offices in New York that read: "Contract signed cheers."[44]

The Diplomatic Advantage of Mixed Bills

The long process of securing the Soviet tour had a palpable effect on programming choices. Initially, Chase and other Ballet Theatre advisors hoped to use the trip to introduce Soviet audiences to populist American choreography, and many saw the ability to do this as the company's primary strength. In 1956, Chase's son, who was serving as the president of the Ballet Theatre Foundation, argued in a letter to the ANTA dance chairperson that the company's American repertory was the primary reason that it should be chosen: "The Ballet Theatre would be especially welcome because it has the widest existing repertory of ballets conveying the spirit of America. Ballets such as *Billy the Kid, Interplay, The Fall River Legend, Rodeo,* and *Fancy Free* would delight the Russian public."[45] In the same year Ballet Theatre's business manager argued that the company could "prove that American ballet is creative and not merely imitative . . . show that American ballet is vital, original and distinctly American in character . . . [and] present a vivid picture of American life in ballets such as *Rodeo, Fancy Free, Billy the Kid* and *Interplay*."[46]

In these early planning phases, Chase repeatedly singled out two works to represent the American side of Ballet Theatre's repertoire: the 1938 *Billy the Kid*, with music by Aaron Copland and choreography by Eugene Loring, and the 1948 *Fall River Legend*, with music by Morton Gould and choreography by Agnes de Mille. Programming for the Soviet tour went through dozens of drafts, and in almost every one Chase included both ballets.[47] That Chase believed so strongly in these two works gives a fuller sense of the way she envisioned both her company and American ballet. Both *Fall River Legend* and *Billy the Kid* were short narrative ballets set in the United States, depicting the type of everyday characters that exemplified populist artwork of the 1930s and 1940s. Their scores incorporated folk tunes and jazz elements. Both were created by white composer-choreographer teams born in the United States. Finally, *Fall River Legend* and *Billy the Kid* were tragedies, revealing dramatic character development through movement.

Chase was not alone in believing that American ballet was best exemplified by *Fall River Legend* and *Billy the Kid*. Both pieces had achieved great critical success on Ballet Theatre's tours of Europe, and *Fall River Legend* was held in particularly high esteem. According to a report of the company's 1950 tour, reviewers in London declared *Fall River Legend*, which dramatizes the Borden family murders, "the first truly great ballet tragedy."[48] During the summer of 1960, Chase declared that "The [ANTA] Panel feels strongly that [*Fall River Legend*] is one of our most important American works."[49]

Chase's plan to present populist American choreography, however, faced resistance both at home and abroad. The ANTA panel, Chase included, worried that by avoiding standard ballet classics such as *Giselle* or *Swan Lake*, Ballet Theatre might imply that American dancers lacked the technique to perform them. Panel members were also nervous that American ballets, often produced by small companies with modest budgets, would seem shabby compared to the lavish spectacles of the Bolshoi Theater.[50]

Other advisors, more familiar with the art scene in the Soviet Union, specifically urged Chase to cut both *Fall River Legend* and *Billy the Kid* from the schedule. As one reason for excluding the works, the experts cited the poor reaction by Soviet officials to a New York Philharmonic performance of *Billy the Kid* during the orchestra's 1959 tour.[51] Conductor Leonard Bernstein had given a speech to the audiences in which he argued that Soviet and American musical styles were very similar. The Soviet officials in charge of the concert, however, never provided Russian translations of Bernstein's remarks. Bernstein had also criticized the Soviet Union on his return to the United States, which angered his Soviet hosts.[52] Whether it was Bernstein's remarks in the Soviet Union, the piece itself, or his criticisms in the United States that caused the poor Soviet reaction to *Billy the Kid*, the event had impressed all of Ballet Theatre's advisors. Later on, during Ballet Theatre's tour, this concern was shown to have merit, when Chase arranged to have her dancers perform a stripped-down version of *Billy the Kid* for local dance professionals in Tbilisi. While the private audience claimed to enjoy the ballet, none of them believed that Ballet Theatre should perform the work for the general public, and some mentioned that they preferred *Rodeo*.[53]

Such serious misgivings about *Billy the Kid* and *Fall River Legend* in the Soviet Union also stemmed from the fact that these ballets violated the conventions of socialist realism. Socialist realist ballets were supposed to inspire the audience through the depiction of heroic individuals. Moreover, Soviet works were supposed to demonstrate that the world was constantly improving, moving through a dialectic struggle into a glorious future.[54] *Billy the Kid* and *Fall River Legend*, which show the tragic fate of violent and largely immoral characters, violated both these principles.[55] English-language dance historians have tended to assume that the Soviet government saw abstraction as the greatest threat coming out of American ballet.[56] As this episode shows, however, the Soviet government was more on guard against ballets with inappropriate plots than abstract works. Goskontsert and other Soviet representatives were far more likely to prevent or discourage American companies from performing ballets with morally ambiguous or sexually provocative narratives than they were to censor abstract ballets, both during Ballet Theatre's 1960 tour and New York City Ballet's tour two years later.

After all the negotiations, Ballet Theatre presented a rotation of three basic programs for its 1960 tour, the details of which could occasionally be shuffled:[57]

    Program I:
    Theme and Variations—music by Pyotr Tchaikovsky, choreography by George Balanchine
    Rodeo—Aaron Copland, Agnes de Mille
    pas de deux from *Swan Lake* Act III (*Black Swan* pas de deux)—Tchaikovsky, Marius Petipa
    Graduation Ball—Johann Strauss, David Lichine

    Program II:
    Les Sylphides—Frédéric Chopin, Michel Fokine
    pas de deux from *Don Quixote*—Ludwig Minkus, Petipa
    Fancy Free—Leonard Bernstein, Jerome Robbins
    Bluebeard—Jacques Offenbach, Michel Fokine

Program III:
Lady from the Sea—Knudåge Riisager, Birgit Cullberg
The Combat—Raffaello de Banfield, William Dollar
Jardin aux Lilas—Ernest Chausson, Antony Tudor
Theme and Variations—Tchaikovsky, Balanchine

As Catharine Nepomnyashchy has observed, Chase's final programming provided a mixture of classical Russian and contemporary American works. Every performance contained at least one selection with a Russian score, and the first two showcased Russian choreography in the form of the pas de deux and *Les Sylphides*.[58] Ballet Theatre could therefore prove that its dancers were as technically proficient at the balletic canon as their Russian counterparts. The company did not, however, abandon the plan to introduce Soviets to American works. Every night, the group performed ballets created in the United States in the mid-twentieth century.

There were also a surprisingly high number of comedies compared to Chase's earlier plans for the tour; one set contained *Rodeo* and *Graduation Ball* and the second *Fancy Free* and *Bluebeard*. In a sense, these comedic ballets allowed Chase and her company to present a version of populist American choreography while at the same time hewing more closely to the dictates of socialist realism. While they were not quite examples of the New Soviet Man, the comedic characters acted in largely moral stories narrated in a method familiar to viewers of Soviet drambalety.

Program III was somewhat different. There was no traditional Russian choreography and no comedy. *The Combat* was the closest thing to a "representative American work" on the program, with choreography by Russian American David Lichine and music by Raffaello de Banfield, a European neoclassicist. Perhaps because of these differences, the third program was performed only six times out of thirty-five total performances. In addition, on the final pass through Moscow, the company performed a modified version of the second program that included *The Combat* in place of *Fancy Free*.[59]

Ballet Theatre began performing these programs in the Soviet Union on September 12, just three and a half weeks after the tour contract was signed.[60] Their first appearance was an open rehearsal for Soviet ballet professionals.[61] The dress rehearsal was followed by a public debut on September 13 at the Stanislavsky and Nemirovich-Danchenko Academic Musical Theater (Figure 2.1).[62] Some of the greatest stars of international ballet, including Ulanova

Figure 2.1 Poster for the American Ballet Theatre's debut performances in the Soviet Union. RGALI f. 2337 o. 2 d. 202. The repertoire listed for the third program was changed following printing.

and Plisetskaya, were in attendance. Political figures also came to the premiere. Although Khrushchev himself did not appear, his wife attended, as did the American ambassador to the Soviet Union. Soviet citizens enthusiastically lined up for their first opportunity to see American ballet. The opening performance was completely sold out.[63]

Following the premiere, Ballet Theatre continued its whirlwind tour. They played for two more nights at the Stanislavsky Theater, then traveled to Tbilisi, Georgia, on September 20, where they gave another twelve performances at the Tbilisi Opera House, each to a sold-out audience of 2,000. Next, the company danced ten times in Leningrad from October 5–12 at the 2,100-seat Theater of the Cultural Cooperative Center, again to sold-out crowds at every performance. From October 15–18, Ballet Theatre performed five times in Kiev at the Theater of the Palace of Culture, filling the 3,000-seat hall at each performance.[64] While in Leningrad and in Moscow, the company was filmed by Soviet TV studios for a live television broadcast.[65]

In each of the theaters, the dancers were accompanied by an orchestra of local musicians, led by Ballet Theatre's own conductor, Kenneth Schermerhorn. The troop also traveled with assistant conductor, Urey Krasnapolsky, pianist Irving Owen, and three American musicians: violinist Jan Tomasov, percussionist Michael Colgrass, and trumpeter Fred Mills. Mills and Colgrass were included to bolster the orchestra for the "jazzy" (in Colgrass's words) sections of *Fancy Free* and *Rodeo*.[66] According to Colgrass, the orchestra provided by the Russians was "the smallest third-rate ballet orchestra any of us had ever seen," because the Bolshoi needed its own instrumentalists for its opera and ballet season.[67] Even though the musicians in the orchestra did not speak English, and Schermerhorn did not speak Russian, there were few language problems during rehearsals.[68]

All of Ballet Theatre's personnel faced an intense and stressful six weeks in the Soviet Union, which came on the heels of an exhausting trip through Europe. The American performers had to conduct themselves under strict rules from both the Soviet and US governments, designed to keep the artists on their best behavior and to limit their access to their surroundings.[69] No Americans were allowed into the city on their own. Everyone was ferried around on the same bus and had to eat all meals together. The food was very bad, with little produce. When Colgrass queried one of the translators about the lack of fruit, she replied that there was typically plenty available in the Soviet Union but there had been "a distribution problem."[70] In addition, the troupe believed itself to be constantly under surveillance. They were accompanied on all outings by a group of Soviet government interpreters, who the dancers assumed were reporting back about their activities.[71] The American State Department advised performers that their hotel rooms in the USSR might be bugged.[72] During the tour, Kenneth Schermerhorn became sick with a terrible cold.[73] In a letter composed in Tbilisi, Chase lamented, "We feel far away and completely out of touch."[74]

The spirits of company members picked up in Leningrad, where they were received with particular enthusiasm by local audiences. In an ANTA report, Payne noted that the Leningrad audiences "understand the American ballets, laugh in the right places, and applaud enthusiastically (even for *Fancy Free*)."[75] Beginning in Leningrad, the troupe was also able to perform with a steady orchestra of musicians on loan from the Bolshoi Theater.[76]

Despite the grueling performance schedule, unfamiliar invasions of privacy, and homesickness, the performers felt a sense of pride in the work they were accomplishing in the Soviet Union, especially the enormity of proving that Americans could really dance. Maria Tallchief recalls in her memoirs an instance in which an old woman came up to her on the street in Moscow, handed her a bouquet of flowers, and said, "Miss Tallchief, we love you." The ballerina believed that the tour was "the pinnacle of [her] career."[77] Colgrass felt that the tour helped promote goodwill between the two countries, giving them an opportunity to meet real Soviet people and vice versa.[78]

According to letters among the Ballet Theatre staff, reports on the tour, and reviews from the Soviet newspapers, the Soviet audiences applauded enthusiastically.[79] The company's opening in Moscow went well. Chase telegrammed back to the Ballet Theatre offices on September 15, "company marvelous form great success."[80] In Tbilisi, the reception was a bit more muted. The audiences there especially favored *Bluebeard*, a satirical ballet choreographed by Michel Fokine to the music of Offenbach.[81] When the company reached Leningrad, they received their first real raves. Chase wrote home that it was a "shame there are no correspondents here, we're such a success."[82]

Chase's programming was an overall success with critics, particularly her combination of American and Russian works. The Russian ballets were by far the most popular; Soviet critics were very pleased to have the opportunity to see Michel Fokine's last ballet, *Bluebeard*, as well as his ultimate rendering of *Les Sylphides*, a work that was still performed in the Soviet Union in an earlier version.[83] Not only did they approve of the American performances of Russian classics, some Soviet critics also expressed open approval for the company's mixture of contrasting ballets on the same program.[84] Theater critic Vadim Gaevsky remarked that while he had felt that *Rodeo* should have been at odds with the classical ballets, in reality "there was no disagreement at all, but rather mutual help and support."[85]

However kind they may have been to their American guests, at no point did the Soviet critics concede that American ballet was as good as their own. Rather, they saw Ballet Theatre's trip to Russia as something of a pilgrimage to ballet's source, and their success as proof of Russian ballet's international triumph. Mikhail Gabovich, in his review for *Sovetskaia kultura*, claimed that Soviet ballet had become the "holy place, the Mecca or Medina for ballet figures of the whole world."[86]

Chase's strategic decision to include so many comedic ballets, such as *Rodeo*, *Fancy Free*, and *Bluebeard*, was relatively successful insofar as it rendered the company more ideologically acceptable and less intimidating. This made it easier for Soviet critics to applaud the American dancers. At the same time, the comedy also meant that reviewers did not generally take the company as seriously, and the resulting tone could be very patronizing.[87] Eteri Gugushvili perhaps summed up the attitude of her fellow Soviet critics to Ballet Theatre's programming best when she wrote, "American Ballet Theatre is young. It is all of twenty years old. And this youth is apparent in everything—in its healthy, youthful playfulness and ease of movement."[88] The Soviet critics applauded American Ballet Theatre, but they did not see the company as a competitor to their own troupes.

American Populist Ballet and Drambalet

Though the long lead-up to the tour had whittled down American Ballet Theatre's populist offerings, the company's mission to present American choreography lived on in two ballets: *Rodeo* and *Fancy Free*.[89] Despite the fact that they represented the specifically American side of the repertory, the aesthetic of these two works was surprisingly reminiscent of Soviet ballets.[90] Like drambalet choreographers such as Leonid Lavrovsky and Rostislav Zakharov, de Mille and Robbins told stories in dance by blending more traditional balletic movement with a type of silent acting.[91] For example, in the opening scene of *Fancy Free*, the three sailors play a game of odds and evens to decide who will pay for the first round of drinks. Their acting for this section is quite stylized and is often stretched to become a dance movement. As the three men turn away from the bar, they lift their legs behind them and spin around. In order to accommodate this type of danced narrative, the scores to *Fancy Free* and *Rodeo* are fairly loose in form, much like Prokofiev's music for *Romeo and Juliet*. In certain scenes, especially those with a great deal of narrative material, Copland and Bernstein string together multiple short themes, each one reflecting the onstage action for that moment.

To some degree, the similarities between the American and Soviet style of ballet can be explained by the similar politics of their creators.[92] This is reflected in the heroes of the two ballets, who are everyday people—cowboys in *Rodeo* and sailors in *Fancy Free*—an element that resonated with Soviet ideology. The two schools, however, also had a common heritage in Russian ballet of the early twentieth century. In particular, two of Ballet Theatre's important early choreographers, Mordkin and Fokine, were connected to actor-director Konstantin Stanislavsky, much like the creators of the drambalet.[93] Mordkin, the Russian dancer-choreographer who founded

Ballet Theatre, had collaborated with Stanislavsky before leaving Moscow.[94] Fokine never worked directly with Stanislavsky, but drew on the director's ideas.[95] Moreover, in addition to becoming one of Ballet Theatre's main choreographers, Fokine also left a strong impression on the work of Robbins and to a lesser extent de Mille.[96] Like their Soviet counterparts, then, these American choreographers adapted much of Stanislavsky's work on realistic acting. Of course, Ballet Theatre's narrative repertoire had other sources and influences that were not Russian. In particular, English choreographer Antony Tudor worked regularly for Ballet Theatre during the first decade of the company's existence.[97] Nevertheless, the influence of Fokine, Mordkin, and Stanislavsky on the early American ballet was palpably felt in *Rodeo* and *Fancy Free*. This connection between the American choreographers and the Russian Stanislavskian heritage was apparent to Soviet critics. In the later 1960s, Soviet critic Natalia Roslavleva wrote to de Mille, telling her, "If ever there was choreography according to Stanislavsky's method, yours is."[98]

Rodeo and *Fancy Free* also mirrored the Soviet drambalety in their emphasis on nationalist gesture and sound. Nationalism was a cornerstone of Soviet aesthetics from the 1930s onwards.[99] During the 1930s and 1940s, national schools of ballet and opera were established in the Soviet republics, and composers and choreographers in these areas were encouraged to create explicitly nationalist styles by drawing on local folk art. Such styles were often supposed to mimic the techniques of nineteenth-century Russian nationalist music and dance. They relied on an essentializing belief that each nationality had a unique character reflected in folk music, but that opera and ballet were universal art forms.[100]

A similar essentializing process undergirded American populist ballet. The creators of these works frequently drew on a variety of folk musics and dances in a quest to create a characteristic American style. For example, *Rodeo* is set in Texas, and the music for the ballet draws on folk songs in order to depict that nationalist setting to the audience. Copland took some of the themes for the music from John A. and Alan Lomaxes' *Our Singing Country* and Ira Ford's *Traditional Music of America*.[101] De Mille's choreography includes folk quotations as well. At one point in the ballet the company performs a square dance, accompanied only by onstage clapping and dance calls.[102] Often the creators of these works appropriated the styles of black artists, even as they crafted a style that was supposed to be read as white. For example, de Mille's hero and heroine, played by white dancers, use tap steps in the final scene of the ballet. The movements undergird *Rodeo*'s place as a nationalist ballet. Yet tap was developed out of the mixing of African and Irish dance traditions, created by black dancers and white minstrel performers.[103] While it is possible that real people living in Texas at the start of the twentieth century might have known the dance form, its inclusion on a stage so purposefully whitewashed illustrates how American artists in the 1940s created this essentializing national style of ballet.

Fancy Free is not steeped in the pastoral like *Rodeo*, but it too uses popular music to evoke American nationalism. Oliver Smith's set for the ballet, a seedy bar behind which one can see the lights of New York, evokes the requisite place; the music and choreography incorporate gestures from jazz and popular dance. The ballet opens with "Big Stuff," a blues song written by Bernstein.[104] Likewise, Robbins introduces elements from jazz and stage dancing into his choreography, including heel clicks, over-the-tops, and cartwheels.

Ironically, then, because *Rodeo* and *Fancy Free* spoke in the same language of essentializing nationalism as the drambalety, they appeared to Soviet audiences to be uniquely American.[105] As the Soviet viewers transliterated their experience of watching American ballet, they had a frame of reference to understand its style and politics. Gaevsky remarked in his review of the company that its ballets had "a specifically American color."[106] In general, the critics were much more favorable about *Rodeo* than *Fancy Free*, perhaps because the latter skirted some of the same issues of propriety as *Fall River Legend* and *Billy the Kid*. Although the main characters in *Fancy Free* are no criminals, the ballet is unapologetic about their pursuit of one-night stands. Gabovich called the women in the ballet "dubious," though he noted with sly approval that Robbins had avoided "open sex" in the production.[107] Moreover, the blues and jazz styles that Bernstein drew on for the score of *Fancy Free* had an ambiguous status in the Soviet Union, sometimes used as a form of mass entertainment and sometimes criticized as the product of the capitalist American market.[108] Undoubtedly, it was this negative press that convinced Ballet Theatre to replace *Fancy Free* with the much more popular *The Combat* in its last performances in Moscow. Nevertheless, many critics had a good word even for *Fancy Free*. Roslavleva claimed that it was full of "energy" and both she and Gabovich praised its "lively humor."[109] *Rodeo* was even better received, in part because its pastoral Americanness fit better with Soviet conceptions of national identity. Dance historian and critic Vera Krasovskaya, writing in Leningrad, applauded both de Mille's expressive characterization and her use of folk art.[110]

Just as Ballet Theatre's populist works presented a comparable style of essentialized nationalism to the Soviet drambalety, so too did the two styles of ballet exhibit a similar approach to gender. Both the American populist ballets and the Soviet drambalety used dance to glorify a type of hypermasculine everyman. In the Soviet Union, this style of masculinity was best exemplified by the performances of Georgian star Vakhtang Chabukiani. Today, Chabukiani is remembered primarily for the men's variations that he performed and choreographed for such ballet classics as *La Bayadère*, *Le Corsaire*, and *Swan Lake*. Chabukiani's variations were filled with huge jumps that conquered the width of the stage.[111] His dancing was not merely technically proficient but also possessed a masculine allure that Maria Tallchief noted in her memoirs: "I had heard of him for years. Renowned not only for his phenomenal technique but because of his fabulous presence, he had a sex appeal—there was no denying it, with his smouldering eyes and pouting smile—that came across onstage."[112] One of Chabukiani's most famous roles was as Jérôme in the original production of Asafiev and Vainonen's *The Flames of Paris*. Jérôme, a worker hero of the French Revolution, is notable for his aggressively flamboyant trick steps; in the coda of his pas de deux, Jérôme jumps high into the air, after which he falls into a kneeling position on the ground and leans back. His movement conquers the full breadth of the stage. Jérôme's physical prowess is echoed in the exaggeratedly militaristic brass music, complete with cymbal crashes.[113]

Chabukiani choreographed as well, creating works such as the 1938 *Heart of the Mountain* and the 1939 *Laurencia*. By the time that Ballet Theatre toured the Soviet Union in 1960, the dancer had largely retired from his performance career to become the director of the Georgian Ballet in Tbilisi.[114] While Ballet Theatre was performing in Tbilisi, Chase hired Chabukiani to train the company in his version of *Giselle*. The first rehearsals went well, and preliminary plans were made to fly the choreographer to the United States to finish training the company in his production and star as Albrecht in the first performances.[115] Sadly, these plans never materialized.

This brief, and ultimately unsuccessful, attempt at collaboration provides an insight into Ballet Theatre's Soviet reception. Chabukiani's manner of dancing was not so different from the male style of performance at Ballet Theatre in 1960. *Rodeo* and *Fancy Free* each paints its own picture of rugged masculinity, with everyday heroes performing broad jumps and spins to heavy brass music, not unlike Jérôme in *Flames of*

Paris. Perhaps the section of *Fancy Free* that best demonstrates the sailors' exaggerated masculinity is the set of three solos in the second half of the work. At this moment, the three sailors and their two female companions are seated at a table in a bar. One by one, the sailors perform a dance to impress the other four characters. The first solo is energetic and over-the-top. The number is taken at an immense clip, with heavy percussion emphasizing almost every beat. In the second half of the number, the percussion switches to the upbeats, pushing the tempo along with even more drive. Over these pounding drums are layered trumpet and trombone solos, which are periodically interrupted by brass fanfares. Onstage, the sailor wildly drinks two beers, performs forward summersaults, and dances on top of the bar. Finally, he jumps off the bar onto the stage, flying through the air with both legs splayed outward. His athletic jumps and musical vigor are absurd, but they also speak, in balletic terms, of his sincere physical prowess. Moreover, they remind the viewer of a younger Chabukiani, who also flew through the air to the pounding of drums and the fanfare of trumpets.

Soviet critics seemed to notice the similarities. Gabovich specifically lauded the men of Ballet Theatre for their masculine way of dancing. He juxtaposed this quality with a style of "androgynous" and "effeminate" movement popularized in the West by choreographer-dancer Serge Lifar.[116] The critic claimed that the Ballet Theatre stars were free of this "crippling" style of male dance.[117] Such language suggests anxiety about the type of work men did in neoclassical ballets, Lifar's preferred style of choreography. In this style of dance, men often dressed in elegant, princely garb and executed small jumps rather than broad leaps. Such language also suggests a coded homophobia, which was heightened in Russia during Khrushchev's premiership.[118] Such homophobia may also explain Soviet ambivalence about *Fancy Free*, which can be read as a potentially queer ballet.[119]

Overall, the strongest sign that Soviet critics accepted *Fancy Free* and *Rodeo* was not any one comment, but rather that the reviewers almost unanimously described the ballets as "contemporary" (sovremennyĭ), a term of praise associated with Soviet art, rather than as "modern" (modernyĭ), generally used to describe Western works. As this indicates, the ballets were generally understood positively within the frameworks of Soviet aesthetics.[120]

The Pas de Deux: Small but Mighty Classics

In addition to showing populist ballets similar to the drambalety, the company also convinced Soviet critics and audiences that American artists had classical virtuosity of the same type showcased by ballet dancers all around the world. Most of the heavy lifting to this end was done by the two pas de deux, one excerpted from *Don Quixote*, the other from *Swan Lake*. By performing these highly virtuosic duets, Ballet Theatre demonstrated that its dancers had technical skills on par with other international stars. Even better, the pas de deux established this fact at extremely low production and transportation costs, since the duets were performed with little scenery. This was not the first time that the short duets had served as a marker of Ballet Theatre's classical credentials. During the company's tour of London in 1946, *Les Sylphides* and the pas de deux from *Swan Lake* ensured that audiences and critics considered the company a ballet ensemble rather than, in Payne's words, "a semiclassical dance company, presenting American musical comedy in pseudo-ballet style."[121]

The full ballets *Swan Lake* and *Don Quixote*, from which these pas de deux were excerpted, were choreographed and performed at St. Petersburg's Mariinsky Theater in the late nineteenth century. *Don Quixote* was choreographed by Marius Petipa to the music of Ludwig Minkus, while *Swan Lake* was choreographed by Petipa and his assistant Lev Ivanov to a score by Tchaikovsky.[122] The pas de deux from both *Don Quixote* and *Swan Lake* were then transported through Western Europe to the United States by a variety of Russian émigré dancers.[123] While there may have been some differences between the Soviet versions of these duets and the Ballet Theatre ones, the overall structure and many of the most virtuosic steps were common to both countries.

When performed in their original ballets, these two duets work as simultaneous choreographic and narrative climax, generally functioning as the consummation of a marriage plot.[124] When performed on their own, however, as they were in the context of the Soviet tour, the pas de deux have a very different function, and to an extent even a different look. Their choreographer, Petipa, was credited with introducing a classical style of ballet that merged Italian bravura technique with French lyricism.[125] In the nineteenth century, when Petipa worked on these ballets, solos could be highly individualized, with the choreography varying from performance to performance depending on the individual strengths of the lead dancers.[126] By 1960, however, such variety had mostly been weeded out of practice in favor of a set of standardized solos that functionally measured the dancers' virtuosity against a common bar.[127]

As in many of Petipa's creations, music and dance combine in these pas de deux to emphasize the virtuosity of the actions onstage. Lifts and difficult balances are often performed at moments of harmonic tension, daring gravity to break the spell and bring the dancer crashing back to earth. The dancers typically execute a single step multiple times to show off consistency and build up tension and excitement. The music is repetitive to complement the repetitive steps, and it cadences frequently, providing a space for the audience to applaud before the dancers move into their next sequence. Perhaps there is no greater example of this latter technique than the coda to the third act pas de deux from *Swan Lake*, in which the lead ballerina famously executes thirty-two *fouettés*, a type of whipped turn that takes an enormous amount of coordination, balance, and physical strength to perform. The music primes the audience for awe: the *fouettés* begin and end at moments of musical cadence, setting this movement up as satisfying, even triumphant. Each *fouetté*, particularly in the second half of the sequence, is timed so that the ballerina's leg whips out exactly on the crashing downbeat of the measure. Throughout, the brass and percussion instruments crash along with enthusiasm.

On Ballet Theatre's 1960 tour of the Soviet Union, the leading performers of the Black Swan pas de deux were Maria Tallchief and Eric Bruhn. The two had worked together previously, and Bruhn had helped convince Tallchief to join the Soviet tour. Tallchief, however, had not performed the Black Swan pas de deux very often. She recalled her concerns about performing this canonical work in front of a Russian audience: "I had been worried about doing the pas de deux all along, imagining the Russians saying, 'Who's this American dancer? What does she think she's doing?'"[128] Despite her fears, opening night was a success. Ulanova and Plisetskaya, the latter of whom was internationally renowned for her *Swan Lake* interpretation, came backstage after the performance to congratulate Tallchief.[129]

The plan to wow Soviet critics with excerpts from the Russian classics paid off. Many reviewers remarked on the dancers' impeccable training, as demonstrated by their mastery of the pas de deux. Bruhn's performances were widely recognized as highly virtuosic, and for the most part Tallchief and Serrano were similarly praised for their classical technique. Vera Krasovskaya claimed in her review for *Leningradskaia Pravda* that Serrano's dance exhibited "true freedom and calm virtuosity."[130] One of the highlights of the tour came in Leningrad during the *Don Quixote* pas de deux, when the applause for Serrano's solo was so overwhelming that she had to perform an encore of her variation.[131]

Not only were Tallchief and Bruhn excellent dancers, but their union onstage symbolized the ballet company's overall blend of American and international profiles. Bruhn was a Danish dancer; while he was a regular performer with Ballet Theatre, he retained his Danish citizenship and performed as a principal dancer with the Danish Royal Ballet as well.[132] Tallchief, who was born in Fairfax, Oklahoma, was an Osage Indian. Her presence in the cast helped solidify the company as genuinely American, despite its international personnel and repertoire. At one point, when the principals were taken to meet Nikita Khrushchev, each of them was announced to him by nationality, either by birth or ancestry. Tallchief was announced only as "American."[133]

The treatment of Tallchief's Native American identity was quite unusual for US cultural diplomacy at the time. Few Native Americans participated in the cultural exchange programs at all, but the State Department's general approach to them mirrored the treatment of other minoritized groups, especially African Americans. These artists were often deployed as a means of counteracting Soviet propaganda about racism in the United States. Such treatment made non-white performers valuable to the State Department. It also subtly reasserted the very minority status of those performers, presenting an image of the United States as a fundamentally white nation that could treat its outsiders benevolently.[134]

Tallchief's case was somewhat different because ballet's position as an American art form was precarious. As American Ballet Theatre's 1960 tour shows, there was a general anxiety in the dance world about whether or not ballet could be perceived as American. As such, Tallchief was presented on tour as the ur American, someone who could not be claimed as an immigrant or the child of one, and thus whose identity and virtuosity could transform ballet into an American art form. This was not the only time that Tallchief's Native American identity had been interpreted this way for the ballet world. In 1954, she appeared on the cover of *Newsweek* with a story calling her "America's Native Dancer" and suggesting that she was the United States' equivalent to Ulanova.[135] Together, the Tallchief-Bruhn collaboration helped demonstrate that America was taking part in an international form of high art while maintaining a unique national identity.

An Uncelebrated Success

After touring in Tbilisi, Kiev, and Leningrad, Ballet Theatre returned to their opening city of Moscow. This time they performed, not in the Stanislavsky Theater, but in the Lenin Palace of Sports, a stadium that held up to 12,000 people.[136] They returned to the capital from a tour that had garnered many more positive reviews and much greater audience enthusiasm than anyone had anticipated. Khrushchev himself attended the final performance and afterwards held a private dinner party for the principal dancers and company leadership.[137] When Chase arrived back at the hotel from the party, she found a gathering of her dancers, who sang in her honor "For she's a jolly good fellow." Chase concluded her journal entry for the day: "*What* an eve! The tour has been fantastic and a really enormous success here—far more than I ever dreamed. Our corps has amazed them and boy, am I proud of them they've all done a marvelous job and I pray we can keep them going. What a finale!"[138]

In order to achieve this startling result, Chase had crafted a set of programs carefully designed with the help of every artistic and political advisor available to her. While Chase originally planned to present exclusively American choreography, the Soviet programs balanced American works with traditional Russian ballets. In order to make these gains, American Ballet Theatre had to give up a certain type of nationalist identity. In a sense, then, Ballet Theatre was not accomplishing the more overtly competitive goals that some Americans wanted out of their cultural diplomacy programs. It is possibly for this reason that the tour has received much less historical attention than New York City Ballet's more overtly aggressive tour of 1962. As we shall see in chapter 4, however, the New York City Ballet's tour was much less subversive than has been previously claimed. Indeed, it seems difficult for cultural diplomacy tours to be subversive, because in order to connect with international audiences, they need to speak a language that the audience is already speaking. By creating such a profile, Ballet Theatre did transform Soviet opinion about the United States. The result, however, was not a reduced appreciation for Soviet values, but rather an understanding of the shared values and humanity between the two countries.

As much as the tour was a success in proving the worth of American dance to Soviet audiences, some aspects of Soviet society had made a positive impression on the American visitors as well. In particular, the American dancers were struck by the value that the arts had in Soviet society. Ballet

Theatre's report on the tour to ANTA described the frustration the company directors felt regarding the differences between the two countries:

> What impressed us was the importance they give to art, and we were important because of our art. I feel sure America can stand up to any country on its product, but unless the country attaches importance and helps to make ballet survive, we will not have the opportunity to create and hold our place in the cultural world.[139]

Ballet Theatre's dual persona—both American and international—revealed similarities between the United States and the Soviet Union. The tour showed the two countries' surprising likenesses, from their essentializing nationalism to their appreciation of ballet itself. These similarities were revealed day in and day out on Ballet Theatre's tour, and though they were rarely overtly recognized, it was these similarities that helped foster the company's best reviews. As such, Ballet Theatre's 1960 tour demonstrates that, while belligerence can secure domestic attention for cultural diplomacy, it is ultimately less effective on the international stage than a more conciliatory approach.

3

A Question of Taste

The Bolshoi Ballet's 1962 Tour of the United States

On September 12, 1962, the curtain of the Metropolitan Opera House rose for the Bolshoi Ballet in the American premiere of Aram Khachaturian's *Spartacus*. As a brass fanfare shook the opera house, legions of dancers dressed as Roman soldiers paraded by a triumphal arch. Young supernumeraries lay down at the front of the stage to welcome the army. Men entered bearing a litter with a beautiful woman draped over it.

It was the middle of the company's second tour of the United States. The first three years of the dance exchange had been marked by a series of stunning successes. American audiences had welcomed Soviet company after Soviet company with open arms. *Spartacus* was supposed to be something special for the Bolshoi's return to North America. Hurok had primed reviewers and audiences with months of press releases advertising the work as "grand," "sensual," and "one of the world's greatest spectacles."[1] The ballet would tell the identical story as Stanley Kubrick's blockbuster hit of the same name, which had taken movie theaters by storm just two years previously. There was every reason to believe, then, that Americans would receive *Spartacus* with the same fervor that they had greeted *Romeo and Juliet* in 1959.

Hardly had the Roman army started marching across the stage, however, when a loud booing began in the audience.[2] The next day's reviews were just as dismissive. *Spartacus*, the golden hope of the Bolshoi's 1962 tour, was deemed a failure after only four performances in the United States and removed from the company's repertoire immediately.

The *Spartacus* fiasco was only one part of the 1962 tour, and there were some brighter moments, but altogether it was a much grimmer outing for the company than its 1959 triumph. American critics still saw all the same flaws in the Bolshoi as before, but these were now magnified owing to two distinct phenomena. First, political tensions between the United States and the Soviet Union, already high in 1959, were stretched even further by 1962. In

Ballet in the Cold War. Anne Searcy, Oxford University Press (2020). © Oxford University Press.
DOI: 10.1093/oso/9780190945107.001.0001.

October of that year, while the Bolshoi Ballet was performing in California, the Cuban Missile Crisis rocked the unsteady relationship. Second, and just as important, the Bolshoi's fellow Soviet ballet company, the Kirov, had toured the United States in 1961. The comparison with the Kirov, perceived by many as the true inheritor of Russia's imperial splendor, magnified problems that American critics had previously seen in the Bolshoi, particularly the company's seemingly unsophisticated style.[3] As the reviews came in for the Bolshoi's 1962 tour, a damning consensus was reached. The Bolshoi simply lacked taste.

Thus, the Bolshoi's 1962 tour unexpectedly collided with the class politics of American performing arts. Ballet as a genre had recently risen in status in the United States. Dance experts and fans were keen to maintain this newfound standing by preserving ballet's reputation as a tasteful, elite art form. In their eyes, the Bolshoi could demonstrate their own sophisticated taste either by displaying their imperial Russian inheritance, like the Kirov, or by following New York trends. *Spartacus* failed to do either, and it was not the only Soviet production received poorly by American audiences in 1962. American reviewers also criticized the Bolshoi's *Swan Lake* for neglecting to preserve the company's Russian heritage.

The one critical success that the Bolshoi had during its 1962 tour was *Ballet School*, which was praised largely for its similarities to the works of George Balanchine. Staged by Asaf Messerer to a mélange of Russian and Soviet light music, the short ballet ostensibly demonstrated the hard work necessary to transform a child dancer into a star of the Bolshoi Theater. *Ballet School* appeared to some American critics as a demonstration that Soviet choreographers had finally abandoned their previous aesthetics in favor of modernist American ones.

The American reception of *Swan Lake*, *Spartacus*, and *Ballet School* shows the interweaving of international and domestic concerns around taste, prestige, and the United States' growing role as a world superpower. The Bolshoi's lack of taste was frequently contrasted with the sophistication of its American counterparts, underlining narratives about Western progress and modernism. American ballet's recently won elite status fed back into beliefs that the United States was destined to run a new ideological empire. Both Americans and Soviets struggled with how to portray such an empire in artistic form, and thus disagreements about the Bolshoi's 1962 repertoire combined anxieties about American empire with concerns about ballet's place as an art form.

The Cuban Missile Crisis and the Empire of Taste

When the Bolshoi Ballet arrived in the United States in 1962, the environment was already icier than it had been three years previously. Tensions between the United States and the Soviet Union had grown increasingly worse during the early 1960s. The two countries struggled over the continuing division of Berlin and the absence of a formal peace treaty with Germany, a situation that came to a dangerous head in 1961 with the construction of the Berlin Wall. The United States and Soviet Union also clashed over influence in the newly independent Cuba. In May 1960, Cuban revolutionary leader Fidel Castro concluded an economic agreement with the Soviet bloc. The United States retaliated with multiple attempts to destabilize the revolutionary Cuban government.[4]

In October 1962, as a response to these threats, Nikita Khrushchev attempted to secure his ally in Cuba by moving nuclear missiles to the island. The US government received confirmation of the incoming missiles on October 14, and American president John F. Kennedy decided to set up a naval blockade of the island to prevent their arrival. When the president informed the American populace about the nuclear missiles and the blockade, there was widespread anxiety and even panic across the country. After two weeks of intense and aggressive talks, American and Soviet diplomats reached an agreement for the removal of the missiles in Cuba in exchange for a public promise from the Americans not to invade Cuba and a secret promise to dismantle the United States' Jupiter missiles in Turkey.[5]

The Cuban Missile Crisis played out in military terms the complicated relationship between the Cold War and the idea of empire, a relationship that would come to the fore artistically with the Bolshoi's 1962 tour. The Crisis was a struggle between the United States and the Soviet Union, and yet it was fought over Cuba. Much of the rhetoric around the Soviet Union's decisions, and to some extent American ones, suggested that they were acting in part for the benefit of the Caribbean nation. Cuban leaders, however, were left out of the negotiations, which focused much more on international military strategy.[6] This exhibits in microcosm the imperial nature of the Cold War, a conflict between two powerful countries both rhetorically dedicated to anti-imperialism yet both with ambitious plans to win over and control the rapidly decolonizing world. As Odd Arne Westad and others have argued, the Cold War attempted to reconfigure the colonial empires of the nineteenth century into two ideological spheres of influence. This could produce a strange ambivalence about the idea of empire; on the one hand, the American and Soviet governments wanted to have the same power as empires of the distant and near past. On the other hand, both superpowers positioned themselves as liberators, friends of decolonizing nations.[7]

The idea of empire therefore played a strange role in Cold War culture, both an enemy and an object of desire. Culturally, in the Soviet-American exchange, both countries worked to depict themselves as the leaders of new cultural empires. At the same time, they imagined themselves as different from empires of the past, less authoritarian and more egalitarian or democratic. During the 1960s, some American leaders, most prominently Kennedy himself, connected the United States' status as a leader in the arts with its worthiness of playing a prominent role in international politics. Perhaps most famously, Kennedy summed this up in a letter to the journal *Musical America* in 1960. The magazine had asked both presidential candidates that year to comment on their views about music and politics, largely foregrounding the issue of cultural diplomacy. Kennedy responded by writing that "There is a connection, hard to explain logically but easy to feel, between achievement in public life and progress in the arts. The age of Pericles was also the age of Phidias. The age of Lorenzo de Medici was also the age of Leonardo da Vinci, the age of Elizabeth also the age of Shakespeare. And the New Frontier for which I campaign in public life, can also be a New Frontier for American art."[8] Taste in the arts thus marked America as a place worthy of inheriting the mantle of great civilizations past.

This vision of America as an international leader in the arts was a key component of the United States' cultural diplomacy program. The State Department focused on sending classical music, ballet, and other elite, European art forms abroad because they would increase the country's international prestige. American Ballet Theatre presented a similar version of American identity during its 1960 tour of the Soviet Union. This was not a patriotic vision of the United States insulated from the outside world. Instead, it was a patriotic vision of the United States as a leader of international art forms. Furthermore, as musicologist Danielle Fosler-Lussier has argued, other countries bought into the same scheme of prestige, demanding that the United States send to them European classical music as a marker that they too were part of an elevated new world order.[9]

Ballet played a growing role in marking the United States' artistic ambitions, but this was a perilously new job for the genre. In the early twentieth century, ballet had an ambivalent position in American class hierarchies.

Sometimes it was played for what dance critic John Martin described as the "ermine-clad" members of society, but at other times it was billed as an art form for the masses.[10] Ballet could be tied to vaudeville, Broadway, and Hollywood. Certain forms of modern dance had more solid associations with the highbrow and were sometimes juxtaposed with ballet as the more serious form of dance. By the 1940s and 1950s, ballet had been established as an elite art form, largely owing to the efforts of such figures as Balanchine and Lincoln Kirstein.[11] In 1949, *Life* magazine published a satirical chart explaining highbrow and lowbrow culture to its readers; they chose an image from Balanchine's *Orpheus* to illustrate highbrow theatrical tastes.[12]

This was the world that the Bolshoi Ballet found when it arrived for its second tour in New York on September 1, 1962, and opened at the Metropolitan Opera on September 6. Their itinerary was longer than in 1959, lasting for nearly three months. The company took stops in New York, Los Angeles, Cleveland, San Francisco, Washington, Detroit, Philadelphia, Chicago, and Boston, before moving on to Canada in December.[13] The Bolshoi brought three full-length ballets, *Swan Lake*, *Giselle*, and *Spartacus*, and also performed a number of gala programs, combining one-act ballets with divertissements. The one-act ballets consisted of Asaf Messerer's *Ballet School*, Leonid Lavrovsky's *Paganini* to music by Rachmaninoff and *Walpurgis Night* to music by Gounod, Fokine's *Chopiniana*, the fourth act from Petipa's *La Bayadère*, and the fourth act from Nina Anisimova's *Gayane*.[14]

Publicly, the Cuban Missile Crisis cast a long shadow over the tour. American audiences were constantly aware of the nuclear threat; the same newspapers covering the Bolshoi's tour also ran daily discussions of the Cuban situation. In the midst of such intense fear, the success of the ballet exchange alleviated some concerns about Soviet-American relations. Newspapers in the United States and the Soviet Union treated the Bolshoi and concurrent New York City Ballet tours as a weather balloon for international relations. Harry MacArthur wrote in the *Evening Star*, "It is reassuring, in view of the events and tensions of recent weeks, to have the Bolshoi Ballet with us once again. Down here at the across-the-footlights level [...] the rapport between Russians and Americans is splendid."[15] Similar sentiments were expressed in the Soviet Union as well. In the months following the Bolshoi's tour to the United States, *Sovetskaia kultura* published an article explaining the importance of cultural exchange. The essay claimed that "In spite of the fact that the winds of the cold war were howling like an Arctic blizzard, the warmth of meetings of the Soviet performers with Americans [...] failed to die out."[16]

Moreover, in November, the Bolshoi became a pawn in the political negotiations, one channel for Kennedy to signal his goodwill to the Soviet government and to demonstrate his powers as a statesman. Though the Soviet and American governments agreed on the key points ending the Crisis in late October, negotiations were still ongoing through November 20 over the possibility of UN inspections of the missile sites and the removal of Soviet IL-28 bombers from Cuba.[17] When the Bolshoi Ballet appeared in Washington during these November negotiations, therefore, the Kennedy family went out of their way to stage as many public appearances with the dancers as possible. John and Jacqueline Kennedy together attended the Bolshoi's premiere in Washington, at which the troupe performed *Swan Lake* (Figure 3.1). In a symbolic gesture, the Kennedys sat across the horseshoe-shaped auditorium

Figure 3.1 The Kennedys arriving at Capitol Theater to see the Bolshoi perform *Swan Lake* with members of the Cabinet and their wives. Hurok is the fourth from the right. Staff Photo, *The Evening Star*, November 14, 1962. Reprinted with permission of the DC Public Library, Star Collection © Washington Post.

from the Soviet ambassador, Anatoly Dobrynin, who arrived with his wife and a party of advisors. Following the opening performance, the Kennedys invited the company to the White House for a special tour and another personal meeting. Jacqueline Kennedy also took her daughter Caroline to one of the troupe's rehearsals, where Maya Plisetskaya presented the little girl with presents, including a canister of film highlights from her career. Caroline Kennedy, who was only four years old at the time, also attended a second performance with a group of friends.[18] After the troupe left Washington, the larger Kennedy family continued to play a role in the Bolshoi's reception. While the company was in Boston, the president's mother invited some of the dancers to a pre-Thanksgiving dinner.[19]

Kennedy and his family presumably lavished so much attention on the Bolshoi in order to signal goodwill to the Soviet government. Indeed, he attended the Bolshoi's Washington performance in order to match a similar appearance by Khrushchev, who had seen an American baritone perform the lead role in *Boris Godunov* at the Bolshoi Theater on October 23, exactly in the middle of the Crisis.[20] Before the events of October 1962, there was no advance warning that the troupe might be graced with the president's presence, nor did any of the Kennedys become involved in hosting the dancers until November. This might simply have been a result of the fact that the troupe was located in New York for the opening of its tour and did not arrive in Boston or Washington until after the Crisis. It seems, however, that the Kennedys took advantage of the Bolshoi's high profile and its fortuitously timed appearances to create more positive public interactions with the Soviet government and its representatives.

While the Cuban Missile Crisis may have had a major impact on the Bolshoi Ballet's reception in the United States, the international political situation was not necessarily foremost on the performers' minds as they toured the country. Instead, the dancers were preoccupied with the day to day life of touring activities, the process of rehearsal, staging, and practice that governed their existence.[21] As always, the tour was hard on its participants, requiring long hours of work and constant performances in stressful living conditions.[22] When they were not performing or rehearsing, the dancers were again given a long sightseeing program to expose them to American culture. In New York, they toured the United Nations and attended a performance by Alvin Ailey American Dance Theater, productions at the Ice Revue and Radio City Music Hall, and two movies.[23] In Washington, DC, the company visited the National Gallery and in Detroit, the Ford museum and plant.

In Boston, they went to a rehearsal of the Boston Symphony Orchestra and met with professors from Harvard University.[24]

Personal and professional anxieties beset many company members. Homesickness played heavily on Lavrovsky and presumably others as well. In one letter from early September, the choreographer wrote to his wife, "In general everything is difficult, and in reality, boring. It already would be better to leave."[25] By September 20, just weeks into the tour, Vasily Pakhomov, the recently appointed director of the Bolshoi Theater, returned to the Soviet Union with choreographer Leonid Yakobson, who was leaving in disgrace following the failure of his production of *Spartacus*.[26] Conductor Yuri Faier also had trouble on tour, due in large part to his failing health. Hurok had to pay Faier's brother to take care of him, and American musicians and Soviet dancers alike complained about his work.[27]

Members of the Bolshoi also came under some pressure in the United States to renounce the Soviet Union, particularly from Rudolf Nureyev, the famous Kirov dancer who had defected the previous year in Paris.[28] Nureyev inserted himself into the Bolshoi's 1962 American trip when he sent Maya Plisetskaya flowers in New York, followed by a note requesting that she join him dancing "in the free world."[29] The incident only brought further scrutiny on Plisetskaya, who had already been subjected to heavy surveillance and pressure from the KGB.[30] Nureyev's actions also provoked some degree of furor within the troupe. One of Hurok's employees wanted to gather a few members of the Bolshoi to meet with Nureyev and apparently discussed the possibility with Yakobson and dancer Maris Liepa. The troupe's administration was not pleased and asked Hurok to send the offending agent away.[31] In the end, all the commotion came to nothing; not one dancer defected.

A different kind of trouble arose around the figure of Galina Ulanova. After retiring from the stage in 1960, the ballerina continued to work at the Bolshoi as a coach. As a result, Ulanova accompanied the troupe when they came to the United States. The tour coincided with the release of *Days with Ulanova*, a book prepared by American photojournalist Albert Eugene Kahn about the dancer's professional and personal life.[32] Ulanova was invited to attend a party in celebration of the book at the New York Public Library, which was also displaying an exhibition of Kahn's photographs.[33] Hurok was concerned that Ulanova's presence and the book's release would distract attention from the Bolshoi's performances, particularly away from Plisetskaya, whom he was now advertising heavily as the prima ballerina of the company.[34] The difficulty was compounded when, shortly after the company's arrival, Ulanova considered giving short performances in California, a decision she almost immediately retracted.[35] Despite Hurok's concerns, however, most focus remained on Plisetskaya.

Taste and the Dream of the Russian Classics

In the tenser Cold War atmosphere of 1962, the ballets that the company performed came under increased scrutiny from American critics, particularly regarding the relationships between taste and the Bolshoi's place in American artistic hierarchies. The two pillars of the Bolshoi's 1962 tour were supposed to be *Spartacus,* the new ballet by Aram Khachaturian and Leonid Yakobson, and *Swan Lake,* which would feature Plisetskaya in her most famous role (Figure 3.2). The latter selection, in particular, should have been an easy triumph for the company, as it had been well received in 1959.

Seeing a full-length *Swan Lake* was an important event for American balletomanes in 1962. Though it may seem surprising given the work's

Figure 3.2 Lily Spandorf's impression of the Bolshoi *Swan Lake* in the United States. Artist: Lily Spandorf, published in: Betty Beale, "President Goes to Bolshoi Ballet," *The Evening Star*, November 14, 1962.

current ubiquity, in the early 1960s no American ballet troupe danced the full *Swan Lake* in its canonical version. Many companies performed the second act, and some, such as American Ballet Theatre, kept a version of the third act pas de deux for gala programs.[36] But the only existing full-length American production at the time had been staged by Willam Christensen in 1940 for San Francisco Ballet. This was based on Christensen's memories of performing the second act, his reading of the libretto, and discussions with Russian immigrants who had seen the ballet decades before. The production departed substantially from the ballet's canonical choreographic text, created in 1895 by Marius Petipa and Lev Ivanov.[37] Thus, the Bolshoi's performances of the work in 1959 and 1962, along with the Kirov's in 1961, were some of the first opportunities that Americans had of seeing the full-length ballet live in its canonical form.

Yet to call any version of *Swan Lake* canonical belies the degree to which the ballet has always been a remarkably fluid work. Tchaikovsky wrote the score for an 1877 production at the Bolshoi Theater, choreographed by Julius Reisinger. This version was never particularly popular and was quickly lost. In 1895, after Tchaikovsky's death, Petipa restaged the ballet for St. Petersburg's Imperial Mariinsky Theater with the help of his assistant, Lev Ivanov, and composer-conductor Riccardo Drigo. It is this latter rendition of the work that is considered canonical, and it is this production against which American critics wanted to measure the Bolshoi and Kirov versions of *Swan Lake* during the 1960s. Even this choreographic text, however, is highly unstable. Within the first few years after its debut, the original choreographers had tinkered with it a number of times. Later in the twentieth century, stagers in both the Soviet Union and the West revised the ballet further. Notations for a relatively early version of the ballet were made at the turn of the century, but these notations only included the steps to twenty-three dances in the ballet, with no arm movements. Furthermore, the 1895 choreography used revised and cut versions of the original 1876 Tchaikovsky score, so anyone trying to stage a complete version of the canonic choreography had to skip some of the canonic music and vice versa.[38] Given that the score and choreography of the ballet have been partially lost and revised so many times, any number of different versions can lay claim to canonical status.

The Bolshoi's *Swan Lake* was based on the Petipa-Ivanov production of 1895, as restaged by Alexander Gorsky in 1901 and again in the early 1920s. The Gorsky choreography was revived by Asaf Messerer in 1956, with changes to Act IV but with the rest of the ballet left intact.[39] The choreography for this Bolshoi production was fairly similar to that performed by the Kirov. Comparing recordings of the Kirov and Bolshoi versions from this era shows that while the Kirov retained a slightly closer relationship to the Petipa original, in reality the two Soviet versions were more similar to each other than either one was to the 1895 production. Many changes to the Petipa version of the famous Act III pas de deux, for example, were shared between the two Soviet theaters.[40]

Most important for an American audience, however, the Kirov and Bolshoi productions differed in the second act, in which Prince Siegfried first encounters Odette by a moonlit lakeside. During the *adagio* at the center of this act, the two lovers are surrounded by dozens of swan maidens. In this section of the ballet, the Bolshoi used the same steps for Odette and Siegfried as the Kirov but changed those for the other swans. In the same act, the Bolshoi also performed an altered version of the "Dance of the Little Swans." In the Kirov version, like the Petipa production, four dancers clasp hands and perform intricate and rapid movements in unison.[41] In the Bolshoi version, there are six swans, not four, and while they begin with similar hands-clasped choreography, they quickly let go of each other and perform new steps.

Such differences over the canonical parts of the ballet were relatively modest. Nevertheless, these small differences between the Bolshoi and Kirov versions made a serious impression on American reviewers, particularly because the second act was the part of the ballet most familiar in the United States. While Plisetskaya and other performers garnered appreciative reviews, the general critical appraisal of the production was fairly lukewarm.[42] Alexander Fried in the *San Francisco Examiner* noted that the Bolshoi's changes to the ballet "were interesting as novelty, but not improvements on the past dance patterns."[43] Claudia Cassidy called the Bolshoi's choreography somewhat "conventional" in comparison to the versions performed by the Kirov and Stanislavsky Theaters, and Allen Hughes argued that the Kirov was more "incandescent," since they had the Petipa-Ivanov choreography.[44]

That American critics valued the Kirov's *Swan Lake* over the Bolshoi's was in keeping with general opinion in the United States about the differences between their two home cities of Leningrad and Moscow. Leningrad, formerly St. Petersburg, had been the capital of imperial Russia, and before the revolution, the Kirov had been named the Imperial Mariinsky Theater. By contrast, the Bolshoi was based in Moscow, the seat of the Soviet government. Western observers often saw Leningrad's imperial nature as a covert sign of its sympathies toward the West, in part because Peter the Great built the city in a European style and in part because the Soviet government had a highly contested relationship with the old capital.[45] For many ballet dancers in the United States, the Kirov's Western connections were personal, as most of the Russian dancers who had immigrated to the West during the early and middle part of the twentieth century had trained and performed there.[46] This point of view was perhaps best summed up by one audience member, Kenneth Rexroth, who wrote into the letters section of the *San Francisco Examiner* to complain about the deficiencies of the Bolshoi:

> Stalin lived in Moscow and got the kind of ballet he liked. The leaps are Olympic and the splits are physiologically unbelievable: if they make a point they underline it three times.
>
> Up in Leningrad the Kirov was a ballet for those rotten diversionists, wreckers and Trotskyite mad dogs—in other words, Western European intellectuals, just like me.[47]

As Rexroth's words indicate, some Americans imagined themselves allies of the Kirov Theater against Moscow, and sometimes even as the inheritors of the Mariinsky's legacy. In a way then, Rexroth's understanding of the Bolshoi and the Kirov was a balletic version of American modernization theory, in which the United States represented the right path of political progress, and the Soviet Union an aberration. In this version of events, the Soviet Union had interrupted the correct evolution of ballet in Russia, and only those artists fleeing the Bolsheviks, first to Western Europe and then eventually to the United States, had properly taken up this abandoned path to the future. The Kirov could thus be an ally of American observers, though it too was only valued insofar as it preserved ballet's past. The future of ballet could only be found in the West.

Rexroth very explicitly related his comparison of the two companies to the question of "taste," which he claimed was "really the point of the whole matter."[48] He argued that the Kirov and its fans possessed this taste, while the Bolshoi, as an extension of the communist leaders, had little. In writing about "taste," Rexroth, like many other American reviewers of the Bolshoi in 1962, implied that it was an ineffable quality, an easily recognizable essence of refinement. As Pierre Bourdieu argues, though, while taste is often conceptualized as an innate capacity for discernment, in reality it is closely linked to educational level and economic class.[49] In remarking on the Bolshoi's taste or lack of taste, then, critics were commenting on its appropriateness or inappropriateness for the audiences assembled to watch.

The tastes of the audiences at the Bolshoi were distinctly upper class, a fact related to the wealth and social standing required to get in the door, particularly in New York and Los Angeles. Hurok's prices were widely considered to be inordinately expensive. In New York, tickets topped out at $15 for regular performances and at $25 for opening night. Resale prices could reach $100, the equivalent of $830 in 2018. As a point of comparison, for the same season the Metropolitan Opera's most expensive tickets sold for a face value of $11.[50] Moreover, Hurok restricted first access to a special list of loyal subscribers.[51] Nonprofit groups sometimes purchased large swathes of seats and resold them at a substantial markup for benefit evenings. Newspapers reported on the who's who of attendees, in some cases describing the audiences' clothing in as much detail as they discussed the dancing.[52] Such audiences expected an artistic display that they would consider commensurate with the status and wealth required to purchase a ticket.

At the same time, it was more than merely cost that gave American audiences such expectations for the Bolshoi. The State Academic Folk Dance Ensemble of the USSR (the Moiseyev Dance Company) had visited the United States in 1958 to widespread acclaim. Their tickets too were extremely expensive, though not quite as dear as those for the Bolshoi, with a face value of $8.05 and an $80 resale value.[53] Because the Moiseyev was a folk troupe, however, perceived as a lower-class genre than ballet, the audiences did not expect the same level of taste that they did from the Bolshoi. Audiences instead applauded the company for its virtuosity, its physical prowess and precision.[54] This does not mean that taste did not play into the Moiseyev's reception; rather, the entire company was judged in advance to be of a lower status than Soviet ballet companies. Indeed, when the company was scheduled to come to the United States, some American dance experts complained that the folk ensemble did not perform a high art genre. They wanted to see the Bolshoi.[55]

This type of hierarchy operated quite differently in the Soviet Union, where, according to the state, there was no difference between high and low culture. Of course, the Soviets did maintain a clear hierarchy that placed the fine arts, including ballet, above television and mass film culture. Nevertheless, the point of this culture, at least propagandistically, was not to maintain distinction between the lower and higher classes but to lift all Soviet citizens up to the point where they could understand the beauty of ballet, the poetry of Pushkin.[56]

Spartacus and the Hollywood Biblical Epics

During the Bolshoi's 1962 tour of the United States, these two models for understanding high culture came into conflict, in no place more than in the reception of the ballet *Spartacus*. In some ways, *Spartacus* had been conceived as the ideal socialist realist ballet. The libretto had been written in the 1930s by Nikolai Volkov, the same author who wrote such important drambalety as *Flames of Paris, Fountain of the Bakhchisarai*, and *Cinderella*. The ballet told the story of Spartacus's slave rebellion in ancient Rome. Volkov gave the work a melodramatic twist by tying Spartacus's eventual downfall to the betrayal of his friend Harmodius. The ballet's rebellion was transparently meant to be a metaphor for the Bolshevik revolution, and Spartacus to stand in for its leaders.

Armenian composer Aram Khachaturian finished the score in 1954. The work was written in the high-Stalinist style of the 1930s and 1940s, full of bombastic chromatic harmonies, syncopated rhythms, and winding lyrical melodies. Nevertheless, despite its seeming perfections for the Soviet stage, *Spartacus* had a long and complex history in the Soviet Union. Following its premiere at the Kirov Theater in 1956, with choreography by Leonid Yakobson, the ballet was produced numerous times by Soviet theaters. The Bolshoi alone staged three different versions of the ballet. The first two of these productions, from 1958 and 1962, were heavily criticized and removed quickly from the Bolshoi stage. Only in 1968, fourteen years after Khachaturian finished the score, did the Bolshoi finally create a version of the work that met with lasting approval. This is the production that is famous with audiences today.[57]

It was the second of these three productions, the Bolshoi's 1962 version, that the company brought to the United States. Yakobson revised his choreography for the Moscow company over the early months of 1962, just in time for the tour. This production of *Spartacus* was highly unusual. The cultural Thaw of the late 1950s and early 1960s opened up possibilities for Soviet choreographers to challenge the tenets of the drambalet.[58] Yakobson's revisions, however, bore little resemblance to those of the other Thaw choreographers, most of whom, such as Igor Belsky and Yuri Grigorovich, were much younger and primarily interested in highlighting music-choreographic relationships.[59]

Yakobson instead hoped to improve the ballet through the use of nationalist gestures. He himself had been trained as a character dancer, a performer who specialized in nationalist or exotic *divertissements*. Yakobson believed that through the application of nationalist dancing he could create more nuanced and realistic ballets.[60] In his 1969 book *Letters to Noverre*, he repeatedly likened himself to eighteenth-century French choreographer Jean-Georges Noverre and early twentieth-century Russian choreographer Michel Fokine, both of whom created more expressive movement by uniting classical and character gestures.[61] In *Spartacus*, Yakobson drew on impressions of Roman art and on the techniques of character dancing to create a style of ballet without pointe shoes, in which the dancers often counterpoised their limbs to one another in a highly fluid manner. Rather than the straight legs and classical *port-de-bras* of nineteenth-century ballet, Yakobson's dancers used bent elbows, knees, and wrists to evoke images of ancient Rome. Yakobson's resulting production earned only lukewarm reviews in Moscow; critics and audiences complained about the work's overreliance on pantomime.[62]

Spartacus's socialist realist credentials were one reason to include the ballet in the Bolshoi's 1962 repertoire, but there was another reason as well. Hollywood epic films featuring ancient Roman and Greek settings dominated the American film market in the 1950s. Yakobson's version of *Spartacus* bore numerous similarities to these films, such as *Ben-Hur*, *The Ten Commandments*, *Quo Vadis?*, *The Robe*, and Stanley Kubrick's film version of *Spartacus*, all of which had made millions of dollars at the box office.[63] Presumably Sol Hurok and the leadership of the Bolshoi had these connections in mind when they selected the ballet for the 1962 tour. Not only did *Spartacus* tell a similar story to the Hollywood epics, but it also resembled those movies in some uncanny ways.

Perhaps the most fundamental connection between *Spartacus* and these American films was the luxurious manner in which they were produced. Both wallowed in expense, a way of demonstrating the massive economic power that could be wielded by Hollywood executives or by the Soviet government. Huge numbers of extras were hired to fill out scenes in movie epics, and advertising often harped on the films' budget totals.[64] Similarly, Yakobson's *Spartacus* used a two-hundred-member cast in order to make the crowd scenes look appropriately grand. In the United States, the company hired American supernumeraries to ensure that the production retained its massive proportions. When advertising the ballet to American audiences, Hurok focused on its size and quoted specific numbers of personnel in order to convey its scale.[65] The impresario claimed that this would give American audiences a chance to sense the "enormous scope of the Moscow stage."[66]

Just as the visuals in *Spartacus* and the Hollywood epics conveyed monumentality, so too did the music. The typical Hollywood film score of the 1950s featured lush orchestrations that evoked a wide sense of scope in similar ways to the movies' immense sets and casts.[67] Such scores often bore similarities to Soviet music of the same era, including *Spartacus*. Khachaturian's ballet score demands a large orchestra and frequently relies on massive brass and percussion sections to create grand effects.[68]

Not only was the production for *Spartacus* immense, it was also self-consciously historic in the manner of the Hollywood epics. In preparation for his version of *Spartacus*, Yakobson spent copious time examining Roman and Greek art at the Hermitage museum.[69] At key moments of the ballet, such as during the death of Spartacus's fellow gladiator, the dancers froze into *bas-relief*, motionless but dynamic *tableaux* that evoked the friezes of ancient Greek and Roman art. Yakobson's attention to historical research echoed the approach of the Hollywood directors, who displayed a consistent concern, not just for historical accuracy itself but for making that historicism legible to audiences. These directors often went to great lengths to assure audiences of research that had gone into their productions, hiring academic consultants and providing voice-overs to explain the historical context.[70]

In staging the Roman empire in such grandeur and historical detail, Yakobson's *Spartacus*, much like Hollywood epics, created a sense of authority that played into Cold War geopolitical concerns. As classicist Maria Wyke argues, Hollywood epic films drew on political tropes connecting American democracy to ancient civilizations. Such comparisons had been used in the national political discourse since the founding of the US government.[71] It is highly notable, however, as many film scholars have pointed out, that the heroes of the Hollywood biblical epics are not the Romans but rather the oppressed peoples of the Roman empire. In *Ben-Hur*, the main character is a leader of the Jewish people. Thus, at the same time that they relied on the authority of ancient Rome to soothe their audience's anxieties about the present, these films also presented the United States as an anti-imperial force.[72] The same ambivalence about empire is present in the Soviet *Spartacus*, in which the slaves serve as symbolic Bolsheviks and yet in which the Roman empire is presented as impressive and authoritative.

Such ambivalence around Cold War empire was also evident in the way that both the Soviet production of *Spartacus* and the American epic films depicted their heroes as allies of ethnic and racial Others. These attempts suggested a parallel to the superpowers' efforts to align themselves with various postcolonial states during the 1950s and 1960s. At the same time that these works present their heroes as allies of marginalized and oppressed characters, they all maintain a racial hierarchy to centralize their white characters and to allow their audiences to take pleasure in Orientalist spectacle. In *Ben-Hur,* for example, the hero allies himself with an Arab sheik. Welsh actor Hugh Griffith, who played the role of the sheik in blackface, won the Academy Award for best supporting actor. While Sheik Ilderim is undoubtedly Judah Ben-Hur's friend, his exotic and lascivious ways also serve to contrast with and therefore highlight Ben-Hur's chaste, Judeo-Christian morality. In the same movie, a group of black dancers perform a primitivist dance at a Roman feast; they are dressed in almost nonexistent costumes and consistently shot in wide frames and at oblique angles that reduce their personhood. While the film associates this display with Roman immorality, it simultaneously encourages the viewer to enjoy it.[73]

Yakobson's production similarly highlighted the ethnic diversity of the slave characters in the ballet, often staging short numbers to portray the different ethnicities of the oppressed slaves. He also probably employed dark skin makeup so that the dancers playing slaves would look racially diverse. While the choreographer tried very consciously to demonstrate the ethnic diversity of the Spartakans, however, he maintained a hierarchy between peripheral, exotic characters and central, white characters.[74] The slaves in the Soviet *Spartacus* were meant to be a metaphor, not just for the Bolshevik revolutionaries, but also for an alliance of communist and postcolonial states in the Cold War. Khachaturian even remarked in an essay on his ballet score that Spartacus could be compared to revolutionaries in Vietnam and Korea.[75]

The peripheral characters in *Spartacus* were often staged in a highly erotic way. The dance of the three slaves at Crassus's feast, for instance, involved two men rubbing their hands up and down a woman's body. In a description of the ballet that Yakobson gave to the artistic advisory committee at the Bolshoi, he recounted the scene in which the concubine Aegina seduces a Roman slave: "Aegina twists her lithe body in languor and voluptuousness. She clings to the slave, she spurns him, inflaming him with passion."[76]

Khachaturian's music for the ballet, much like many Hollywood biblical epic scores, creates a contrast between Spartacus's relatively clear-cut, militarized melodies, and the winding, chromatic woodwind lines used to depict exotic women in the ballet.

Yakobson's lewd dances and scandalously short costumes inflamed debates about immorality at the Bolshoi that had been simmering as a result of Khrushchev's political Thaw. Many Soviet citizens saw the political changes as a relaxation of socialist morality.[77] It was these same debates around sexuality that compelled Goskontsert to discourage American Ballet Theatre from performing *Billy the Kid* and New York City Ballet from showing *Afternoon of a Faun* and *The Cage* during their tours of the Soviet Union. Members of the artistic advisory committee at the Bolshoi were divided about the appropriateness of Yakobson's choreography to the stage.[78] During one of the artistic committee meetings, Yakobson gave his explanation for his highly sexualized dances:

> The morals at these [Roman] feasts were such that it is now impossible to speak of them. That which we wanted to show—it is trivial in comparison with what was then at the feasts, but from our point of view, it is perhaps a bit too much.[79]

Much like the Hollywood filmmakers, Yakobson thus justified the presence of the erotic by assigning it to the Romans, the villains of the story.

While Yakobson's production ostensibly condemned the Romans for their sexual deviancy and exploitation of other ethnic groups, however, the viewers were drawn into a sensual visual experience in which they were encouraged to take pleasure in that same exploitation. In both the Soviet Union and the United States, these epic stories encouraged their intended audiences to imagine their own country as the heroic ally of newly independent postcolonial nations. Yet in both cases, the artistic effect was to emphasize the moral authority and historical centrality of the United States and the Soviet Union, and in both cases the viewer was encouraged to indulge in exoticist fantasies.

Spartacus thus echoed many aspects of American Hollywood epics, reflecting deep similarities across the Iron Curtain, from American and Soviet anxieties about sexuality, to the geopolitical goals of the two countries, to their shared concerns about empire. Yet because of these very similarities, the Bolshoi's performances of Yakobson's *Spartacus* were perhaps the greatest artistic disaster of the early Soviet-American cultural exchange. The New York audiences booed loudly on opening night, and critics followed with excoriating reviews.[80] Allen Hughes bemoaned in the *New York Times* that "the fact that one of the greatest ballet companies in the world would invest so much talent, time, money, and, presumably, belief in the staging of a dull pageant is simply beyond understanding."[81] By the week after its American premiere, it was clear that *Spartacus* was a flop. Hurok canceled the ballet's final three performances in New York, replacing it with a production of *Giselle* and two triple bills that would include *Ballet School*.[82] The cancellation and the derision in the press were very hard on Yakobson. Maya Plisetskaya, who stood firmly by the production, recalled in her memoirs: "Only after the last performance of *Spartacus* in New York [...] did Yakobson sit down on the metal stool in my dressing room at the Met and break out into silent weeping. Large, heavy tears dropped from his blue eyes."[83]

There is a palpable tension between the American reception of *Spartacus* and the joy that many of the ballet's participants and viewers took from it. Plisetskaya was an unwavering supporter of Yakobson's work. American dancers Rosie Novellino-Mearns and Wendy Perron, who were both teenage supernumeraries in 1962, have written about the excitement they felt for the ballet as well. Moreover, a number of American reviewers described the work as joyful or over-the-top in a pleasing way.[84] Something, however, bothered these American audiences enough to pan the production despite its charms. It is likely that part of the problem that Americans had with the production was the way it strangely mirrored the geopolitics of Hollywood epic films.[85] Allen Hughes remarked, "Perhaps parallels can be drawn between the story and events in Russian history that give the work a special patriotic or ideological appeal for Russians it does not have for us."[86]

More than politics, however, the aesthetic comparison between the Bolshoi *Spartacus* and Hollywood films was distasteful to New York audiences because it was a sign that the production failed to fit into ballet's designated place in their aesthetic hierarchies. Over and over again, reviewers compared the ballet *Spartacus* to Hollywood sword-and-sandal epics, but the comparisons were not flattering. According to Allen Hughes, the music was "very much in the style of Hollywood sound tracks, and this may be significant, for the work as a whole represents a sadly disappointing attempt to do something that Hollywood manages better."[87] The critical dismissal of the Bolshoi *Spartacus* reflected a similar reaction on the part of film reviewers to Hollywood epics. While audiences flocked to films such as *The*

Ten Commandments, mid-century critics were generally quite cool to them. Often, the very spectacle that defined the genre could undermine its artistic credibility.[88]

New York dance critics' negative reaction to the Bolshoi *Spartacus* thus mimicked the reaction to Hollywood epics, in particular because the Bolshoi's style of production already played into similar concerns. Dance reviewers objecting to the expense and decoration in the Bolshoi *Spartacus* echoed film critics but also harkened back to the American reception of *Romeo and Juliet* in 1959 as a production "only communists can afford."[89] Similarly, the comparison resonated with American beliefs that the Bolshoi was hopelessly old-fashioned, because some also felt that Hollywood epics were passé.[90] Many of the American critics compared the Bolshoi's *Spartacus* specifically to Cecil B. DeMille's epic films of the 1920s and 1930s rather than to the more recent spate of such blockbusters.[91] P. W. Manchester of the *Christian Science Monitor*, for instance, remarked that "Sad to say, it is a bore on a colossal scale; the kind of spectacle which old silent movies did very much better."[92]

The concerns about *Spartacus* and the Hollywood epics played into the already overwhelming preoccupation with ballet's status as an elite art form. Critic after critic lamented *Spartacus*'s lack of taste. For example, Jean Battey wrote in the *Washington Post, Times Herald* that "it is the heavy-handed portentousness, the outright schmaltz and the overdone emotionalism that make 'Spartacus' so tasteless."[93] Similarly, Perron has pointed to the production's eroticism as its greatest problem, arguing that this was "not catering to good taste."[94]

Despite widespread condemnation of the ballet on the grounds of taste, certain viewers indicated that the ballet was enjoyable if not respectable. Not only do both Novellino-Mearns and Perron describe their excitement to take part in the production, but many 1962 critics discussed their fondness for it along with their disapproval. Walter Terry remarked in his review of *Spartacus* that "it is great fun every now and again to have a mad feast, rather like one who diets permitting himself the abandon of a butterscotch sundae (with nuts) (with cream too) (and marshmallows)."[95] Los Angeles critic John Chapman also enjoyed *Spartacus*, describing it as "a wide-screen orgy in three-dimensional technicolor."[96] Chapman believed quite firmly that price factored into the American reaction to *Spartacus*, writing "anybody who pays $15 for one ticket is bound to take ballet as seriously as a death in the family."[97] Chapman's words suggest how much class and ballet's newly elite status in New York fueled concerns about *Spartacus*. If ballet were not taken in such a serious light, related to its new highbrow status and expensive tickets, American audiences might have reacted better to the relatively populist work, just as American filmgoers welcomed *Ben-Hur*.

In the end, it was the very connection to the Hollywood epics, the connection that must have seem so promising before the tour, that doomed Yakobson's balletic *Spartacus* in the United States. It is possible to speculate on an alternate past in which the Bolshoi did not scrap *Spartacus* after three performances but instead took it on the road to its other cities: Los Angeles, Cleveland, San Francisco, Washington, Detroit, Philadelphia, Chicago, and Boston. Possibly, in these cities, farther away from the concerns of the New York critics about ballet's status, the production would have found kinder reception, audiences who could have recognized the emotional and kinetic power of Khachaturian's score, the subtlety and charisma of Plisetskaya's performance as Phrygia, and the aesthetic innovations of Yakobson's *bas-relief* scenes—and perhaps could have enjoyed the sight of two hundred people on a stage filled with lush Roman spectacle.

The Success: *Ballet School*

The class-based nature of the *Spartacus* critique comes into sharper relief in the context of the Bolshoi's one major success from its 1962 tour: the new one-act *Ballet School*, a work created specifically for the Soviet-American cultural exchange tours. Hurok, after attending the graduation exercises of the Moscow Choreographic Academy, requested that the Bolshoi bring something similar to the United States for its tour. In response, Messerer choreographed a ballet that would show the growth of a dancer in the Soviet system, starting as a young child and eventually blossoming into a principal in the company.[98] *Ballet School* opens with small children performing warm-up exercises at the *barre*. These children are eventually replaced by members of the *corps de ballet*, who begin doing basic steps as well, gradually increasing the speed and complexity of their combinations. The work ends with a series of virtuosic feats from the company's biggest stars; in 1962, Maya Plisetskaya, Nikolai Fadeyechev, Ekaterina Maximova, Vladimir Vasiliev, and Mikhail Lavrovsky wowed audiences with their jumps, turns, and lifts. Throughout the ballet, Messerer himself stayed on stage, playing the role of the teacher (Figure 3.3).[99]

Figure 3.3 Messerer directs children onstage in *Ballet School*. Screen capture from film of a performance of the work on the stage of the Bolshoi Theater.

In order to depict the full education of a Soviet dancer, *Ballet School* required the participation of about twenty young children. Because transporting and then caring for Soviet students for twelve weeks in a foreign country was unfeasible, the Bolshoi employed a small group of local children in each of their destination cities. Before arriving in a tour city, the company would release a press announcement calling for young dancers to audition, often specifying the appropriate ages or heights—children with classical ballet training, between the ages of ten and thirteen, and between 4 foot 5 inches and 4 foot 9 inches. These young people would perform basic ballet movements for Soviet observers. Hundreds of students arrived for each of the auditions, hoping to appear onstage with the famous troupe. Messerer, who was the Bolshoi's head ballet coach, conducted the final part of the auditions himself. The winning children rehearsed briefly with the company before appearing in the final productions.[100]

In its structure and design, *Ballet School* closely resembled Danish choreographer Harald Lander's *Études*, which he created for the Royal Danish Ballet in 1948.[101] Indeed the works are so similar that it seems highly probable that Messerer had seen *Études* before choreographing his own work.[102]

It is almost certain that Hurok had it in mind when he requested the ballet, a canny move, since American Ballet Theatre had restaged *Études* in the United States just the year before to general praise.[103] Both ballets are danced on an empty or near empty stage, devoid of any setting beyond a few *barres* used in the opening section. Both pieces are structured around the minute-by-minute accounting of a ballet class, beginning with simple work at the *barre*, then proceeding to work on the floor, first center *adagio*, then turns and jumps. Both works also end in a flurry of virtuosity.

While the two ballets are structured similarly and have a very similar look, however, they depart from each other rather sharply in their aesthetic aims, a contrast that is most apparent from their musical settings. In general, *Études* is the more concentrated, almost proto-minimalist work, with long stretches of repetitive, atomized movement, while *Ballet School* treats its dancers as human characters, emphasizing full body expression. The score to the Western ballet, *Études*, is a set of piano études by Carl Czerny, orchestrated by Knudåge Riisager.[104] For an overture, the orchestra plays minutes upon minutes of scales. These simple musical exercises didactically inform the audience of the ballet's subject: the steps performed by the dancers will be similar to the scales practiced by a musician. The style of the piano études, the atomized chunks of musical information that are repeated again and again, also reflects the style of the choreography. In the opening scene, a line of women at the *barre* perform *tendus, ronds de jambe, battements,* and *développés,* all exercises that utilize one leg moving out to the side, front, or back, often in the air. The stage is entirely black and the women are lit only around their legs, so that it seems as if the legs are moving independently. The women are entirely dehumanized, separated from the mechanical processes of their bodies. Throughout, the almost invariably emotionless music separates the viewer from the dancer, making the figures onstage appear doll-like rather than human.

The Bolshoi's *Ballet School*, in contrast, presents its characters as human actors. This is reflected in the score, which was arranged from dances by Glazunov, Liadov, Liapunov, and Shostakovich.[105] Most of the musical selections are frothy nineteenth-century pieces, often with a lyrical melody carried over an unobtrusive, steady accompaniment. These pieces help connect the audience with the dancers onstage, granting their movements a more humanizing element. A greater emphasis is placed on the dancers' musicality and on their entire bodies; while the ballerinas are spotlighted in their work at the *barre*, mimicking Lander's *Études*, at no point does that lighting cut out any part of their bodies. For instance, in an early *barre* sequence of *Ballet School*, the ballerinas perform a series of extensions, during which the string section of the orchestra swells in sweeping melodies.[106]

One of the goals of staging *Ballet School* on tour was to demonstrate the stunning virtuosity of the Bolshoi's lead principals, who showed off their most impressive steps in the final moments of the ballet. P. W. Manchester wrote that "at one point the stage seemed to be filled with boys and girls running across it at top speed, the girls thrown into the air and caught again in flight, and all smiling away as though it were the simplest thing in the world."[107] The end of the ballet looks like a dozen codas from a nineteenth-century ballet stitched together. Multiple women perform long series of *fouettés*, sometimes stationary and sometimes charging across the stage. At one point a handful of ballerinas perform hops on pointe.[108] By staging these stunning technical elements in one ballet, each performed hard on the heels of the last, the Bolshoi could emphasize the depth of its talent. This assemblage of virtuosity was one aspect of the Soviet company that was intimidating to its American viewers. American ballet troupes were in general much smaller than their Soviet counterparts, and they had fewer stars. In 1959, American critics had frequently noted that the second and third Bolshoi casts were often as good as the first-night casts, demonstrating the enormous wealth of Soviet talent.[109]

Messerer's decision to display the Bolshoi dancers as virtuosic and human subjects, rather than as Lander's machines, reinforced the ballet's dramatic purpose, to demonstrate the hard work involved in becoming a Bolshoi dancer. The emphasis on hard work, seen on stage in the reproduction of the dancers' daily drills, correlated with the aggrandizement of heroes and celebrities in the Soviet Union. Athletes were often touted in Soviet publications as examples of the New Soviet Man, a near-superhuman ideal promised in propaganda as the everyman of the future. Articles about these athletes emphasized their daily training regimes as evidence that a scientific approach to work could transform human nature.[110] *Ballet School* did something similar in demonstrating a scientific approach to dance training that ended in a virtuosic display of the Soviet subject. The work was appropriate enough to Soviet sensibilities that when the company returned to Moscow, they kept *Ballet School* in their repertoire under the title *Class Concert*.[111]

However much *Ballet School* may have furthered Soviet policies, many American critics transliterated *Ballet School* firmly through the lens of Balanchine and Lander's work. Critics, particularly those located in the

Northeast, complimented the Bolshoi for showing its dancers unadorned, and for celebrating movement for movement's sake. Walter Terry described it as a celebration of the dancers' exertions, but he also compared *Ballet School* directly to Balanchine's oeuvre, and praised it for contrasting so sharply with the Bolshoi's narrative fare.[112] John Chapman called *Ballet School* the "masterpiece" of the season.[113]

Critics who were not full-time dance specialists or who lived further away from New York were less likely to read *Ballet School* as an attempt at abstract neoclassicism and more likely to take the production at face value, accepting it as a demonstration of Soviet educational methods. Allen Hughes, for instance, who at the time wrote for the *New York Times* primarily as a music critic, praised the work as a depiction of a ballet class.[114] Similarly, Alexander Fried of the *San Francisco Chronicle* approached the ballet as a pedagogical display, even complaining that it could lead audiences to believe that "sheer acrobatics" were the pinnacle of the Bolshoi's abilities.[115] Of course, the critics also enjoyed the fact that American children were performing with the great Bolshoi Ballet. Indeed, the decision to use American children in the production, though done for practical reasons, also provided the company with excellent publicity. Because *Ballet School* required an audition and rehearsal period before the performances, the Bolshoi's arrival in every city was heralded over a week in advance with newspaper articles about this process.[116]

The split within the American critical reading of *Ballet School* was another reflection of the ballet critics' concern with taste. The New York dance critics were concerned with fitting *Ballet School* into their parameters of highbrow modernist ballet, while other American critics were happy to let the ballet stand as a testament to the hard work of ballet dancers or a demonstration of superb virtuosity.

Transliteration and Reconciliation in the Bolshoi's 1962 Tour

Owing to the excellent reception of *Ballet School* and the continuing support for the company's dancers, then, the Bolshoi's 1962 tour achieved a moderate success. The full tour could be seen as an important victory for reconciliation at a time when military and conventional diplomatic relations between the two countries were at their worst.[117] The Bolshoi's 1962 achievements in the face of the Cuban Missile Crisis represent the height of the exchange's ability to foster real goodwill between the nuclear superpowers.

Nevertheless, the tour did demonstrate an area of strain between the two countries, as each aspired to lead the new twentieth-century empire. The need to provide artistic accomplishments that would justify such an international position both fueled domestic concerns about ballet and made the art form useful to cultural exchange programs. Critics, particularly those in New York, hoped to make American ballet an international leader in its field, and they anticipated doing this through elite, modernist styles. As we will see again in chapter 4, ballet's newly highbrow status in the United States and its usefulness to the American government in cultural exchange were strongly tied together. In promoting this type of ballet for the United States, American critics felt the need to denigrate Soviet ballet as tasteless, lacking the class that they hoped their own art would display.

The tour also showed how much differing expectations for ballet could confound plans for the cultural exchange. When the Bolshoi arrived in the United States in 1962, no one in the company would have guessed that the big success of the tour would be *Ballet School*, that *Spartacus* would flop, and that *Swan Lake* would garner only grudging praise for the dancers. But that was because no one in the Soviet troupe had imagined how an elite American audience would transliterate those works. To these viewers, *Ballet School* did not seem like end-of-the-year exercises for schoolchildren, but rather like Balanchine's neoclassical works. *Swan Lake* did not seem an unassailable classic, but rather like a pale imitation of the Kirov's imperial splendor. *Spartacus* did not seem like a heroic tale told through dance but rather like a Hollywood epic film. In the end, it was the tastes of American audiences that determined the worth of Soviet dance in the United States.

American critics and audiences understood the Soviet works through their own prisms of experience, and they were perfectly eager to recast Soviet ballets in American terms when those ballets were a triumph. At the same time, a similar process was working out on a greater scale with the New York City Ballet's tour of the Soviet Union. The success of that company with Soviet audiences was tremendous, but much like their American counterparts, the Soviet critics drew their visitors' performances into debates over the merits of domestic ballet.

4

"Ballet Is a Flower"

New York City Ballet's 1962 Tour of the Soviet Union

Over the course of October and November 1962, just as the Bolshoi Ballet was touring the United States, New York City Ballet was performing to packed halls across the Soviet Union. From the futuristic Kremlin Palace of Congresses in Moscow to the elegant Kirov Theater in Leningrad, the company was greeted by cheers, bravos, and thunderous clapping. In city after city, by audience after audience, New York City Ballet was welcomed enthusiastically.

However gratifying they were, such exuberant ovations came as a great surprise to American participants and observers of the tour, who had feared critical and popular outcry against the company. New York City Ballet's choreographer, George Balanchine, was famous as an innovator of neoclassical, abstract ballets. Moreover, he had left the Soviet Union in 1924 for the West. American experts had assumed that he and his company would be sharply criticized in the Soviet Union. Instead, Balanchine and his works were welcomed with open arms.

New York City Ballet's 1962 tour of the Soviet Union has garnered far more scholarly attention than any other encounter from the Cold War ballet exchange. There are understandable reasons. The tour took place, like its counterpart, during the Cuban Missile Crisis. It was also the first time that Balanchine returned home to the Soviet Union following his emigration in 1924. Finally, the warm welcome extended to Balanchine and his company so confounded American expectations that it seemed to demand an explanation. Previous scholarly accounts have mostly evaluated the tour from an American perspective, according to American historical narratives and primarily using American sources. They thus generally place the tour either in the context of Balanchine's development as a choreographer or the United States' triumph in the Cold War.[1] The major exception is dance historian Clare Croft's *Dancers as Diplomats,* which discusses the experiences of the New York City Ballet dancers. Croft concludes that the American and Soviet dancers had a great deal in common with one another and that the conflicts raised by the tour have been overemphasized.[2] This is an important step in understanding the events as they were lived by the participants, and Croft's work complicates the triumphalist narratives about Balanchine's success in the Soviet Union.

Nevertheless, the tour's reception still needs to be re-examined, and it is better understood through exploration of Soviet sources and in the context of Soviet history than through an American lens. New York City Ballet arrived in Moscow at the height of the Thaw, when choreographic symphonism was replacing the drambalet on Soviet stages. But this change did not happen instantaneously or by fiat. Like most cultural shifts during the Thaw, it was the subject of sustained debate.[3] Because New York City Ballet arrived in Moscow during this time of transformation, the company's repertoire was evaluated by Soviet critics in the context of the ongoing arguments about the old and new styles of ballet.

In placing Balanchine's works in this new context, the Soviet critical essays on Balanchine demonstrated the deep similarities between the new Soviet and American choreographic styles of the 1950s and 1960s. At the heart of both was an emphasis on music. Thus, Soviet ballet experts and casual audiences alike were to some degree prepared to understand Balanchine's work, and the language of official Soviet aesthetics could easily be applied to the analysis of the New York City Ballet repertoire. Most reviewers discussed Balanchine's works in a positive, appreciative tone.

Nevertheless, there were also areas in which these similarities broke down; this happened not so much on the side of choreography, but in the realms of reception and philosophy. A neoclassical Balanchine ballet might look very similar to a choreographic symphonic work, but the Soviet audience understood it very differently from an American one. While Soviet critics admired Balanchine's choreography, they argued frequently and firmly against his artistic philosophies, which he laid out in interviews with Soviet publications. The key disagreement between Balanchine and his hosts centered on music's meaning. These arguments had their roots in nineteenth-century philosophy and criticism, filtered through Cold War politics. On the American side, Balanchine argued that music had no meaning, and that therefore any ballet that responded directly to its score would do so in terms of formalism and pure aesthetic experience. On the Soviet side, most critics argued that music had definite meaning and that dance should translate this interior content into choreography. The resulting conflict in understanding shaped New York City Ballet's reception in the Soviet Union.

New York City Ballet and Its Relationship to the State Department

George Balanchine (1904–1983) was one of the most important figures of twentieth-century ballet. He grew up in St. Petersburg, Russia, and trained there at the ballet section of the Imperial Theater School. Balanchine began choreographing in the early 1920s. In 1924 he left Russia for Western Europe, performing in Germany and England before arriving in France, where he worked for Diaghilev's Ballets Russes.[4] In 1933, Balanchine moved to the United States at the behest of American impresario Lincoln Kirstein, and together they founded the School of American Ballet (SAB), along with a performing troupe to showcase student talent in Balanchine's works. During the 1930s, Balanchine also choreographed for a number of Broadway and Hollywood musicals. Though the school's original ballet troupe fell apart in 1940, six years later Balanchine and Kirstein established a new company in connection with SAB. The group was renamed New York City Ballet in 1948.[5]

As early as the 1940s, Kirstein and Balanchine were already involved with the State Department's cultural diplomacy program. In 1941, Kirstein led a troupe touring Latin America in execution of the United States' Good Neighbor policy.[6] During the 1950s, with the establishment of New York City Ballet, the relationship deepened. From 1955 to 1960, Kirstein sat on the ANTA dance panel.[7] Along with American Ballet Theatre, New York City Ballet was one of the companies most frequently chosen for State Department–funded tours. Though Kirstein recused himself from direct votes on his company, his presence on the board almost certainly helped secure funding.[8] At one meeting of the panel, Kirstein claimed that New York City Ballet needed the steady income from State Department tours to survive.[9] Moreover, Balanchine and his fellow administrators were often eager to reach out to the State Department to suggest new collaborations between the organizations. For a short period, Balanchine staged ballets with foreign companies through the auspices of the State Department, framing the activities as "donations" from the US government. In the 1960s, New York City Ballet also helped sponsor participants in the State Department's "reverse flow" program, which allowed foreign artists to spend time in the United States.[10]

Balanchine's and Kirstein's efforts to work in collaboration with the State Department seem to have been motivated by both sincere feelings of patriotism and opportunism. Balanchine and the company certainly benefited from the relationship. Not only did money from exchange tours help sustain the company, but Balanchine was also able to ask local embassies and consulates for assistance when traveling abroad.[11] At the same time, Balanchine possessed heartfelt patriotism for his adopted country, of which he became a citizen in 1940.[12] More than one of his ballets from the 1950s tapped into post–World War II patriotic fervor, including *Stars and Stripes*, a work set to the marches of John Philip Sousa.

Despite the company's close and productive relationship with the State Department, Kirstein and Balanchine were initially reluctant to tour the Soviet Union on behalf of the United States. Balanchine's personal concerns about returning to his homeland and his staunchly anti-Soviet politics fueled this decision, but there were also practical reasons to be anxious. Balanchine had left the country in the 1920s, surely creating ill will toward him in those who had stayed. Moreover, his relatively abstract, storyless ballets contrasted sharply with the spectacular, realist aesthetic of the drambalet. Rather than plot, Balanchine's works were structured around a careful matching of choreography to musical score. When the possibility of an American ballet tour of the Soviet Union was discussed at the ANTA panel in December 1957, Kirstein informed them that New York City Ballet would not take part. His explanation was that, in addition to concerns about Balanchine's politics, they felt that the Soviet government would criticize their company for its modernist musical choices and lack of costumes and sets.[13] Again, a year later, Kirstein expressed concern that he did not want to enter a "slugging match" with Russia.[14] Thus, though personal reasons probably played a role, Kirstein and Balanchine also wanted to protect their company from what they saw as the certainty of bad Soviet reviews.

Kirstein and Balanchine remained opposed to a New York City Ballet tour of the Soviet Union up through the end of the 1950s. In 1961, however, Kirstein abruptly did an about-face and began campaigning for State Department officials to grant New York City Ballet a European and Soviet tour. Despite having resigned from the ANTA panel in 1960 in order to avoid a conflict of interest, Kirstein still had a great deal of influence with the people managing the State Department's cultural exchange programs. That year, he traveled to Washington, DC, to meet with bureaucrats in the State Department, whom Kirstein asked to arrange a Soviet tour for New York City Ballet. The meeting seems to have been successful. At this point, though, the ANTA panel had become more hesitant to approve the tour. While they greatly admired New York City Ballet, some members had planned on recommending either Jerome Robbins's Ballets: U.S.A. or Martha Graham's company.[15] Kirstein's new pressure succeeded in part because it was supported by the Soviets themselves, who were more enthusiastic about hosting New York City Ballet than Robbins's company.[16] In 1962, representatives of the two governments signed a new cultural exchange agreement specifying that New York City Ballet would tour the USSR over the following year.[17]

Once the new agreement had been signed, however, and much to the surprise of the State Department, Kirstein and Balanchine demurred again, claiming that they would only send the company on a Soviet exchange if it were part of a larger tour including the countries of Western Europe. Balanchine announced in a meeting with State Department representatives that "the only reason the Company would accept the Russian tour would be as a means of getting to the major capital cities of Europe."[18] Since New York City Ballet had been unable to raise the money for such a trip, Kirstein and Balanchine asked the State Department for the requisite funds to make up the deficit. Balanchine also demanded that the length of the Soviet tour, set at eight weeks, be reduced to five or six, since he considered spending time in the Soviet Union to be a "hardship" assignment, where the company would have poor food and accommodations.[19]

Unsurprisingly, the State Department was enormously reluctant to hand over the funds requested, which came to approximately $80,000. In the end, it was Sol Hurok who financed this section of the tour. Hurok was concerned that if the New York City Ballet tour fell through, the Soviet government would be unwilling to send the Bolshoi Ballet to the United States.[20] He therefore gave New York City Ballet $25,000 to help finance their tour in Europe, money that he agreed would not be returned, even if their performances turned financial profit.[21]

Soviet and American Models for Understanding Music and Dance

The Soviet government's eagerness to invite New York City Ballet was the first sign that Kirstein and Balanchine were mistaken in their earlier anxieties about the company's official reception in the USSR. Unbeknownst to most American observers, Balanchine's neoclassical ballet greatly resembled the new choreographic symphonism in the Soviet Union, particularly in his highly musical approach to ballet. Both Balanchine's style and choreographic symphonism grew out of developments in early twentieth-century Russian ballet, particularly those of choreographers Michel Fokine, Leonid Massine, and Fyodor Lopukhov. Rather than always commissioning new music for their works, Fokine, Massine, and Lopukhov often created ballets to previously composed instrumental works, most of which had never been intended for the stage. They were inspired to work in this manner in part by modern dancer and choreographer Isadora Duncan, who at the turn of the century began performing to works of the classical musical canon. Ballet choreographers continued this practice in the early twentieth century. Fokine, for example, created the ballet *Scheherazade* to Rimsky-Korsakov's symphonic suite of the same name. A decade later, in the Soviet Union, Lopukhov used the music of Beethoven's Symphony No. 4 for a work titled *Magnificence of the Universe*, which was supposed to depict the origins of the cosmos.[22]

In the Soviet Union, the music-based style of ballet pioneered by Lopukhov in *Magnificence of the Universe* fell out of favor in the 1930s with the rise of the drambalet. However, as de-Stalinization progressed in the mid-1950s, the ballet theaters of the Soviet Union returned to some of their earlier musical and choreographic aesthetics. As Christina Ezrahi describes in *Swans of the Kremlin*, Lopukhov was briefly reinstated as the head of the Kirov Theater in 1955. He became a leader of choreographic symphonism, commissioning many important works from the new movement's young artists.[23]

Balanchine was also deeply influenced by Lopukhov. He had performed with Lopukhov in Petrograd before immigrating to Paris, and he credited the older choreographer with demonstrating that symphonies could be used for dance.[24] Balanchine was also well acquainted with the works of Leonide Massine, who created a number of "symphonic ballets" to pre-existing instrumental music during the 1930s and 1940s.[25] Like these choreographers, Balanchine centered his repertoire on classical instrumental music; he created ballets to pieces including Ravel's *La valse*, J. S. Bach's Concerto for Two Violins, Bizet's Symphony No. 1 in C Major, and Tchaikovsky's Piano Concerto No. 2.[26]

Despite their deep similarities and common heritage, American and Soviet choreographers had very different models for conceptualizing the relationship between music, dance, and narrative. Balanchine's way of understanding meaning and music was ultimately descended, over a long period of time, from the ideas of nineteenth-century music critics, most prominently Eduard Hanslick. Hanslick promoted "absolute music," that is to say, music without any narrative or programmatic associations. He glorified a type of listening that prioritized active thinking about musical form and denigrated any attempt to connect stories to instrumental compositions. In the twentieth century, Hanslick's ideas found favor with Western modernist composers. These composers were reacting in part to the politics of World War II and the Cold War and to the type of propagandistic art that the Nazi and Soviet governments funded. Concerned that any type of programmatic content could be associated with Soviet or Nazi politics, these composers argued that only absolute music could be truly free.[27]

Like these modernist composers and philosophers, Balanchine believed that narrative was foreign to music, and thus to musical dance. He and the American critics who admired his ballet extrapolated from this idea to suggest that musicality and narrative were opposed to one another. American dance critic Edwin Denby wrote that "The more ballet turns to pantomime, the less intimate its relation to the music becomes; but the more it turns to dancing, the more it enjoys the music's presence, bar by bar."[28] This model for understanding dance can be depicted as a continuum, with narrative at one end and music at the other (Figure 4.1). The more musical a ballet was, under this system of thought, the less narrative, and vice versa.

The Soviets, by contrast, conceptualized meaning and narrative as something filling music. This content could then be translated into dance (Figure 4.2). This model was clearly grounded in Soviet ideology, which suggested

Ballet

Narrative ←——————————→ Music

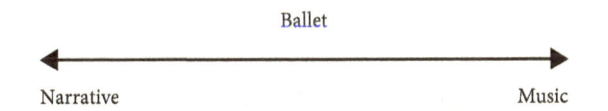

Figure 4.1 The American Cold War paradigm for understanding the relationship between music, narrative, and dance.

```
Narrative/Content
      |
      v
    Music                   Narrative/Content
      |                        |       |
      |                        v       v
      v                      Music   Dance
    Dance
```

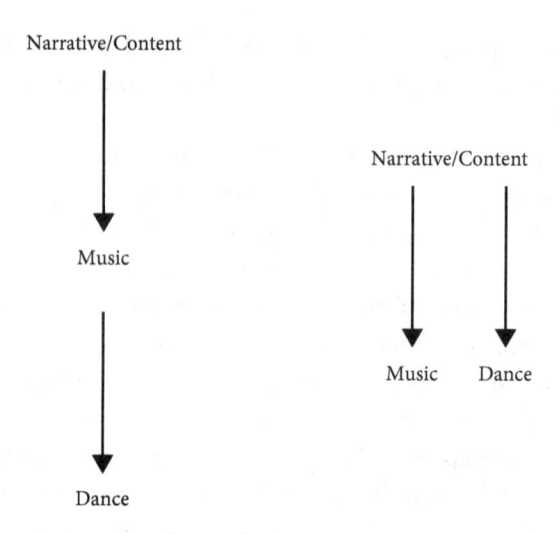

Figure 4.2 Two Soviet paradigms for understanding the relationship between music, content, and dance.

that art should have one correct meaning, or "content," clearly discernible by an audience. During the 1930s and 1940s, content was defined in very limited terms; under this system of thought each ballet would only have one clear, easily readable narrative. Ballets would be crafted so that both music and dance flowed from the content of a libretto. These beliefs were sharpened in juxtaposition to the development of abstract modernism in the West. The more that Western artists advocated for formalist art, the more Soviet bureaucrats pushed back against it.[29]

During the Thaw, supporters of the choreographic symphonist movement began pushing against the narrow reading of "content" as narrative. They argued that good dance should take its content from the music, rather than simply from an external libretto. Moreover, some argued that good dance could reflect a broad range of content, including philosophical and spiritual, the type of content that they believed was also inherently present in classical forms of instrumental music such as the symphony, suite, or concerto. This did not mean that the choreographic symphonists promoted abstract dance. Rather, they promoted a highly musical form of ballet that would draw on and interpret the meaning already present in music.[30]

Balanchine developed his understanding of musical abstraction in conjunction with his new style of choreography, in which minute changes in musical form were reflected very closely in the dance. He often accomplished this by matching specific performers, steps, or stage layouts with musical themes. For example, the form of his 1947 neoclassical ballet *Symphony in C* (originally titled *Le Palais de Cristal*) very closely matches its score, George Bizet's Symphony No. in C Major. The first movement of Bizet's symphony is in sonata form, with an arpeggiated first theme presented in the strings and a lyrical second theme first presented in the oboe. In Balanchine's choreography, the first theme is danced by eight women from the corps, arranged in two lines at the back of the stage in a V-shape, with one soloist dancing in front of each line. They perform a series of small steps and *tendus*. As the music modulates, the dancers move more frequently across the stage. The entrance of the second theme is marked by the entrance of the principal soloist for the movement. Part of her choreography for this second theme includes a circle of turns in arabesque. In the development section, fragments of the second theme appear, accompanied by the horn section. During these entrances three men come on for the first time, accompanying the three soloists onstage in a series of turns. Thus, Balanchine preserves the thematic material of the choreography for the second theme—the turns—while adding new dancers to match Bizet's new instruments.[31]

During the recapitulation of this movement, the first theme is matched, not by a return of the original steps, but by a return to the same stage position, with eight dancers at the back in a V-shape. This time, the male soloists perform a series of small jumps to the first theme. When the second theme comes back in the recapitulation, the lead ballerina again enters and performs spins with her partner. The choreography thus very closely matches the musical form and rewards a similar type of structural listening to that advocated by Hanslick in the nineteenth century.

Soviet choreographic symphonists often treated music in a similarly structural way, matching musical themes or textures with performing forces onstage. Unlike Balanchine, however, the choreographic symphonists did not separate out this type of musical choreography from narrative. For example, choreographer Igor Belsky's 1961 *Leningrad Symphony* narrativizes Shostakovich's Seventh Symphony. In creating the ballet, Belsky dramatized the music's program by matching mimetic gestures closely to the formal structure of the score. The ballet uses the first movement of the symphony to depict an idyllic life shattered by invading Nazis; the movement's incessant melodic ostinato is choreographed with a series of interlocking and constantly repeating dance motifs for the invading troops. The agonized countermelodies are given to the tormented Soviet characters.[32] When the

106   BALLET IN THE COLD WAR

Kirov toured in the United States in 1961, they performed Belsky's *Leningrad Symphony,* which intriguingly was retitled *Shostakovich's 7th Symphony* in the American programs, presumably in attempt to sound more like Balanchine's works.[33]

In some works, such as *Symphony in C,* Balanchine shied away from the type of mimetic gestures that Belsky used, but in other ballets, such as his 1934 *Serenade,* he embraced them. *Serenade* is an ethereal ballet choreographed to Pyotr Tchaikovsky's 1880 Serenade for Strings.[34] The music is unified by the use of a motto, a theme that appears throughout the symphony rather than just in one movement. In Serenade for Strings, the motto theme is a slow homophonic descent. It plays at the opening and closing of the first movement and again at the close of the fourth. Throughout the ballet *Serenade*, the motto theme is always choreographed for the entire female corps standing in nearly the same unusual stage pattern: seventeen women in flowing white dresses arrayed in a double diamond (Figure 4.3).[35] At the opening of the

Figure 4.3 The double diamond formation associated with motto theme in Balanchine's *Serenade*. The dancers standing on the right side are standing outside the frame. From *New York City Ballet in Montreal, Vol. 1. Serenade,* Choreography by George Balanchine © The George Balanchine Trust.

first movement, the dancers in this arrangement all perform a series of very basic gestures in unison, mirroring the slow, prayer-like atmosphere of the music.[36]

When this motto theme returns in the conclusion of the first movement, the dancers hold their opening poses, but there is an empty place on stage, in the front position of the left diamond. A soloist walks in from the wings, as though she has arrived late to the stage and is trying to figure out her place in it. She settles into the empty spot and proceeds to perform the gestures from the ballet's opening; at the same time, the rest of the women perform new choreography, in which they slowly process offstage, leaving the soloist alone. The choreography dramatizes the repetition of the motto theme. Unlike *Symphony in C*, *Serenade* appears to have a narrative. Yet the musical form is illuminated just as sharply by the choreography.

Despite the importance of the motto theme to the score and to Balanchine's realization of it, in the concluding two movements Balanchine alters the structure of Tchaikovsky's music to prioritize narrative closure over formal closure. The original Tchaikovsky score places the slow movement, marked "Elegy," third, followed by a brisk "Tema Russo." When Balanchine originally choreographed the ballet in 1933, he skipped the "Tema Russo" movement, adding it only in 1940.[37] When he added the "Tema Russo" back into the ballet, however, he made it into a new third movement, choosing to keep the "Elegy" in the final place, though adding a male soloist. Adding the "Tema Russo" last would have provided a formal symmetry to the ballet, since the movement ends with a late reappearance of the motto theme. Instead, Balanchine decided to retain his more melancholic, poetic close from the 1934 version.

In this "Elegy" movement, Balanchine maintains his attention to musical form, but he does so by interpreting that form in a narrative way. The music to the "Elegy" is in ternary form, framed by a theme that is halting, its phrases constantly cut off in strange places. In the ballet, the movement opens with a female soloist lying collapsed on stage. She is the same dancer who earlier had appeared late to the second double diamond formation. A man crosses the stage to reach this fallen woman, accompanied by a soloist referred to by New York City Ballet dancers as the "dark angel." As the man crosses the stage, this dark angel stands behind him, covering his eyes. When this same theme returns later in the movement, the characters of the fallen soloist, the male soloist, and the dark angel come back. The man clutches the hand of the female soloist, this time lowered again to her fallen position onstage, while the dark angel hides behind him, her arms stretched out to provide him wings (Figure 4.4). At a particularly intense moment in the music, the angel begins to flap her wings; it looks as if the man himself is a winged creature. By dramatizing the returning musical theme, Balanchine does illustrate the form of the score, but he does so through narrative rather than in opposition to it.

There were multiple works like *Serenade* in the New York City Ballet repertoire, ballets in which Balanchine used mimetic gesture and story to illuminate the form of the music. These pieces, including *La valse* and *Western Symphony,* mirrored very closely some of the choreographic symphonic works created by Soviet artists at approximately the same time. Balanchine's colleague Jerome Robbins, two of whose ballets were performed on tour, also tended to create works along these lines. The fourth movement of his *Interplay,* for example, stages a game between two teams of dancers as a way to dramatize the music's repetitive phrase structure.

Figure 4.4 Male soloist, female soloist, and "dark angel" in the final movement of Balanchine's *Serenade.* From *New York City Ballet in Montreal, Vol. 1. Serenade,* Choreography by George Balanchine © The George Balanchine Trust.

There were many signs leading up to the tour that the Soviet government was relatively unconcerned about Balanchine's abstraction. To start, Hurok actively encouraged the State Department to include New York City Ballet in the 1962 exchange.[38] Moreover, once ANTA had approved the company's participation and the American and Soviet representatives had signed off on the exchange, two officials from Goskontsert flew to the United States to decide which of the New York City Ballet works could be performed in the USSR. The list that they eventually approved included almost all of Balanchine's ballets and coincided fairly closely to a recommended repertoire list that had been produced by the ANTA dance panel.[39] The two officials only excluded four ballets from the New York City Ballet repertoire: Balanchine's *Ivesiana* and *Orpheus* and Jerome Robbins's *Afternoon of a Faun* and *The Cage*.[40] Their choices suggest that Goskontsert and the Ministry of Culture were much more concerned about keeping out New York City Ballet's sometimes frank sexuality than they were in forbidding Balanchine's abstraction. Indeed, three of their four forbidden ballets had clear narratives.

In their report back to the Ministry of Culture, the Soviet officials noted Balanchine's tendency toward abstraction but dismissed it as a relatively unimportant issue, writing, "Balanchine declares that he is an advocate of 'pure art' in ballet and loves to stage dances on music without a subject. However, . . . [he] does not repudiate the realistic school of ballet and, despite a strong modernist influence, he tries to preserve in his work the classic legacy of Russian ballet."[41] Their comments would prove to be highly representative of the ways that Soviet experts framed Balanchine's art.

American and Soviet Aesthetics Brought Into Dialogue

New York City Ballet arrived in Moscow on October 6, 1962. The dancers' feet had hardly touched the tarmac when the debates over abstraction were set off, not by the Soviets, but by Balanchine himself. A radio interviewer greeted the choreographer by exclaiming, "Welcome to Moscow, home of classic ballet!" Balanchine reportedly replied, "I beg your pardon . . . Russia is the home of romantic ballet. The home of classic ballet is now America."[42] This comment would set the tone for Balanchine's subsequent interviews with Soviet media outlets. The choreographer frequently claimed in these interviews that his ballets were superior because they were abstract, works that were intended to address the beauty of dance and nothing else. In an interview with *Sovetskii artist*, Balanchine argued that ballet should be more than a simple "illustrator" of literary works, no matter how elevated the source.[43] Presumably this was intended as a criticism of drambalet adaptations such as *Romeo and Juliet*. Instead, Balanchine argued, ballet "can speak about itself by itself and for itself." He continued, claiming, "Ballet is flowers, it is beauty, it is poetry, and one should speak of it only in terms of aesthetics, if one must speak of it at all."[44] This last statement, in particular, clearly touched a nerve with Soviet critics, many of whom would go on to quote it in their reviews.

Much as he did in his radio interview, Balanchine constantly returned to the ideology of modernization, opposing the newness of his approach with the conservatism of Soviet ballet. When asked about his purpose in Moscow in another interview, Balanchine responded with language that emphasized the forward-looking nature of his artistic project. He claimed that he wanted to "acquaint Soviet viewers with the distinctive features of American dance, with our quests and our discoveries. After all, art [...] should always live and grow, and it is for this reason that we are seeking the course of choreography's further evolution."[45] With such statements, Balanchine likely knew that he was provoking the Soviet ballet establishment. Indeed, Nancy Reynolds, a dance historian who was personally acquainted with him, wrote of his press interviews in the Soviet Union that "if I know him, with somewhat diabolic intent—[Balanchine] thus provided a platform wide open to attack."[46]

Balanchine's attempt to distance his work from Soviet aesthetics was sharply at odds with the approach taken by the State Department. Following common practice for the cultural exchange program, the American Embassy in Moscow released a short Russian-language booklet describing the company's history and style in an attempt to educate local audiences.[47] Copies of this booklet found their way into the personal archival collections of at least two different ballet experts in Moscow, the critic Natalia Roslavleva and the dancer Akiva Diner.[48] It seems therefore to have had at least moderate circulation among the Soviet ballet elite.

The embassy booklet attempted to make Balanchine's ideas more palatable to a Soviet audience, in particular soft-pedaling the importance of abstraction in his work. While the booklet did mention the dodecaphonic modernist ballet *Agon*, it described the piece only as "difficult," avoiding any mention of the ballet's potentially controversial aspects, such as its abstraction or twelve-tone score. The booklet focused on Balanchine's recent *Midsummer Night's Dream* and *Western Symphony*, both of which shared some similarities with the Soviet drambalety. *Midsummer Night's Dream*, as a full-length narrative ballet based on a Shakespearean subject, would seem similar in topic and structure to Soviet works such as *Romeo and Juliet*. *Western Symphony*, with a score that drew on American folk tunes and dancers dressed in cowboy outfits, may have appealed as an example of the essentialized nationalism prominent in drambalety. This was the same style of nationalism that made *Rodeo* so popular in the Soviet Union in 1960, a fact that representatives at the American Embassy would certainly have remembered.[49] The cover of the embassy booklet featured a picture of Diana Adams and Nicholas Magallanes in *Western Symphony*, dressed up in cowboy and saloon girl outfits (Figure 4.5).[50]

The program notes for the company's performances were almost as conciliatory as the embassy booklet. While the notes drew attention to Balanchine's innovations, including plotless ballet, they also underlined some of the aspects of choreography that aligned with Soviet artistic values. For instance,

Figure 4.5 American Embassy in Moscow, "News of American Culture" brochure. *Western Symphony*, Choreography by George Balanchine © The George Balanchine Trust. Programs of New York City Ballet, RGALI f. 2966 o. 1 d. 454 l. 47.

they mentioned that Balanchine's works sometimes expressed the "national character of the music," using *Scotch Symphony* and *Western Symphony* as examples.[51] The program notes also pointed out that Balanchine had choreographed some narrative works, including *La Sonnambula,* one of the ballets being performed on the Soviet tour. The program notes even attempted to make the modernist *Agon* more acceptable by emphasizing the connections between the score and seventeenth-century music, rather than pointing out its ties to serialist composition.[52]

Soviet audiences had their first opportunity to see these works for themselves on October 9, 1962, when New York City Ballet opened its tour of the Soviet Union at the Bolshoi Theater. All tickets were sold out in advance.[53] After opening night, the company moved its performances to the Kremlin Palace of Congresses, a larger theater that had been built inside the walls of the Kremlin itself to house the meetings of the full Communist Party.[54] After its performances in Moscow, the company went on to perform in Leningrad (October 31–November 8), Kiev (November 11–18), Tbilisi (November 21–25), and Baku (November 28–December 1).[55] By all accounts the performances were sold out, and the audiences cheered enthusiastically, even wildly.[56] According to one anecdote, during a performance of *Donizetti Variations,* Edward Villella was greeted with such fervent applause that he repeated his solo, breaking a company policy that forbade encores.[57]

For Balanchine, despite the success, the trip to the Soviet Union was emotionally taxing. It was the first time he had returned to Russia or seen his family since his departure in 1924. Balanchine's brother, composer Andrei Balanchivadze, met the company at the airport in Moscow, and there was reportedly an emotional reunion.[58] According to Balanchine's biographer, Bernard Taper, however, even this meeting proved to be a source of strain. The two siblings had not been in contact since the choreographer's emigration, and, moreover, Balanchine did not approve of his brother's music. Taper recounts that Balanchine began to have nightmares about being trapped in Russia, and eventually skipped the company's performances in Kiev, choosing instead to return to the United States for a week of rest before rejoining the company in Tbilisi.[59]

Surprisingly, New York City Ballet's trip remained relatively unaffected by the Cuban Missile Crisis. According to Clare Croft's interviews with members of the company, some felt anxiety about the political situation, and many remembered having to leave the embassy quickly at times to avoid protestors. Nevertheless, much like the Bolshoi dancers in the United States, their days were mostly occupied not with politics, but with rehearsals and performances that gave little extra time for broader concerns.[60]

There were two difficult confrontations between company dancers and Soviet citizens that pointed to the ongoing political tensions. During one of the protests outside the American Embassy, someone put his cigarette out on Kay Mazzo's arm. Later, Shawn O'Brien was arrested for filming scenes in a public park with his 8 mm camera. O'Brien was held and questioned in a nearby building for four and a half hours. He was eventually released and the film was returned to him, but Hans Tuch, the company's State Department handler, was outraged that the Soviet police would hold an American performer for such a long time without notifying US authorities.[61] While this was the only incident involving a run-in between the American dancers and the Soviet police, these two fairly aggressive interactions between the dancers and their Soviet hosts speak to the tense and suspicious atmosphere of the Cold War.

As they toured the major cities of the Soviet Union, New York City Ballet's appearances were noted constantly in the Soviet press. In newspaper after newspaper, reviewers wrote long and involved accounts of the company's performances. It seemed that everyone in the Soviet dance world, from composers and choreographers to dancers and historians, had an opinion to express about Balanchine and New York City Ballet. As usual in the exchange, these critics transliterated their experience of viewing the new works through the prevailing domestic debates about ballet.

In the case of New York City Ballet's 1962 tour, Soviet experts transliterated the performances through the ongoing disagreements over the shift from drambalet to choreographic symphonism. Though acceptance of choreographic symphonism was increasing in the years leading up to the 1962 tour, not all members of the Soviet ballet establishment approved of it. Those artists who were still devoted to the drambalet aesthetic opposed choreographic symphonism vehemently, and in the ballet world, the period of the Thaw was marked by intense debates between proponents of the two styles. Such arguments were characteristic of the Thaw era, which saw public debate over many topics, including literature and music. Indeed, historian Nancy Condee has identified formalized debate, or "ritual combat" between the old and the new, as one of the key aspects of Thaw culture.[62]

In these debates, the side of the drambalet was taken up primarily by its choreographers. Leonid Lavrovsky defended the style in a public 1962 essay by using the earlier, more narrow definition of content as narrative.

According to Lavrovsky, the choreographic symphonists, or as he called them proponents of the "world of agitated feelings," rejected content in the ballet and therefore were dangerously close to treading down the same path as Western ballet.[63] Lavrovsky's opinions, however, were not shared by everyone in the Soviet ballet world, and by the mid-1960s, he had entirely lost his fight against the choreographic symphonists. He was replaced in 1964 by Yuri Grigorovich as the head choreographer of the Bolshoi ballet.[64] Moreover, even Lavrovsky, despite his rhetoric, embraced choreographic symphonism to some degree with his ballet *Paganini*, which the Bolshoi performed on their 1962 tour of the United States. *Paganini*, set to Rachmaninoff's *Variations on a Theme by Paganini*, used the music's variation form to lay out a series of semi-narrative scenes.[65]

Balanchine's works provided fodder for this debate. Dancer Alexander Lapauri opened his review of Balanchine's troupe with the statement, "Without doubt, NYCB's performances [...] are an important artistic event. And, like any event, it creates its admirers and opponents. And where there are two sides, there arises argument, and in argument is born truth."[66] Such a belief in the power of debate reflects the atmosphere of the Thaw, and it is a fair summary of the company's Soviet reception.

Reynolds has suggested that the 1962 reviews of New York City Ballet were censored.[67] Her interpretation accords with the model of Soviet censorship as it was understood by Americans up through the early 1990s, which conceptualized the process as top-down, with the Party general-secretary directly imposing his will on all published material. Historian Samantha Sherry's more recent work emphasizes the multi-person nature of censorship as practiced in the post-Stalin period. During this time, the Soviet censorship board (Glavlit) was encouraged to act in partnership with the editorial boards of journals, rather than above them.[68] Moreover, as sociologist Alexei Yurchak has argued in *Everything Was Forever until It Was No More*, even though public political acts and public discourse became increasingly frozen during the late Soviet period, this unchanging discourse paradoxically opened up places for Soviet citizens to express themselves creatively by creating a variety of new meanings for old acts and words.[69] The transformation of the word "content" in Soviet ballet discourse represents a case of the phenomenon that Yurchak describes. By following certain rigid discursive strictures, Soviet reviewers demonstrated their political orthodoxy, yet within those strictures the critics could express a variety of opinions.

The account of Russian dance historian Elizabeth Souritz, who was one of New York City Ballet's Soviet reviewers in 1962, supports this interpretation. In an article published in 2011, Souritz described the tone that the government encouraged for the New York City Ballet reviews. She claimed that the reviewers were encouraged not to insult Balanchine and his company, for fear of creating an international incident and riling up American reviewers against Soviet companies. At the same time, reviewers were to assert the superiority of Russian ballet.[70] Just as Souritz describes, a careful search through the Soviet reviews shows that they were largely positive, though they tried to co-opt Balanchine as a figure of Russian rather than American culture. I would add that the reviews almost all contain some direct affirmation of realism or rejection of abstraction, and this statement may have been understood as necessary in discussing Balanchine's works. Within the strict constraints that Souritz describes, however, critics expressed a broad array of opinions on the strengths and weaknesses of the company and on Balanchine's style of choreography. Editors may have encouraged their critics to write certain things about the company, but it is unlikely that the government exerted direct pressure on the reviewers. Indeed, Souritz recounts knowing about the preferred tone of the reviews by having read the first review of the company that appeared in *Pravda*, not through any direct censorship process.

It is important to acknowledge that the critics may have censored themselves. At the same time, though, as Souritz herself asserts, we should not assume that the reviews were lies any more than we can assume they were purely truthful. Souritz even claims that rereading the article she herself wrote in 1962, she is surprised at her ignorance but thinks that the opinions probably were her own at the time.[71] As Yurchak claims:

> What tends to get lost in the binary accounts is the crucial and seemingly paradoxical fact that, for great numbers of Soviet citizens, many of the fundamental values, ideals, and realities of socialist life (such as equality, community, selflessness, altruism, friendship, ethical relations, safety, education, work, creativity, and concern for the future) were of genuine importance, despite the fact that many of their everyday practices routinely transgressed, reinterpreted, or refused certain norms and rules represented in the official ideology of the socialist state.[72]

In the end, we cannot know for certain whether the reviewers believed in their hearts what they published in Soviet papers. What we can observe is what the Soviet critics wrote. The accounts of New York City Ballet did not dismiss Balanchine but rather co-opted his artwork. In numerous long, carefully argued essays, they refashioned Balanchine's aesthetics for the debates ongoing in Soviet ballet at the time.

Overwhelmingly, Soviet critics praised Balanchine first and foremost for his innovation, his "original choreographic vocabulary" and "compositional fantasy," as Khachaturian wrote in his review of the company.[73] Critic Maria Sabnina remarked, "It is impossible not to be delighted by his inexhaustible imagination."[74] Balanchine's works often introduced unorthodox movement into the balletic vocabulary, using sharply bent wrists and knees and emphasizing the hips. Many of these gestures came originally from African American dance styles, which Balanchine was familiar with from his years working on Broadway.[75] These movements, as original as they were to Americans of the 1950s, may have been even more startling for a Soviet audience, largely unfamiliar with the black dancers who influenced Balanchine. Moreover, the drambalet choreographers had tended to emphasize novelty in story-telling techniques rather than movement vocabulary. As early as 1952, at least one Soviet ballet expert had written with some acerbity on the repetition of classical steps in drambalety, so it is perhaps unsurprising that Balanchine's choreography seemed particularly rich in this area to his Soviet viewers.[76] In addition to praising Balanchine for his originality, the Soviet critics were also uniformly impressed with the "impeccable classical technique" of the New York City Ballet dancers.[77] Gerber remarked that "it is impossible not to recognize the high professional mastery of the American artists, their sharp technique, their clean performance of difficult, virtuosic combinations."[78]

Many of the Soviet critics attributed New York City Ballet's technical prowess to Balanchine's time in the Leningrad Dance Academy rather than to the American nature of his enterprise. Historian and reviewer Anna Ilupina, for instance, asserted that the entire character of the New York City Ballet could be attributed to Balanchine's Russian birth and education.[79] The claims to New York City Ballet's Russianness were not completely unfounded, since Kirstein and Balanchine's School of American Ballet, where most of the New York City Ballet dancers had studied, boasted a number of Russian-trained teachers.[80] In the publicity leading up to New York City Ballet's tour, the School of American Ballet had been mentioned multiple times as one of

Balanchine and Kirstein's great accomplishments in the United States and as one of the main reasons that the company was so successful.[81]

The Soviet critics, however, constantly emphasized and exaggerated Balanchine's connections to Russia. More than just attributing the technical excellence of his dancers to Balanchine's Russian training, many Soviet critics counted all of Balanchine's works and actions as part of a Russian ballet school.[82] Sabnina, who was one of the staunchest defenders of Balanchine's works in the Soviet press, remarked as an opening gambit in her review, "[Balanchine's biography] confirms the fact that all the major developments of contemporary foreign choreography are directly or indirectly connected with the Russian school and its traditions."[83] Balanchine was quite angered by these claims. Indeed, according to Clare Croft's interviews, Balanchine bristled at every attempt on the part of the Soviet government to claim him and instead tried to emphasize that he was Georgian by birth and American by choice.[84]

The excellence of New York City Ballet's dancing and Balanchine's choreography did force Soviet critics to take American ballet more seriously than they had done following Ballet Theatre's 1960 tour. There were no more patronizing comments in the reviews about the dancers coming on a pilgrimage to the home of ballet. Moreover, it even led to concern that the USSR could perhaps be falling behind the West in ballet. In the year following New York City Ballet's tour there was an All-Union Choreographic Conference, a country-wide gathering of ballet experts to discuss the future of the art form. At this 1963 meeting, a few experts expressed concern, in the wake of Balanchine's visit, that American ballet had possibly caught up to or surpassed the Soviets. Some even suggested that they should study examples of Western choreography, though no one at the meeting wholeheartedly endorsed Balanchine's style.[85]

While the 1962 Soviet reviewers were near unanimous in their praise for Balanchine's originality and the technical excellence of the New York City Ballet dancers, they varied wildly on the validity of Balanchine's aesthetic models. Those Soviet critics who supported the drambalet over choreographic symbolism unsurprisingly took a strictly negative view of Balanchine's works. This opinion was most fervently expressed by Rostislav Zakharov, one of the founding choreographers of the drambalet school. While Zakharov claimed he appreciated the talent of the New York City Ballet dancers and the innovation of certain movements in Balanchine's works, he attacked Balanchine for the lack of content in his ballets.[86]

Zakharov's position, however, was an outlier. Most Soviet critics did not reject Balanchine's aesthetics out of hand. Perhaps the largest group, including Gerber and historians Boris Lvov-Anokhin and Natalia Roslavleva, found ways to praise Balanchine's works while still asserting the superiority of choreographic symphonism. This group focused on the difference between what they saw as inner and outer features of music. They argued that Balanchine had not succeeded in conveying the content of the music, claiming instead that he succeeded only in translating the superficial or exterior features of the score. Gerber, for example, wrote that Balanchine demonstrated great musicality in his works but objected that "music is not just a musical and rhythmic design that the choreographer strives to dance out. . . . It has definite content that reflects the worldview of the composer. It expresses a wide range of thoughts and feelings."[87] In Gerber's view, Balanchine failed to take into consideration the emotional and intellectual content of the musical scores.

The distinction between the interior content and exterior features of a musical score allowed these writers to criticize some aspects of Balanchine's works while still defending the choreographic symphonists and their models, Fokine and Lopukhov. In his review for *Nedelia*, Lvov-Anokhin recognized the musicality of Balanchine's works but drew an unfavorable comparison between Balanchine's *Serenade* and Fokine's *Chopiniana*. Lvov-Anokhin argued that while *Chopiniana* "embodies the music's soul, the same cannot always be said of Balanchine's *Serenade*."[88] Similarly, dance critic and historian Natalia Roslavleva used her review of Balanchine's works to defend plotless dance, particularly in the works of Fyodor Lopukhov. Again, Roslavleva drew a distinction between the exterior facets of music, which she argued Balanchine expressed well, and the inner content of music, which she felt he had failed to convey.[89]

A final group of Soviet critics was more vocally in favor of Balanchine's choreography. These writers, led by dancer Mikhail Gabovich, celebrated Balanchine's achievements as a form of choreographic symphonism. They used the same distinction between the interior and exterior facets of music but claimed that Balanchine managed to transmit both parts of the music through choreography. Gabovich argued that works by composers such as Mozart, Tchaikovsky, Ravel, Prokofiev, and Stravinsky already had internal content. By embodying and reinterpreting that music so vividly onstage, Balanchine's art also expressed valid content, whatever the choreographer himself might say on the matter. Gabovich additionally argued that the classical dance vocabulary itself conveyed a kind of content by exploring the workings of the human body. While Gabovich was Balanchine's staunchest supporter in the Soviet press, Maria Sabnina and Olga Lepeshinskaya also argued that Balanchine had transmitted musical content in his ballets.[90]

Nevertheless, even critics such as Sabnina or Gabovich, who found ways to support Balanchine's works within the parameters of choreographic symphonism, also rejected some of his statements in the Soviet press.[91] While Gabovich lauded Balanchine and his ballet, he argued against Balanchine's claims that ballet needed to be abstract and that his neoclassical style was the only path forward for dance. Instead, Gabovich called for artistic understanding between proponents of the drambalet, of choreographic symphonism, and of Balanchine's style. Gabovich maintained that both plotted and plotless works of ballet had validity. Comparing Belsky to Balanchine, Gabovich pointed out their differences while writing that "Both styles have a right to existence, just as much as other genres of great [. . .] choreography."[92]

That Sabnina and Gabovich, despite their overall admiration for Balanchine, still felt a need to address Balanchine's statements in the *Sovetskii artist* interview is an indication of the degree to which Balanchine's artistic philosophy and his works were conflated in the Soviet reception of New York City Ballet's 1962 tour. Many of the newspaper and journal critics, including Lapauri, Sabnina, Gabovich, and Lepeshinskaya, directly referenced Balanchine's *Sovetskii artist* statements in their reviews, demonstrating that the article had been widely read, widely discussed, and was considered an integral component of Balanchine's appearance in the Soviet Union.[93]

The Soviet Reception of *Agon* and the American Reaction

For the most part, Soviet critics praised Balanchine's works, whether whole heartedly in the manner of Gabovich and Sabnina, or with caveats, as in the writings of Roslavleva and Lvov-Anokhin. Nevertheless, there were two ballets on the New York City Ballet programs that did not meet with the approval of any Soviet critics: *Agon* and *Episodes*. Both were set to serialist scores, by Igor Stravinsky and Anton Webern, respectively. Both featured dancers in practice clothes of leotard and tights on an empty stage, and both incorporated many of Balanchine's most drastic changes to choreographic technique. Of these aspects, the twelve-tone music was by far the most objectionable to Soviet critics.

During the 1930s and 1940s, representatives of the Soviet government had repeatedly railed against Western music, particularly by modernist composers. This criticism came to a head in 1948, when Western music was denounced at the shake-up of the Union of Composers. At this meeting, Tikhon Khrennikov, the newly named head of the Union, criticized works by Stravinsky, Hindemith, Krenek, Berg, Britten, Messiaen, and Menotti, arguing that Western composers used "a conglomeration of wild harmonies, a reversion to primitive savage cultures."[94] In the 1960s, such vehement disapproval of Western modernism was no longer the norm. As musicologist Peter Schmelz discusses in his book, *Such Freedom If Only Musical*, the cultural Thaw led to a broadening of taste in the Soviet Union and the gradual reintroduction of some Western composers to the Soviet music scene.[95]

By 1962, however, these new attitudes toward Western modernism were only in their infancy. Moreover, even during the period of greater acceptance, there was still deep ambivalence or hostility on the part of major Soviet musical institutions to twelve-tone composition. Stravinsky had come under sharp criticism from Soviet musicologists during the late 1950s and early 1960s for his new allegiance to the dodecaphonic system. In 1958, musicologist Izrail Nestev wrote a critical response to the Stravinsky-Craft interview "35 questions and 35 answers," in which the composer argued that musical form was related to mathematics. Two years later, musicologist Iurii Keldysh published an article about Stravinsky in which he condemned the music of *Agon* in some detail.[96]

Since the Soviet critics who supported Balanchine did so based on his musicality, the quality of the score itself was central to their arguments. For Balanchine's works set to composers such as Bizet, Tchaikovsky, Prokofiev, or even Stravinsky in his neoclassical period, the close connections between music and dance could justify the ballets within the confines of Soviet aesthetics. For serial works, however, the close relationship between music and dance condemned them. Stravinsky's analogy between art and mathematics was particularly antithetical to choreographic symphonists, and Soviet criticisms of *Agon* almost uniformly employed metaphors about science or mathematics to deride the work. Lvov-Anokhin described it as "choreographic geometry, algebra, chemistry, the audacious 'fission of an atomic nucleus' in dance, anything at all, only not inspiration, not art if we take that to be the expression of living human emotions."[97] Even Gabovich called the work cold and mathematical, arguing that the performers "did not dance so much as solve difficult problems with their legs (to their credit without the aid of a slide rule)."[98] Gabovich felt that Balanchine had choreographed Stravinsky's score because of its difficulty rather than its artistic worth.[99] Such mathematical criticisms may have reflected knowledge of Stravinsky via Soviet musicologists, but they also responded to the ballet's elaborate structure. *Agon* is ordered around the grouping and regrouping of twelve dancers—four male soloists, four female soloists, and four female members of the corps. These twelve dancers form various combinations onstage— the four men together, the eight women together, six pairs, and so forth. This grouping and regrouping of the dancers, which draws attention to the number twelve's many divisors, could plausibly have a "mathematical" or "geometric" quality.[100]

Soviet critics also took issue with the ballet's sterile, dispassionate qualities. The dancers in *Agon* perform in a relatively detached style, making few overtly emotional gestures and using calm and unmoving facial expressions. Sabnina criticized the ballet for being "dry" and lacking emotion.[101] Critics had similar objections to *Episodes*, another work with a serialist score choreographed in much the same manner as *Agon*. Roslavleva argued that "even in the atomic age, the subject of art will be man." She ended her assessment of the piece by asking hopelessly, "what world is opened to us by the 'higher mathematics' of *Episodes*[?] It is not easy to answer."[102]

The only section of *Agon* that met with the approval of Soviet critics was the pas de deux, precisely because it contrasted so much with the rest of the ballet. Instead of the sharp, separated articulations that characterize the rest of the music, the majority of the pas de deux uses long, held notes. The parts are repeatedly marked *espressivo*, and at one point even *dolce espressivo*. The music opens with the violin and viola each leaping up and down over an octave, slipping between dissonance and consonance with one another. As instrumental parts grate against each other, the piece develops a sense of emotional strain. Meanwhile, onstage, the dancers engage in an erotic *adagio*. In a classical pas de deux, this section would feature the man showing off the woman's best extensions and balances. Here, that practice is pushed to its limits, as the man stretches the woman's body out into sexually suggestive poses (Figure 4.6).[103] Often, these stretches draw attention to the woman's pelvis, as during a lift in which the woman opens her legs up in a V-shape toward the audience. The two dancers are almost constantly in physical contact, bodies draped across one another or hands clasped as they contort into various seemingly unfeasible figures. The combination of music and dance suggests an intense sensuality. The ending of the pas de deux is particularly

Figure 4.6 Allegra Kent and Arthur Mitchell performing *Agon* in Moscow, 1962. From *Amerikanskiy balet v Moskve*. Choreography by George Balanchine © The George Balanchine Trust.

dramatic, as the man kneels and the woman drapes herself over his body, a gesture that is reminiscent of the *Pietà*.

To the Soviet critics, this duet compensated for the problems they had previously found with *Agon*, most particularly its rejection of human emotion and character. Lvov-Anokhin, who was scathing regarding the rest of the ballet, wrote of the pas de deux, "The laborious thinking out of form gives way to stirring plastic expression of extremely strained and complex, but at the same time natural and therefore excellent, human emotion."[104]

That the Soviet critics admired the *Agon* pas de deux, however, cannot be attributed entirely to Balanchine's work. Much of the credit must be given to the performers, Arthur Mitchell and Allegra Kent, who were beloved by Soviet audiences. What positive things the Soviet reviewers had to say about the ballet were almost always discussed as evidence of Kent and Mitchell's talents. Sabnina thought that Kent's "exciting lyricism" was such that even in "aimless" dances such as *Agon,* the dancer performed "poetically, with inspiration."[105] Similarly, Zakharov wrote that Mitchell "immediately won the sympathy of our viewers with his exceptional plasticity, his manner of dancing, and his genuine spirituality. He dances freely and easily, with a beautiful, noble manner."[106]

As Clare Croft has discussed, the fact that Mitchell was the only black dancer in the company put him in a particularly sensitive position. He was marked as separate from the rest of the troupe and worshiped, almost fetishized, by the Soviet audience. Croft documents that the ANTA panel hoped to use Mitchell's presence as a token to distract foreign observers from race problems in the United States; Mitchell's astounding performances in the Soviet Union and his celebrity status there helped them accomplish this goal. But American newspaper coverage of the tour tended to discount Mitchell's importance to the company's success, choosing instead to focus on Balanchine's abstract ballets. Indeed, since the American newspaper critics and the ANTA dance panel believed so strongly that Balanchine's ballets were totally abstract, they thought that works such as *Agon* inherently could not comment on race relations. Modernist works thus seemed to the ANTA dance panel and the State Department a perfect form in which to package blackness for a foreign audience. As Croft describes, however, Mitchell's presence and his performance in *Agon* defied this thinking, foregrounding racial difference and the hegemonic white construction of the ballet company and of American cultural diplomacy in general.[107]

A re-examination of the 1962 Soviet reviews largely supports Croft's reading. Soviet reviewers were not at all taken with Balanchine's practice clothes style, particularly *Agon*. They were, however, enthralled by Kent and Mitchell as performers. While Mitchell was a particular favorite with critics, however, he was not the only American dancer who found fans in the Soviet Union. Many of the company's performers were singled out in reviews for their astounding technique, including Kent, Melissa Hayden, and Edward Villella.[108] Video footage of the performances also suggests that the Soviet audiences were excited by the company's virtuoso dancers. During a performance of *Western Symphony* that was recorded for Soviet television, it is possible to hear the audience cheering for Arthur Mitchell and applauding rhythmically in the middle of Gloria Govrin's solo, a sign of great admiration in Russian dance culture.[109]

In this way, the Soviet reception of New York City Ballet in 1962 resembled the American reception of the Bolshoi Ballet in 1959. In both instances, reviewers were much quicker to praise the dancers than to praise choreography, although the Soviet reviewers were much kinder to Balanchine and Robbins than the American reviewers to Lavrovsky and Grigorovich. For both sides, the dancers seemed to be regarded as a politically neutral group to praise, while discussions of choreography were fraught with anxieties.

Tellingly, a full report of the Soviet reviews never reached the United States. American newspapers, particularly the *New York Times* and *New York Herald Tribune*, were eager to print news of New York City Ballet's success, but were willing to forgo nuance in order to foreground the company's accomplishments. John Martin, who had just retired as the *New York Times* dance critic, traveled to the Soviet Union with New York City Ballet in order to cover their progress. The *New York Herald Tribune* and other American newspapers also published frequently on New York City Ballet's tour.

Their reporting constantly exaggerated the conflict between New York City Ballet and the Soviet dance establishment. In the weeks leading up to New York City Ballet's tour in the Soviet Union, the New York papers frequently reminded their readers of the clash between the Soviet and American styles. While the company was in the Soviet Union, John Martin repeatedly referenced the revolutionary nature of Balanchine's ballets, claiming in a review of October 31 that

> The [Soviet] public, accustomed to productions larger and louder than life consisting of a full evening of swashbuckling stories punctuated by designedly applaudable bursts of bravura, was required to make a major adjustment in the face of this repertory made up entirely of dancing shaped along musical lines and without drama or spectacle.[110]

Following the first performance, the American newspapers generally reported on the enthusiastic applause from the audience, but as a few critical comments appeared in Soviet newspapers, the American reporters expressed confusion and frustration at their lack of appreciation for Balanchine's works. Many of the American reporters seemed to regard Moscow reviews as wildly unfavorable, though, as we have seen, most were actually positive. At the same time, so much had been written in the United States about the purportedly revolutionary nature of Balanchine's choreography in the USSR that any positive response from Soviet audiences or critics was regarded as, in Martin's words, "something of an esthetic revolution."[111] The genuine applause from the Soviet audiences, the excitement about both Balanchine and the New York City Ballet performers, all of which really existed, were reinterpreted in the American press to be a rejection of Soviet ballet, even a sign of political rebellion.

On November 25, 1962, Walter Terry published selections of Mikhail Gabovich's second review of New York City Ballet in an article entitled "A Revelation for Russians." In it, Terry quoted selectively from Gabovich's essay to demonstrate how well Americans were performing in the ballet exchanges. According to Terry, Soviets were beginning to recognize that "Russian ballet, choreographically speaking, is way behind the times."[112] To him, Gabovich's article was evidence of the impact that Balanchine was having in the Soviet Union, a sign that "the ballet revelation induced by Balanchine is going to lead to ballet revolution within the cultural life of the Soviet Union."[113] Terry's triumphant language brought forward all the positive points that Gabovich made about Balanchine's style of dance, yet stripped them of context. In particular, Terry did not quote any of Gabovich's writing from the final section of his article, in which he argued that Balanchine's style should be allowed to exist alongside choreographic symphonism and drambalet. Rather than an argument for aesthetic tolerance, Terry's version of Gabovich's "Dance Panorama" seems to be a recognition of Balanchinian (and American) exceptionalism.

Gabovich's Flowers

In its unedited form, Gabovich's original article is one of the critical highlights of the Soviet-American exchange. In a meeting so filled with misunderstandings and failed translations, Gabovich's writing stands out for his insights into Balanchine's work. The review on New York City Ballet and Balanchine delved deeply into the company's strengths and into the choreographer's style. Gabovich praised the polyphonic arrangements that Balanchine created and celebrated the lack of outwardly bravura dancing.

So acute was his understanding of Balanchine that Gabovich's review is probably the source of an aphorism that is now almost universally associated with Balanchine: "See the music, hear the dance." While Balanchine has occasionally been credited with the saying himself, it has long been known that the choreographer took many of his most famous phrases from other writers. Thus far, the accepted wisdom is that Balanchine lifted this phrase from a review published by the American Glenway Wescott in December 1963. In the article, Wescott wrote, "Suddenly I *see* the music; suddenly

I *hear* the movements of the dancers."[114] But a full year prior, in November 1962, Gabovich wrote in his review of New York City Ballet, "[Balanchine] truly 'sees' music and 'hears' dance."[115] Given that Balanchine's version more closely matches Gabovich's phrasing than Wescott's, it is more likely that the choreographer saw the original remark in Russian.

While Terry's version of Gabovich was a work of American triumphalism, the Soviet author himself was much more balanced. In the final paragraphs, he called for greater artistic acceptance of New York City Ballet's style in the Soviet Union, but he also defended Soviet ballet from Balanchine. Gabovich quoted the choreographer's claim that "Ballet is a flower," and responded:

> That is quite right, even the symbolic comparison with beautiful flowers. Yes, the flowers that Albrecht holds in his hands as he walks towards Giselle's grave are beautiful. But three times lovelier are the sadness, the anguish and the repentance felt by the man who kneels and scatters white flowers on the grave. Man and flowers, that is the poetic symbol of romantic ballet.[116]

Gabovich's answer to Balanchine draws on the heritage common to them both, citing the quintessential Romantic ballet, *Giselle*, which was created in 1841 by composer Adolph Adam and choreographers Jean Coralli and Jules Perrot. In pointing out the power of the moment when Albrecht lays flowers on Giselle's grave, a moment portrayed purely in pantomime, Gabovich argued for the relevance of narrative ballet to the future of the art form.

Even more, with this argument Gabovich drew attention to the way that flowers function as a symbol of heavy significance in *Giselle*. In one moment they are a naive promise of love, in the next a sign of mourning, in the next a symbol of the witch queen's power. By digging into Balanchine's metaphor, Gabovich implied that even the coldest cut flowers can carry intense symbolic and emotional resonance for audiences. In doing so, Gabovich agreed with Balanchine's claim that ballet was a flower but denied the implication that ballet's beautiful motions were devoid of meaning. Perhaps to some audiences, a flower was a flower, but to others it would be filled with significance.

In comparing ballet with flowers, then, Gabovich's article could be an argument for the very flexibility of meaning that lay at the heart of the Soviet-American exchange, and in particular of New York City Ballet's Soviet reception. Just as the flowers in *Giselle* take on different meanings depending on the context, so too do ballets take on different meanings to different audiences. While to Balanchine, *Serenade* might be a pristine rose, an object of serene beauty to its audience, to others the same ballet might be a heartbreaking poem about death and resurrection, to others a reminiscence of a forgotten waltz. To some audiences, *Agon* was a masterly combination of serialism and choreographic form. To others it was a math problem and to still others a story about race relations in the United States. Not only did the ballets take on different meanings, but different audiences could experience viscerally different things depending on which elements of the ballet they paid attention to. The thrilling overlay of musical and choreographic form in Balanchine's works, for example, comes through more strongly for audience members who know to listen and look for those connections. For those who are not listening for the music's form, perhaps what they notice is the movement of the dancers' hips or the tense partnering.

Through these confusions and discombobulations of meaning, the Soviet critics and audiences did not fail to understand New York City Ballet. They simply transliterated the visiting works into a new alphabet. To Balanchine, his works explored the formal, abstract properties of great classical music. For many of the Soviet Union's dance community, the same works could participate in their own debates about choreographic symphonism and dramballet. As such, Balanchine's visit may have tipped the scales toward the choreographic symphonists, but not, as Terry suggested, because everyone in the Soviet Union gave up on story ballets when they saw abstract choreography. Rather, the experience of seeing Balanchine's works underlined the multiplicity possible in ballet, the many meanings that each individual work could have. The visit did not close down an argument between American and Soviet styles of ballet. Rather it furthered the very practice of debate at the heart of the Thaw.

Epilogue

Exchange in the Twenty-first Century

In 2011, the Bolshoi Theater hired South Dakota–born David Hallberg as a principal dancer, making him the first American to occupy the highest rank in the Moscow company. Momentarily, ballet was in the national spotlight. Interviewing the dancer for his Comedy Central TV show, Stephen Colbert jokingly needled Hallberg, claiming, "Americans don't defect to go to the Bolshoi, the Russkies defect to come here." When Hallberg gently reminded Colbert that the Cold War was over and assured him that he would continue to dance with American Ballet Theatre, Colbert quipped, "American Ballet Theatre and the Bolshoi at the same time . . . so you're a double agent!"[1]

The Bolshoi's decision to hire Hallberg was seen in the United States as a triumph, a sign that American performers had finally caught up to their Russian counterparts.[2] In Moscow, he was initially welcomed warmly by audiences and dancers alike.[3] A few months after joining the company, however, Hallberg was cast as the lead for the re-opening of the Bolshoi's historic stage, which had just undergone a six-year, hundreds-of-millions-of-dollars renovation.[4] Casting him in such a politically important performance elicited sharp criticisms, particularly from celebrity dancer Nikolai Tsiskaridze, who complained that the decision was an insult to Russian ballet.[5] Following Tsiskaridze's remarks, Russian fan responses were somewhat more critical of Hallberg, though many commenters on the Russian-language internet forum *Balet i opera* continued to defend him vigorously.[6]

Hallberg's welcomes, both frosty and warm, illustrate the continuities and changes in the world of ballet over the past fifty years. During the Cold War, ballet performances could be political events. The Soviet-American exchanges were organized by the American and Soviet governments with the goal of enhancing each country's position in a network of military, economic, and ideological struggles.

Not only was the organization of the tours deeply political, but the reception was as well. As audiences observed foreign ballets, they did so through

Ballet in the Cold War. Anne Searcy, Oxford University Press (2020). © Oxford University Press.
DOI: 10.1093/oso/9780190945107.001.0001.

the prisms of their own experiences. They transliterated what they saw from a foreign choreographic language into their own alphabet. By drawing performers into domestic debates about dance, consciously or not, these audiences exerted power in the exchanges. When the New York City Ballet performed Balanchine's *Symphony in C* in Moscow, critics interpreted it as a work of choreographic symphonism. To those Soviet writers, then, the piece commented on the inheritance of Russian ballet and the content of the musical score. As such, it reinforced beliefs about the superiority of Russian dance and the need for humanist content in art, while still demonstrating that a company from the United States had produced impressive dancers and works. Similarly, American audiences applauded Messerer's *Ballet School* in 1962 because it reminded them of the works of Balanchine. The ballet alleviated concerns about Soviet-American competition in the Cuban Missile Crisis, but it simultaneously gave Americans the impression that they were already victorious in the cultural Cold War.

Though the direct political function of ballet exchanges, and thus transliteration, has changed since the 1960s, American and Russian audiences still see ballet in remarkably different ways. These differences still have political implications. In today's ballet world, companies and dancers are more likely than ever to tour abroad. Yet despite the increasing frequency of such tours, the ballets performed continue to be read and understood through the lenses of local aesthetics and politics. In 2014, the Bolshoi Ballet toured New York City and Washington, DC, performing *Giselle, Swan Lake, Don Quixote,* and *Spartacus,* the final work presented in Yuri Grigorovich's 1968 production. Many American commentators accused the Bolshoi of being conservative, drawing on Cold War–era criticisms of the Russian company.[7] Alastair Macaulay wrote in the *New York Times*, "Returning to New York after nine years, the Bolshoi Ballet [. . .] seems keen to prove that it has reverted to the ghastly artistic torpor it enjoyed in the last two decades of the Soviet era."[8]

Other comments reflected the mid-twentieth-century concern with the Bolshoi's level of taste. In the *New Yorker,* Joan Acocella introduced *Spartacus* to her readers in a short essay that predicted, "New York's former-Soviet community will no doubt be out in full force. They are faithful dancegoers. But Russians aren't the only people who like things big and vulgar."[9] Numerous posters on the English-language internet forum *Ballet Alert!* complained about the "dirty" pointe shoes worn by the Russian dancers.[10] Of course, as during the Cold War, this type of rhetoric was not limited to the American side. Macaulay's criticisms were devoured by the readership of *Balet i opera,* most of whom responded to the *New York Times* articles with outrage, a few disparaging American culture writ large in light of the reviews.[11]

The rhetorical anger that the tours inspired online and in print directly contradicted the atmosphere at the performances themselves. I saw the Bolshoi twice during their 2014 performances in New York, in *Don Quixote* and *Spartacus*. The applause was generous and effusive, and I was particularly struck by the audience response during *Spartacus*. The atmosphere started out slightly muted. In the middle of the second act, however, something seemed to snap, and the crowd became boisterous and excited. When the curtain came down on Maria Vinogradova, stretching her arms out to the ceiling in an expression of Phrygia's pain, the audience screamed and cheered, a raucous noise that reminded me of accounts of the Bolshoi's performances in 1959.[12] The company was scolded in the press for being old-fashioned and tasteless, while in person, crowds cheered with abandon.

In addition to the continuing tradition of touring companies, star dancers and choreographers are increasingly independent agents, staging their own individual tours in the summer or making frequent trips to perform as guests with other companies.[13] Thus, unlike performers during the Cold War, artists now can have careers spanning the United States and Russia at the same time.

Perhaps the most prominent such figure is choreographer Alexei Ratmansky. Ratmansky was born in the Soviet Union and trained as a dancer at the Bolshoi Choreographic Academy. During the 1980s and 1990s, he performed globally: in the Ukrainian National Ballet, the Royal Winnipeg Ballet, and the Royal Danish Ballet. Ratmansky led the Bolshoi Ballet from 2004 to 2009, when he left to become the Artist in Residence at American Ballet Theatre.[14] Nevertheless, he continues to work with the Bolshoi. In other words, much like Hallberg, he flits back and forth over the artistic and geopolitical lines of the Cold War.

In many of his works, Ratmansky continues the traditions of both the choreographic symphonists and American neoclassicism, treading a fine line between the two styles and interpretations of choreography. Many of his ballets blend elements of abstract and narrative choreography, including *Russian Seasons, Namouna: A Grand Divertissement,* and *Pictures at an Exhibition*, all choreographed for New York City Ballet. Ratmansky interprets the music along formal lines but using mimetic gestures that can suggest a narrative. In *Russian Seasons,* for example, set to a Leonid Desyatnikov score with soprano and string orchestra, Ratmansky's choreography realizes formal elements of the music and often suggests a plot that reflects the lyrics sung by the soprano.

However, the lyrics and their translations are never provided to the English-speaking audience in New York. To many, therefore, the ballet seems to have no story. To others, it is clearly narrative. Ratmansky's works thus thread the gap between Russian and American schools of choreography, allowing them to be interpreted very differently by different audiences. Essentially they are works that operate in multiple, carefully defined languages.[15]

Ratmansky's story, like Hallberg's, is a tale of how much the Cold War shapes ballet today. Ratmansky blends Soviet and American balletic sensibilities, but his audiences in Russia and the United States view his ballets differently. Hallberg traverses both sides of the old Iron Curtain, and those actions are freighted with political weight from the Cold War. The lenses of the Cold War continue to define how American and Russian audiences experience ballet. Far from a universal language, ballet is an art form with unique dialects all over the world. Moreover, the political conflicts that lay at the heart of the Soviet-American exchanges have not stopped playing a role in the way ballet is created and consumed all over the world. The Cold War continues to shape and define ballet. It will do so until we reevaluate both the politics of the twentieth century and the art form itself.

Note on Abbreviations

The following abbreviations have been used:

ABECA	The Bureau of Educational and Historical and Cultural Affairs Historical Collection, Special Collections Division, University of Arkansas Libraries
CAh	Houghton Library at Harvard University
GARF	State Archive of the Russian Federation
GABT	Bolshoi Theater (State Academic Bolshoi Theater)
Museum of GABT	Bolshoi Theater Museum
NYp	New York Public Library for the Performing Arts
RGALI	Russian State Archive of Literature and Art
RGANI	Russian State Archive of Contemporary History

Notes

Introduction

1. This scene is reconstructed from interviews with Judith P. Zinsser and Marina Kondratieva and newspaper accounts of the Madison Square Garden performances. Judith P. Zinsser, Interview with Author, November 14, 2014, Iowa City, IA. Marina Kondratieva, Interview with Author, May 14, 2013, Bolshoi Theater, Moscow. Margaret Lloyd, "Farewell to the Bolshoi," *Christian Science Monitor*, May 16, 1959. Walter Terry, "Two Ballet Companies Will Draw 16,000 Fans in Single Evening Here," *New York Herald Tribune*, May 10, 1959. "Bolshoi Ballet Flies in on Tour," *New York Times*, April 13, 1959. "A Record 13,000 See Bolshoi at Garden," *New York Herald Tribune*, May 13, 1959. "Ballet Fans Wait in Rain 7 Hours," *New York Times*, April 11, 1959. Illiustrirovannye programmy gastrolei Bol'shogo teatra v Pol'she i SShA. S uchastiem L. M. Lavrovskogo. 1959–1960, RGALI f. 3045 o. 1 d. 317.

2. Geoffrey Allen Pigman argues that diplomacy is composed of two halves: representation and communication. The studies of cultural diplomacy that focus on the presenting country explore the first half of that equation: representation. In this book, I will focus equally on communication. *Contemporary Diplomacy: Representation and Communication in a Globalized World* (Cambridge, UK: Polity Press, 2010).

3. Danielle Fosler-Lussier, *Music in America's Cold War Diplomacy* (Oakland: University of California Press, 2015), 2. David Caute, *The Dancer Defects: The Struggle for Cultural Supremacy during the Cold War* (Oxford: Oxford University Press, 2003), 1–16. Justin Hart, *Empire of Ideas: The Origins of Public Diplomacy and the Transformation of U.S. Foreign Policy* (Oxford: Oxford University Press, 2013), 2–5. Nigel Gould-Davies, "The Logic of Soviet Cultural Diplomacy," *Diplomatic History* 27, no. 2 (2003): 193–214.

4. Svodnyĭ plan po kul'turnym sviaziam SSSR s kapitalisticheskimi stranami na 1959 godakh, and Note from TsK KPSS, November 14, 1958, Zapiski Gosudarstvennogo komiteta po kul'turnym sviaziam s zarubzhnymi stranami, RGANI f. 5 o. 36 d. 54 ll. 8, 13–20.

5. Gould-Davies, "The Logic of Soviet Cultural Diplomacy," 205–206.

6. Prilozhenie No. 1 k prikazu Ministra kul'tury SSSR ot 23 avgusta 1958, No. 590, Polozhenie o Gosudarstvennom kontsertnom ob"edinenii SSSR, RGALI f. 648 o. 7 d. 269 l. 31

7. Carol A. Hess, *Representing the Good Neighbor: Music, Difference, and the Pan American Dream* (Oxford: Oxford University Press, 2013), 3–4. Justin Hart argues that the US public diplomacy project began as early as 1935. *Empire of Ideas*, 2.

8. Uta G. Poiger, *Jazz, Rock, and Rebels: Cold War Politics and American Culture in a Divided Germany* (Berkeley: University of California Press, 2000), 1–30. Jessica C. E.

Gienow-Hecht, *Transmission Impossible: American Journalism as Cultural Diplomacy in Postwar Germany 1945–1955* (Baton Rouge: Louisiana State University Press, 1999), 1–11. David Monod, *Settling Scores: German Music, Denazification, and the Americans, 1945–1953* (Chapel Hill: University of North Carolina Press, 2005), 1–11.

9. Fosler-Lussier, *Music in America's Cold War Diplomacy*, 12–13. Emily Abrams Ansari, "'Masters of the President's Music': Cold War Composers and the United States Government" (PhD diss., Harvard, 2009), 30–31.
10. Monod, *Settling Scores*, 6–7.
11. ANTA was an organization dedicated to the promotion of American theater. It was established in 1935 by Congress as part of the New Deal. The ANTA dance panel was made up of twelve to fifteen members from the dance community, mostly choreographers, administrators, and critics. The panel primarily selected modern dance and ballet companies to participate in the tours, with a smattering of folk dance and contemporary dance included as well. Naima Prevots, *Dance for Export: Cultural Diplomacy and the Cold War* (Hanover, NH: Wesleyan University Press, 1998), 37–40.
12. Danielle Fosler-Lussier and Eric Fosler-Lussier, "Database of Cultural Presentations: Accompaniment to *Music an America's Cold War Diplomacy*," version 1.1, last modified April 1, 2015, http://musicdiplomacy.org/database.html, accessed April 4, 2017.
13. Gould-Davies, "The Logic of Soviet Cultural Diplomacy," 196–200. Vladislav Zubok and Constantine Pleshakov, *Inside the Kremlin's Cold War: From Stalin to Khrushchev* (Cambridge, MA: Harvard University Press, 1996), 36–54. Vladimir O. Pechatnov, "Soviet-American Relations through the Cold War," in *Oxford Handbook of Cold War Studies*, ed. Richard H. Immerman and Petra Goedde (Oxford: Oxford University Press, 2013), 107–123.
14. Caute, *The Dancer Defects*, 30. Kiril Tomoff, *Virtuosi Abroad: Soviet Music and Imperial Competition during the Early Cold War* (Ithaca, NY: Cornell University Press, 2015), 16. O kul'turnykh sviaziakh s Soedinennymi Shtatami Ameriki, RGANI f. 5 o. 36 d. 86 l. 163. Michael Sy Uy, "Performing Catfish Row in the Soviet Union: The Everyman Opera Company and *Porgy and Bess*, 1955–56," *Journal for the Society for American Music* 11, no. 4 (2017): 470–501. Nicholas J. Cull, *The Cold War and the United States Information Agency: American Propaganda and Public Diplomacy, 1945–1989* (Cambridge, UK: Cambridge University Press, 2008), 165.
15. Prevots, *Dance for Export*, 23–26, 44–52, 71.
16. Fosler-Lussier, *Music in America's Cold War Diplomacy*, 171–176. See chapters 2 and 4 for more on ANTA selections.
17. Caute, *The Dancer Defects*, 3.
18. Jessica C. E. Gienow-Hecht, "*The World Is Ready to Listen*: Symphony Orchestras and the Global Performance of America," *Diplomatic History* 36, no. 1 (2012): 23–25. Fosler-Lussier, *Music in America's Cold War Diplomacy*, 200–203.
19. Report, Ministry of Culture to TsK KPSS, June 13, 1958, RGANI f. 5 o. 36 d. 56 l. 12. Tomoff, *Virtuosi Abroad*, 18–19.
20. Nancy Reynolds, "The Red Curtain: Balanchine's Critical Reception in the Soviet Union," *Proceedings of the Society of Dance History Scholars* (Riverside: University

of California Riverside, February 14–15, 1992), 47–57. Yale Richmond, *Cultural Exchange and the Cold War: Raising the Iron Curtain* (University Park: Pennsylvania State University Press, 2003), 125. Jennifer Homans, *Apollo's Angels: A History of Ballet* (New York: Random House, 2010), 376–379. Fosler-Lussier criticizes this line of argument. *Music in America's Cold War Diplomacy,* 166–167. Somewhat on the converse side of this argument, historian Cadra Peterson McDaniel argues that the Soviets used cultural diplomacy to indoctrinate American viewers. *American-Soviet Cultural Diplomacy: The Bolshoi Ballet's American Premiere* (Lanham, MD: Lexington Books, 2015), xix–xxiv.

21. Fosler-Lussier, *Music in America's Cold War Diplomacy,* 171. Stéphanie Gonçalves has also discussed the difficulty of achieving reciprocity in the British-Soviet ballet exchange. "Ballet, Propaganda, and Politics in the Cold War: The Bolshoi Ballet in London and the Sadler's Wells Ballet in Moscow, October–November 1956," *Cold War History* 19, no. 2 (2019): 171–186.

22. For example, State Department officials tried to prevent the ANTA panel from using the tours as means of supporting American companies financially. ANTA Dance Panel Meeting Minutes September 25, 1958, NYp, ABT, Folder 3393.

23. Harlow Robinson, *The Last Impresario: The Life, Times, and Legacy of Sol Hurok* (New York: Viking, 1994), 18, 64–76, 136–138, 154–162, 207, 214–220.

24. O kul'turnykh sviaziakh s Soedinennymi Shtatami Ameriki, RGANI f. 5 o. 36 d. 86 l. 163.

25. Memo of Conversation, Coombs and Dr. Rainink, November 1, 1961, ABECA, Box 50, Folder 75. Also, Report, Corden, "Performing Arts," ABECA Box 51, Folder 5. Report to TsK KPSS from Ministry of Culture, October 19, 1959, RGANI f. 5 o. 36 d. 86 ll. 195–196.

26. Tickets for the Bolshoi's New York performances in 1962 topped out at $15. Rosalyn Krokover, "At 'Met' in Park," *New York Times,* September 2, 1962. According to measuringworth.com, the income value of this figure would be $302 in 2019. *Measuring Worth,* accessed April 24, 2020. Maya Plisetskaya, *I, Maya Plisetskaya,* trans. A. Bouis (New Haven, CT: Yale University Press, 2001), 206–217. The Soviet government had strict rules in place in order to preserve as much foreign currency as possible from the exchange. Memo, TsK KPSS, 1958, RGANI f. 5 o. 36 d. 56 ll. 12–15.

27. Estimated Weekly Budget of Expenses for Tour, including Europe and Russia; Letter from Onysko to E. B. Carter at ANTA, April 22, 1960; Letter, Onysko to Carter, December 2, 1960, NYp, ABT, Folders 3397 and 3404.

28. Memo of Conversation, Coombs and Dr. Rainink, November 1, 1961, ABECA, Box 50, Folder 75.

29. "Bolshoi to Give New Works Here," *New York Times,* June 5, 1962.

30. Discussions with Hurok and B. N. Krylova, September 8–9, 1958, RGALI f. 2329 o. 8 d. 907 ll. 9–10. Memo to Bohlen from Frank G. Siscoe, August 18, 1961, ABECA, Box 50, Folder 75.

31. Croft, *Dancers as Diplomats,* 66–72. Christina Ezrahi, *Swans of the Kremlin: Ballet and Power in Soviet Russia* (Pittsburgh, PA: University of Pittsburgh Press, 2012), 137–168.

32. Michael E. Latham, "Introduction: Modernization, International History, and the Cold War World," in *Staging Growth: Modernization, Development, and the Global Cold War*, ed. David C. Engerman, Nils Gilman, Mark H. Haefele, and Michael E. Latham (Amherst: University of Massachusetts Press, 2003), 1–18.
33. Mark Everist, "Reception Theories, Canonic Discourses, and Musical Value," in *Rethinking Music*, ed. Nicholas Cook and Mark Everist (Oxford: Oxford University Press, 1999), 378–402. Hans Robert Jauss, "Literary History as a Challenge to Literary Theory," trans. Elizabeth Benzinger, *New Literary History* 2, no. 1 (1970): 7–37.
34. Scholars of cultural diplomacy, including David Caute, have issued calls for research that uses non-American or transnational sources. Caute, *The Dancer Defects*, 613–614. Carol Hess has demonstrated the effectiveness of using a transnational body of sources in cultural diplomacy research, employing both English- and Spanish-language sources to explore the United States' relationship with Latin America in the mid-twentieth century. *Representing the Good Neighbor*. Recent scholarship on colonialism has also focused on the communication and cultural translations that happen between different groups. Julian Go, for example, has discussed how elites in Puerto Rico and the Philippines "domesticated" American colonial cultural tutelage. Go further discusses the fact that colonizers and colonized did not share the same meaning for the same symbols, and that these differences in meaning shaped the colonial encounter. *American Empire and the Politics of Meaning: Elite Political Cultures in the Philippines and Puerto Rico during U.S. Colonialism* (Durham, NC: Duke University Press, 2008). See also Gienow-Hecht, *Transmission Impossible*. Some scholars of translation have applied the theories of reception and reader-response to their field, and these efforts perhaps form the closest analogy to the cultural diplomacy event. Nevertheless, in the act of translation there is a single point of contact between the literary work and its foreign audience, the translator. The translation itself can be read by its audience as a literary work in their own tradition. In a cultural diplomacy performance there are a multitude of reactions. Friederike von Schwerin-High, *Shakespeare, Reception and Translation: Germany and Japan* (London: Continuum, 2004), 1–9.
35. I take the term "interpretive strategies" from the work of Stanley Fish, even though Fish is invested more in a theoretical approach to reception than a historical one. Stanley Fish, *Is There a Text in This Class? The Authority of Interpretive Communities* (Cambridge, MA: Harvard University Press, 1980), 1–17, 147–173.
36. Tim Scholl argues that the term symphonism "carries no literal or denotative meaning. Instead, it serves as a floating signifier to indicate nothing more than the presence of an absence: the lack of 'bad' ballet music." Scholl's claim, however, is based on an analysis of the restaging of *Sleeping Beauty*, not a new work, in the mid-1950s, before the genre of choreographic symphonism really took off. Both Christina Ezrahi and I have refuted Scholl's statements. Ezrahi argues that choreographic symphonism was a code term for complex, abstract choreography, while I see it as a signifier that Soviet ballets of the 1950s and 1960s reworked the relationship between movement and music. Ezrahi discusses the shift to choreographic symphonism in great detail, particularly

focusing on developments at the Kirov. Tim Scholl, *"Sleeping Beauty": A Legend in Progress* (New Haven, CT: Yale University Press, 2004), 85. Ezrahi, *Swans of the Kremlin*, 116. Anne Searcy, "The Recomposition of Aram Khachaturian's *Spartacus* at the Bolshoi Theater, 1958–68," *Journal of Musicology* 33, no. 3 (2016): 388–395.

37. Balanchine was not alone in this shift; Leonid Massine, Serge Lifar, and others experimented with similar ideas. They drew on the experiments of Fyodor Lopukhov, Isadora Duncan, and Ruth St. Denis. Stephanie Jordan, *Moving Music: Dialogues with Music in Twentieth-Century Ballet* (London: Dance Books, 2000). Irene Alm, "Stravinsky, Balanchine, and Agon: An Analysis Based on the Collaborative Process," *The Journal of Musicology* 7, no. 2 (Spring 1989): 254–269. James Steichen, *Balanchine and Kirstein's American Enterprise* (Oxford: Oxford University Press, 2019), 57–60. Julia Phillips Randel, "Dancing with Stravinsky: Balanchine, *Agon, Movements for Piano and Orchestra,* and the Language of Classical Ballet" (PhD diss., Harvard University, 2004).
38. I discuss the complexities of the situation in greater detail in chapter 4.
39. Fosler-Lussier, *Music in America's Cold War Diplomacy,* 205–218.
40. Joseph S. Nye Jr. *Bound to Lead: The Changing Nature of American Power* (New York: Basic Books, 1990), 31–32. Nye, *Soft Power: The Means to Success in World Politics* (New York: Public Affairs, 2004), x–xi, 11–15, 35–55. Gienow-Hecht and Fosler-Lussier both suggest more complex ways of analyzing the relationship between soft and hard power that rely on the roles assumed by artists in the exchange. Gienow-Hecht, *"The World Is Ready to Listen,"* 17–19. Fosler-Lussier, *Music in America's Cold War Diplomacy,* 216–217.
41. Danielle Fosler-Lussier and Eric Fosler-Lussier, "Database of Cultural Presentations: Accompaniment to *Music an America's Cold War Diplomacy*," version 1.1, last modified April 1, 2015, http://musicdiplomacy.org/database.html, accessed October 27, 2017. There were two later American tours to the Soviet Union that fall outside the confines of this study: American Ballet Theatre's return trip in 1966 and New York City Ballet's second tour in 1972. The Soviets sent the Bolshoi and Kirov in a near constant rotation during the 1960s and 1970s. The United States's later decision to use fewer ballet companies seems to have been constant across countries of destination, not just to the Soviet Union.

Chapter 1

1. Walter Terry, "Bolshoi Ends Run at Met to Ovation Inside and Out," *New York Herald Tribune*, May 10, 1959. Letter from Lavrovsky to Chidson, May 9, 1959, RGALI f. 3045 o. 1 d. 195 l. 39.
2. Robert Greskovic, "Don't Blame the Dancers," *Wall Street Journal*, July 22, 2014. Joan Acocella, "Man of the People," *New Yorker*, July 20, 2014. McDaniel, *American-Soviet Cultural Diplomacy*. Homans, *Apollo's Angels,* 341–395. For more on this ongoing critical reception, see the Epilogue.

3. Ezrahi, *Swans of the Kremlin*, 72–73. Natalia Roslavleva, *Era of the Russian Ballet* (London: Victor Gollancz Ltd., 1966), 28. Simon Morrison, *Bolshoi Confidential* (New York: W. W. Norton, 2016), 9–11.
4. Plisetskaya, *I, Maya Plisetskaya*, 139–140. January 1934 saw the first appearance by Soviet dancers in the United States. Vakhtang Chabukiani and Tatiana Vecheslova performed in New York City. John Martin, "The Dance: Art in New Russia," *New York Times*, January 7, 1934. Saniã Davlekamova, *Iã ne khotela tantsevat'* (Moscow: Ast Press SKD, 2005), 171–172. Ezrahi, *Swans of the Kremlin*, 137–168.
5. *Newsweek*, April 13, 1959.
6. A small selection: *Newsweek*, April 13, 1959. "Child Aid Group Planning Benefit at Bolshoi Ballet," *New York Times*, April 8, 1959. "Ballet Benefit Planned by Child Study Association," *New York Herald Tribune*, April 9, 1959. "Who Is Blocking Bolshoi from S.F.?" *San Francisco Chronicle*, April 16, 1959.
7. John Martin, "Dance: Please!" *New York Times*, April 12, 1959.
8. "Ballet Fans Wait in Rain 7 Hours," *New York Times*, April 11, 1959. "Ballet Rush at Garden," *Daily News*, April 11, 1959.
9. "Bolshoi Ballet Opening Tonight," *New York Times*, April 16, 1959.
10. Inez Robb, "Undaunted Daughter Still a Patriot despite Those Soviet Dancers," *New York World Telegram and Sun*, May 13, 1959.
11. Advertisement, *New York Herald Tribune*, April 6, 1959.
12. Harrison E. Salisbury, "Ulanova Arrives for Bolshoi Ballet's Tour," *New York Times*, April 8, 1959. "Bolshoi Ballet to Take Off for Tour of U.S., Canada," *New York Herald Tribune*, April 6, 1959. "Bolshoi Ballet Flying to N.Y.," *New York Herald Tribune*, April 12, 1959. Financial Records for 1959 Tour, RGALI f. 648 o. 7 d. 882.
13. Robert Alden, "Dancers Deplore Flooring at 'Met,'" *New York Times*, April 14, 1959.
14. Letter from Lavrovsky to Chidson, April 19, 1959, RGALI f. 3045 o. 1 d. 195. The company toured during the old Metropolitan Opera House's final decade of use.
15. Letter from Lavrovsky to Chidson, April 19, 1959, RGALI f. 3045 o. 1 d. 195.
16. Kondratieva, Interview with Author, Bolshoi Theater, Moscow, May 14, 2013.
17. Robert Alden, "Bolshoi Girl Stars on Tour of City," *New York Times*, April 20, 1959. Farnsworth Fowle, "Bolshoi Dancers Relax at the Zoo," *New York Times*, April 27, 1959. Edith Evans Ashbury, "'West Side Story' Plays Host to Frolicsome Bolshoi Dancers," *New York Times*, April 30, 1959.
18. Iurii Fedorovich Faĭer, *O sebe, o muzyke, o balete* (Moscow: Vsesoiuznoe izdatel'stvo sovetskiĭ kompozitor, 1970), 420–424. Kondratieva also recalled meeting with a woman she had known as a small child. Kondratieva, Interview with Author, Bolshoi Theater, Moscow, May 14, 2013.
19. The stage of the old Metropolitan Opera House was 63 feet wide, and the DC Capitol Theater 55 feet wide. Richard L. Coe, "Bolshoi May Pass Us By," *Washington Post and Times Herald*, April 1, 1959.
20. Betty Beale, "Part of the Bolshoi to Be Presented Here," *Evening Star*, April 22, 1959.
21. Cholly Angeleno, "Socialites Throng Opening of Ballet," *Los Angeles Examiner*, May 20, 1959. "Star-Studded Audience Cheers Bolshoi on Coast," *New York Post*, May 20, 1959. "Russ Bolshoi Ballet Will Dance Here," *Los Angeles Examiner*, February 27, 1959.
22. Letter from Lavrovsky to Chidson, May 22, 1959, RGALI f. 3045 o. 1 d. 195, l. 49.

23. Kondratieva, Interview with Author, Bolshoi Theater, Moscow, May 14, 2013. Letter from Lavrovsky to Chidson, May 5, 1959, RGALI f. 3045 o. 1 d. 195.
24. Memo by Chief of Department of Culture TsK KOSS Polikarpov and Head of Section of Bureau Yarustovsky, March 5, 1959, RGANI f. 5 o. 36 d. 99 l. 19. Plisetskaya, *I, Maya Plisetskaya*, 204–205.
25. "Bolshoi Ballet Bows on Coast," *New York Times*, June 7, 1959. "Bolshoi Expected to Gross Over $2,000,000 on Tour," *New York Post*, May 8, 1959.
26. Milt Freudenheim, "Bolshoi Ballet's U.S. Premiere a Dazzling Smash," *Chicago Daily News*, April 17, 1959.
27. Terry, "Bolshoi Ends Run at Met to Ovation Inside and Out."
28. Letter from Lavrovsky to Chidson, May 9, 1959, RGALI f. 3045 o. 1 d. 195 l. 39.
29. Kondratieva, Interview with Author, Bolshoi Theater, Moscow, May 14, 2013.
30. "Biggest Audience," *Telegraph and Morning Post*, May 14, 1959.
31. Roslavleva, *Era of the Russian Ballet*, 229–236. Ezrahi, *Swans of the Kremlin*, 253. V. Bogdanov-Beresovsky, *Ulanova and the Development of the Soviet Ballet*, trans. Stephen Garry and Joan Lawson (London: Macgibbon and Kee, 1952).
32. "Russian Ballerina to Tour U.S.," *Long Island Star-Journal*, March 19, 1959. "Galina Ulanova: Long-Awaited Visitor Arrives," *New York World Telegram and Sun*, April 11, 1959.
33. John Martin, "Bolshoi Dancers in 2d Highlight," *New York Times*, May 1, 1959. Walter Terry, "Bolshoi Ballet," *New York Herald Tribune*, May 1, 1959. Walter Sorell, "Bolshoi 'Giselle' New Experience" (from Museum of GABT 1959 Scrapbook); Jean Battey, "Music to My Ears," *Washington Post; Saturday Review*, May 16, 1959 (from Museum of GABT 1959 Scrapbook).
34. Milt Freudenheim, "Bolshoi Ballet's U.S. Premiere a Dazzling Smash," *Chicago Daily News*, April 17, 1959.
35. Walter Terry, "Bolshoi Ballet Hailed in Debut at the Met," *New York Herald Tribune*, April 17, 1959.
36. Sumiko Higashi, *Stars, Fans, and Consumption in the 1950s: Reading Photoplay* (New York: Palgrave Macmillan, 2014), 27–45.
37. Bogdanov Beresovsky, *Ulanova and the Development of the Soviet Ballet. Galina Ulanova: The Making of a Ballerina*, translated from Russian by S. Rosenberg (Moscow: Foreign Languages Publishing House)
38. Judith Crist, "Ulanova Here for U.S. Tour," *New York Herald Tribune*, April 9, 1959.
39. Anatole Chujoy, "Moscow Bolshoi Ballet Is Sensation in New York," *Dance News*, May 1959.
40. Plisetskaya, *I, Maya Plisetskaya*, 6, 9–11, 32–42.
41. Plisetskaya, *I, Maya Plisetskaya*, 133–167, 191–198.
42. Numerous documents from the planning phases of the tour list Plisetskaya as one of the major figures. She was going to star in the first cast for *Swan Lake*, and the Bolshoi was preparing biographies about her to be printed in English for fans. Her name is on the list for hotel rooms. A list of artists going to London from an unknown date then has Plisetskaya's name crossed off. GABT Order No. 275 June 28, 1956; Plan for Rehearsals on Stage of London Theater, September 1956; Preparation of Materials for Press; Printing for Tour of Bolshoi Ballet Theatre in London; Repertoire of the Guest Tour in London October 1956; Program Contents for Ballets, RGALI f. 648 o. 7 d. 473

ll. 4, 20, 26, 27, 28, 29. List of Workers of the Bolshoi Theater, Taking Part in Tour of London; Letter from Director of GABT to Shashkin, June 20, 1956; Letter from Director of GABT to Shashkin July 2, 1956, RGALI f. 648 o. 7 d. 474 ll. 1, 70, 86.

43. The reported reason for Plisetskaya's staying in the USSR during the 1956 London tour was to keep up the level of dancing in Moscow. In 1958, however, the Bolshoi was closed for renovations and did not need anyone to stay home. Mikhail Chulaki, then director of the Bolshoi, wrote a letter to the Ministry of Culture requesting that some other job be found for the dancer while the Bolshoi performed in the West, suggesting a tour to Bulgaria, Czechoslovakia, and Poland. In the end, this request seems to have been effective, as a special smaller tour to Czechoslovakia starring Plisetskaya was approved. Letter from Chulaki to Ministry of Culture, Mikhailov, May 7, 1958. Approval of trip to Czechoslovakia, starring Plisetskaya and A. Makarov, RGALI f. 648 o. 8 d. 88.

44. This Georgy Zhukov was not the famous general. Zapis' besedy b/sh Zhukov i Iurok, February 24, 1959, RGALI f. 2329 o. 8 d. 1234 l. 40.

45. Stenogramma besedy G.A. Orvida s sovetskimi i zarubezhnymi zhurnalistami o predstoiashchikh gastroliakh baletnoi truppy v SShA i Kanade, March 20, 1959, RGALI f. 648 o. 7 d. 308.

46. Telegram, April 9, 1959, RGALI f. 2329 o. 8 d. 1234 l. 80. This is a request to speed Plisetskaya's visa through in order for her to come with the other dancers.

47. Plisetskaya may have also been helped by Shchedrin's meeting with a KGB agent to convince them that Plisetskaya would not defect, as well as Sol Hurok's adamant insistence that Plisetskaya should be included in the tour. Plisetskaya, *I, Maya Plisetskaya*, 182–183, 188–197. According to Morrison, Olga Lepeshinskaya also made a case for Plisetskaya at the Communist Party organization within the Bolshoi. Morrison, *Bolshoi Confidential*, 344–345.

48. Walter Terry, "Hurok Assured Plisetskaya Will Join Bolshoi in U.S.," *New York Herald Tribune*, 1959 Tour Scrapbook, Museum of GABT. Walter Terry, "Bolshoi Ballet in U.S.A.," *New York Herald Tribune*, April 12, 1959.

49. Higashi, *Stars, Fans, and Consumption in the 1950s*, 107–128.

50. John Martin, "Stone Flower," *New York Times*, May 5, 1959. "Bolshoi's Treasury of Ballet Highlights Cheered at Shrine," *Mirror News*, May 22, 1959. Patterson Greene, "'Swan Lake' Thrills Audience," *LA Examiner*, May 23, 1959. "Direct from Moscow—Russia's Best," *Newsweek*, April 13, 1962. Leonard Lyons, "The Lyon's Den," *New York Post*, April 15, 1959.

51. Ed Sullivan, "Little Old New York," *Daily News*, May 8, 1959.

52. "Maya Plisetskaya," *Vogue*, November 1, 1959.

53. Miles Kastendieck, "Brilliance by Bolshoi," *New York Journal American*, May 5, 1959. Winthrop Sargeant, "Musical Events: A Stunner," *New Yorker*, May 16, 1959.

54. This type of mixed repertoire was central to the entire Soviet cultural diplomacy program. In 1961 the Ministry of Culture took steps to ensure that more Soviet artists touring abroad would combine classical works designed to show off their mastery of performance with newer works written by Soviet composers. The ballet theaters were held up as an example of how to carry out this type of programming successfully.

Spravka o repertuare teatrov, khudozhestvennykh kollektivov, artisticheskikh grupp i solistov, vyezzhaiushchikh zarubezh, RGALI f. 2329 o. 3 d. 1192 ll. 31–41.

55. David Nice, *Prokofiev: From Russia to the West, 1891-1935* (New Haven: Yale University Press, 2003), 5–6, 25–60, 146–165, 320–337.
56. Simon Morrison, *The People's Artist: Prokofiev's Soviet Years* (Oxford: Oxford University Press, 2009), 6–7, 30–31. Leonid Maximenkov, "Prokofiev's Immortalization," in *Sergey Prokofiev and His World*, ed. Simon Morrison (Princeton: Princeton University Press, 2008), 298–299.
57. Morrison, *The People's Artist*, 247–295.
58. Quoted in Boris Schwarz, *Music and Musical Life in Soviet Russia*, enlarged ed. (Bloomington: Indiana University Press, 1983), 219. Kiril Tomoff, *Creative Union: The Professional Organization of Soviet Composers, 1939-1953* (Ithaca, NY: Cornell University Press, 2006), 122–151.
59. Morrison, *The People's Artist*, 341–392.
60. Morrison, *The People's Artist*, 72.
61. Ezrahi, *Swans of the Kremlin*, 156–159.
62. Maximenkov, "Prokofiev's Immortalization," 303–307.
63. The Prokofiev biography in this program was translated from the biography used in Russian programs. Illustrated Program Bolshoi, RGALI f. 3045 o. 1 d. 326 l. 48. Russian version appears in Program for *Stone Flower*, Stone Flower Collection, Museum of GABT.
64. Illustrated Program Bolshoi, RGALI f. 3045 o. 1 d. 326 l. 48.
65. On nineteenth-century ballet: Marian Smith, *Ballet and Opera in the Age of Giselle* (Princeton: Princeton University Press, 2000), 97–123, 176–177. Lynn Garafola, "Russian Ballet in the Age of Petipa," in *The Cambridge Companion to Ballet*, ed. Marian Kant (Cambridge: Cambridge University Press, 2007), 151–163. On drambalet: N. Chernova, "Balet 1930–1940kh godov," in *Sovetskiĭ baletnyĭ teatr*, ed. V. M. Krasovskaia (Moscow: Iskusstvo, 1976), 106–154. Yuri Grigorovich, "Traditsii i Novatorstvo," in *Muzyka i khoreografiia sovremennogo baleta*, ed. I. V. Golubovskiĭ (Leningrad: Muzyka, 1974), 7–14. Roslavleva, *Era of the Russian Ballet*, 229–254. Chernova and Grigorovich actually use the term "choreodram" for this type of ballet, a term that seems to have been as widespread as drambalet. However, as drambalet has already entered the English-language literature, I continue to use it here.
66. Pauline Fairclough, *Classics for the Masses: Shaping Soviet Music Identity under Lenin and Stalin* (New Haven: Yale University Press, 2016). David Hoffmann, *Stalinist Values: The Cultural Norms of Soviet Modernity, 1917-1941* (Ithaca, NY: Cornell University Press, 2003), 163.
67. Konstantin Stanislavski, *My Life in Art*, trans. and ed. Jean Benedetti (New York: Routledge, 2008). Rose Whyman, *The Stanislavsky System of Acting* (Cambridge: Cambridge University Press, 2008).
68. Lynn Garafola, *Diaghilev's Ballets Russes* (Oxford: Oxford University Press, 1989), 19–24. Tim Scholl, "The Ballet Avant-Garde II: The 'New' Russian and Soviet Dance in the Twentieth Century," in *The Cambridge Companion to Ballet*, ed. Marian Kant (Cambridge: Cambridge University Press, 2007), 212–223.

69. Ezrahi, *Swans of the Kremlin*, 54.
70. As Katerina Clark argues, this period saw authors and cultural critics trying to shape socialist realism as a style with highly individualized characters rather than monumental composite figures. "Shostakovich's Turn to the String Quartet and the Debates about Socialist Realism in Music," *Slavic Review* 72, no. 3 (Fall 2013): 573–589.
71. Roslavleva, *Era of the Russian Ballet*, 254.
72. This is of course following the early version of the ballet in which Prokofiev gave the work a happy ending. The happy ending version was criticized heavily at the Bolshoi Theater, so Prokofiev changed the plot but kept much of the same music. Morrison, *The People's Artist*, 34–40.
73. Sergei Prokofiev, *Romeo and Juliet: A Ballet in Four Acts* (New York: Bellwin Mills, 1979?). Sergei Prokofiev, *Romeo i Dzhul'etta. Arranged for Piano by L. T. Atovm'iana* (Moscow: Gosudarstvennoe Muzykal'noe Izdatel'stvo, 1946).
74. As Marian Smith has pointed out, ballet composers used leitmotifs well before Wagner. Marian E Smith, "Orchestra as Translator: French Nineteenth-Century Ballet," in *Cambridge Companion to Ballet*, ed. Marian Kant (Cambridge: Cambridge University Press, 2007), 141.
75. Morrison, *The People's Artist*, 32.
76. Morrison, *The People's Artist*, 49, 106–110. Lavrovsky, "Balet 'Romeo i Dzhul'etta' Istoriia spektaklia," RGALI f. 3045 o. 1 d. 145.
77. Choreographic analysis of *Romeo and Juliet* in this paper is informed by two video sources. The first is the film version of *Romeo and Juliet* directed by Lavrovsky and L. Arnstam from 1954. It stars Galina Ulanova and Yuri Zhdanov. The other is a film of the stage production at the Bolshoi from 1976, staring Natalia Bessmertnova as Juliet and Mikhail Lavrovsky, the choreographer's son, as Romeo. I combined this with impressions from seeing the ballet performed at the Mariinsky Theater in St. Petersburg. *Romeo and Juliet* performed by the Bolshoi Ballet, directed for film by L. Arnstam and Leonid Lavrovsky, 1954 (Video Artists International, 2003). *Romeo and Juliet* performed by the Bolshoi Ballet, 1976 (Kultur, n.d.). *Romeo and Juliet*, performed by the Mariinsky Ballet (St. Petersburg: Mariinsky Theater, June 8, 2010).
78. William Shakespeare, *Romeo and Juliet*, ed. Jonathan Bate and Eric Rasmussen (New York: Modern Library, 2007), Act I, Scene 4.
79. Lavrovsky, "'Romeo i Dzhul'etta' Rezhisserskaia ėkspozitsiia baleta S S Prokof'eva, postavlennogo v leningradskom teatre opery i baleta i. Kirova. Stenigraffa," March 10, 1939, RGALI f. 3045 o. 1 d. 4.
80. Lavrovsky, "'Romeo i Dzhul'etta' Razhisserskie zametki k baletu S S Prokof'eva, postavlennomu v Leningradskom teatre operi i baleta im. Kirova," 1939, RGALI f. 3045 o. 1 d. 5.
81. Costume designs for *Romeo and Juliet*, RGALI f. 2336 o. 1 d. 81. Set designs for *Romeo and Juliet*, RGALI f. 2336 o. 1 d. 26.
82. Lavrovsky, "'Romeo i Dzhul'etta' Rezhisserskaia ėkspozitsiia baleta S S Prokof'eva."
83. Lavrovsky, "'Romeo i Dzhul'etta' Razhisserskie zametki k baletu SS Prokoef'eva." Morrison, *The People's Artist*, 107, 110.

84. V. F. Svin'in et al., *Stalinskie premii: dve storony odnoĭ medali. Sbornik dokumentov i khudozhestvenno-publitsisticheskikh materialov* (Novosibirsk: Svin'in i Synov'ia, 2007), 743.
85. Immanuel Wallerstein, *After Liberalism* (New York: New Press, 1995), 72–85. Latham, "Introduction: Modernization, International History, and the Cold War World," 1–22.
86. Nicholas Timasheff, *The Great Retreat: The Growth and Decline of Communism in Russia* (New York: E. P. Dutton and Co., 1946). David L. Hoffmann, "Was There a 'Great Retreat' from Soviet Socialism?: Stalinist Culture Reconsidered," *Kritika* 5, no. 4 (Fall 2004): 651–674.
87. Matthew E. Lenoe, "In Defense of Timasheff's *Great Retreat*," *Kritika* 5, no. 4 (Fall 2004): 723.
88. Emily Genauer, "Bourgeois Decor at Bolshoi, with Men in Prudish Tights," *New York Herald Tribune*, April 26, 1959.
89. Walter Terry, "Bolshoi Ballet Hailed in Debut at the Met," *New York Herald Tribune*, April 17, 1959.
90. Miles Kastendieck, "Spectacular the Word for Bolshoi Ballet," *New York Journal-American*, April 17, 1959.
91. Louis Biancolli, "Bolshoi's Dazzling 'Romeo' Thrills 1st-Nighters at Met," *New York World Telegram and Sun*, April 17, 1959.
92. John Martin, "The Dance: Lavrovsky," *New York Times*, April 26, 1959. On April 26, 1959, Martin dedicated his weekly dance column solely to Lavrovsky, calling him the third star of the Bolshoi, in the same rank as Ulanova and Prokofiev. Martin noted that *Romeo and Juliet* was "a characteristic creation of the *contemporary* Soviet ballet" [emphasis mine]. The column praised Lavrovsky for his "superb dramatic instinct" and "enormous invention," especially in the form of the "highly acrobatic lifts [that are] not for the purpose of exhibiting virtuosity but for the communication of emotional states that transcend the ordinary dimensions of normal experience." Lavrovsky himself read the article and was delighted by it, writing back home to his wife that this was one of the best reviews he had received in his life. Letter from Lavrovsky to Chidson, undated, RGALI f. 3045 o. 1 d. 195 l. 17.
93. Emily Genauer, "Bourgeois Decor at Bolshoi, with Men in Prudish Tights," *New York Herald Tribune*, April 26, 1959.
94. John Chapman, "Bolshoi Ballet a Very Great One," *Sunday News*, April 26, 1959.
95. Thomas R. Dash, "New York Is Conquered! But Only by Bolshoi's Art," *Women's Wear Daily*, April 17, 1959.
96. Irving R. Levine, "Khrushchev's Prettiest Propaganda," *This Week Magazine*, April 19, 1959.
97. Levine, "Khrushchev's Prettiest Propaganda."
98. Ezrahi, *Swans of the Kremlin*, 148–156. Gonçalves, "Ballet, Propaganda, and Politics in the Cold War," 184. As Ezrahi points out, the criticisms about Soviet ballet's conservatism were relatively moderate in England, particularly with reference to *Romeo and Juliet*.

99. The Bolshoi's visit to London was covered substantially in the American press, with articles appearing frequently in the *New York Times* about fan and critical reaction. The negative reactions, however, were not printed as much in the American coverage. "Bolshoi Dancers Arrive in London," *New York Times*, October 2, 1956. "London Acclaims Bolshoi's 'Romeo,'" *New York Times*, October 4, 1956. "New Queue for Bolshoi," *New York Times*, October 21, 1956.
100. Marina Balina, "Introduction," in *Politicizing Magic: An Anthology of Russian and Soviet Fairy Tales*, ed. Marina Balina et al. (Evanston, IL: Northwestern University Press, 2005), 105–121.
101. Stone Flower Libretto, RGALI f. 648 o. 5 d. 901.
102. Morrison, *The People's Artist*, 349.
103. Stone Flower Libretto, RGALI f. 648 o. 5 d. 901.
104. Sergei Prokofiev, *Skaz o kamennom tsvetke*, in *Sobranie sochinenii*, Vol. 12–13 (Moscow: Gosudarstvennoe Muzykal'noe Izdatel'stvo, 1962).
105. Peter J. Schmelz has discussed this shift with regards to classical music. Peter J. Schmelz, *Such Freedom, If Only Musical: Unofficial Soviet Music during the Thaw* (Oxford: Oxford University Press, 2009).
106. Ezrahi, *Swans of the Kremlin*, 118–136.
107. Christina Ezrahi has also discussed this shift in her book *Swans of the Kremlin*, though she sees it more as a reversion to nineteenth-century classical aesthetics than I do. Ezrahi, *Swans of the Kremlin*. V. M. Krasovskaia, "V seredine veka," in *Sovetskii baletnyi teatr*, ed. Krasovskaia (Moscow: Iskusstvo, 1976), 218–290. . Sokolov-Kaminskii, *Sovetskii balet segodnia* (Moscow: Izdatel'stvo 'Znanie', 1984). For more on the argument about content, see chapter 4.
108. Choreographic analysis is informed by two video recordings of the Bolshoi, one starring Ekaterina Maximova and Vladimir Vasiliev from 1979 and the other starring Nikolai Dorokhov and Liudmila Semenyaka from 1990; and by one live performance at the Stanislavsky Theater in Moscow, March 2, 2013, starring Aleksei Lyubimov and Natalia Somova. *Stone Flower*, performed by the Bolshoi Ballet, directed for film by Valery Gorbatsevich, 1979 (VAI 2007). *Stone Flower*, performed by the Bolshoi Ballet, directed for film by Motoko Sakaguchi, 1990 (Arthaus Musik, 2005). *Stone Flower*, performed by the Stanislavsky and Nemirovich-Danchenko Moscow Music Theater (Moscow, March 2, 2013, afternoon).
109. Sergei Prokofiev, *The Tale of the Stone Flower*, with the Orchestra of the Bolshoi Theatre, conducted by Gennady Rozhdestvensky (Melodiia, 2005). Sergei Prokofiev, *The Tale of the Stone Flower*, with the BBC Philharmonic Orchestra, conducted by Gianandrea Noseda (Chandos, 2003).
110. Mikhail Gabovich, "Obraz baletnogo spektaklia," *Sovetskaia kul'tura*, April 11, 1959.
111. Grigorovich was made artistic director of the Bolshoi in 1964, and he held this position until 1995.
112. "Prem'era baleta 'Kamennyi tsvetok' v Bol'shom teatre," *Sovetskaia kul'tura*, March 7, 1959.

113. Dmitri Shostakovich, "Kamennyĭ tsvetok v Bol'shom teatre," *Muzykal'naĭa zhizn'*, no. 5 (1959), *Stone Flower* Collection, Museum of GABT. Shostakovich regularly signed pieces that were ghost-written by others, so there is a possibility that he did not write this article, though he did sometimes write his own reviews of musical events. Laurel Fay, *Shostakovich: A Life* (Oxford: Oxford University Press, 2000), 173–174.
114. Paul Robeson, "Serdechno blagodariŭ vas, druz'ia, za udovol'stvie," *Sovetskii artist*, March 11, 1959.
115. Margaret Lloyd, "Welcome the Bolshoi Ballet!" *Christian Science Monitor*, April 2, 1959.
116. Osgood Caruthers, "Russians Cheer Bolshoi Ballet That Breaks Classical Pattern," *New York Times*, March 9, 1959. Claudia Cassidy, "On the Aisle: Bolshoi Ballet Picks Provocative Time for 1st American Tour," *Chicago Sunday Tribune*, March 15, 1959. "Direct from Moscow—Russia's Best," *Newsweek*, April 13, 1959. Cassidy notes that *Stone Flower* looks more modern and that the dancers have a new kind of freedom, "the kind George Balanchine talks so eloquently about." *Newsweek* claims that the ballet features simple backdrops and abstract designs instead of cumbersome traditional scenery, and states that while foreign critics have pointed out similarities with Western ballet, Bolshoi director Orvid and dancers are "reluctant to admit it."
117. John Martin, "Dance: Bolshoi Ballet," *New York Times*, March 22, 1959.
118. The comparison with Radio City Music Hall gives an early example of the concept of "taste" playing into the Bolshoi's reception in the United States. This will be discussed at greater length in chapter 3. Miles Kastendieck, "Brilliance by Bolshoi," *New York Journal American*, May 5, 1959.
119. John Martin, "Ballet: 'Stone Flower,'" *New York Times*, May 5, 1959. Walter Sorell, "Bolshoi—Unforgettable," *Providence Sunday Journal*, May 17, 1959.
120. Jay S. Harrison, "The Music," *New York Herald Tribune*, May 5, 1959.
121. Walter Terry, "Bolshoi Ballet Hailed in Debut at the Met," *New York Herald Tribune*, April 17, 1959.
122. Kastendieck, "Brilliance by Bolshoi."
123. Elizabeth Grosz, *Volatile Bodies: Towards a Corporeal Feminism* (Bloomington: Indiana University Press, 1994), 14.
124. Jennifer Fisher, "Tulle as Tool: Embracing the Conflict of the Ballerina as Powerhouse," *Dance Research Journal* 39, no. 1 (Summer 2007): 5. Fisher speaks of today's ballet world, but anecdotally her point rings true for the 1950s as well in both the Soviet Union and the United States. In 1959, Lucia Chase was still in charge of American Ballet Theatre, along with Oliver Smith. But Lincoln Kirstein and George Balanchine ran New York City Ballet, soon to be joined by Jerome Robbins. Lew Christensen was in charge of the San Francisco Ballet. The situation was equally stark in the Soviet Union, where most major choreographers (Lavrovsky, Belsky, Grigorovich, Yakobson, and Chabukiani) were men.
125. Robert D. Dean, *Imperial Brotherhood: Gender and the Making of Cold War Foreign Policy* (Amherst: University of Massachusetts Press, 2001). K. A. Cuordileone, *Manhood and American Political Culture in the Cold War* (New York: Routledge,

2005). Andrea Friedman, "The Smearing of Joe McCarthy: The Lavender Scare, Gossip, and Cold War Politics," *American Quarterly* 57, no. 4 (2005): 1105–1129.
126. Milton R. Bass, "The Lively Arts," *Berkshire Eagle*, May 14, 1959.
127. "Bolshoi Ballet on Tap for U.S. Tour," *Washington Daily News*. "Bolshoi Dancers Arrive for Tour," *Long Island Daily Press*, April 13, 1959. "Bolshoi Ballet Arrives to Open Eight-Week Tour of U.S. and Canada," *New York Times*, April 13, 1959. "Bolshoi Ballet Flies In, Met by Ecstatic Hurok," *New York Herald Tribune*, April 13, 1959.
128. Drew Pearson, "Communist Ballets... and Bullets!" *New York Mirror*, May 20, 1959.
129. Kimberly A. Williams, *Imagining Russia* (New York: State University of New York Press, 2012).
130. Inez Robb, "Undaunted Daughter Still a Patriot despite Those Soviet Dancers," *New York World Telegram and Sun*, May 13, 1959. On "conquering": Dash, "New York Is Conquered!". Patterson Greene, "Bolshoi 'Romeo' Magnificent," *Los Angeles Examiner*, May 20, 1959.

Chapter 2

1. Letter from Onysko, April 8, 1960, New York Public Library (NYp), American Ballet Theatre Collection *MGZMD 49, Folder 3162. Seymour Topping, "Ballet Theatre Opens in Moscow," *New York Times*, September 14, 1960. Report on European Tour, NYp, ABT, Folder 3187.
2. Programs USSR, September 8, 1960, NYp, ABT, Folder 3183.
3. Programs USSR, September 8, 1960, and Proposed Repertoire for Europe March 11, 1960, NYp, ABT, Folder 2465. List of people filed with Air France Itinerary, NYp, ABT, Folder 3154.
4. Christopher Endy, "Power and Culture in the West," in *Oxford Handbook of the Cold War*, ed. Richard Immerhan et al. (Oxford: Oxford University Press, 2013), 329–330. Vanessa R. Schwartz, *It's So French: Hollywood, Paris, and the Making of Cosmopolitan Film Culture* (Chicago: University of Chicago Press, 2007), 159–198. Barnhisel also points to Cold War modernism as something international that "like the military and economic alliances being forged through the North Atlantic Treaty Organization and the Marshall Plan, served to knit the West together, with the United States leading the way." Greg Barnhisel, *Cold War Modernists: Art, Literature, and American Cultural Diplomacy* (New York: Columbia University Press, 2015), 11.
5. For a full bibliography on the New York City Ballet tour, see chapter 4. The only scholarly work fully addressing the 1960 ABT tour is Catharine Nepomnyashchy, "American Pioneer: American Ballet Theatre's 1960 Tour of the USSR," *American Ballet Theatre*, http://www.abt.org/insideabt/USSRtour_1960.asp#_ednref8, accessed June 8, 2015. The only book to address the two tours in equal amounts is Prevots, *Dance for Export*, 75–89.
6. Charles Payne, *American Ballet Theatre* (New York: Alfred A. Knopf, 1978), 12–4, 28–36, 129. Alex C. Ewing, *Bravura! Lucia Chase and the American Ballet Theatre*

(Gainesville: University of Florida Press, 2009), 25–46. For more on Russian dominance of ballet in the United States, see James Steichen, *Balanchine and Kirstein's American Enterprise* (Oxford: Oxford University Press, 2018). Lynn Garafola, "Making an American Dance: *Billy the Kid, Rodeo,* and *Appalachian Spring*," in *Aaron Copland and His World*, ed. Carol Oja and Judith Tick (Princeton: Princeton University Press, 2005), 124–126.

7. Business disagreements also factored into the break with Hurok. Payne, *American Ballet Theatre,* 54–55, 99, 125–129, 139–142, 159, 168. Ewing, *Bravura!,* 48–49, 84–97, 128.
8. Payne, *American Ballet Theatre,* 20–25, 31–32, 105–106, 138. Ewing, *Bravura!,* 5–71, 84–97. Jack Anderson, "Lucia Chase of Ballet Theater is Dead," *New York Times,* January 10, 1986.
9. Payne, *American Ballet Theatre,* 166.
10. Ewing, *Bravura!,* 168.
11. Prevots, *Dance for Export,* 37–43.
12. ANTA Dance Panel Meeting Minutes, October 17, 1957; December 19, 1957; October 18, 1956, NYp, ABT, Folders 3384 and 3388. One of the major conflicts for American ballet companies during the 1930s and 1940s was to hold on to their status as ballet companies while seeming American. For more on this, see Charles Payne, *American Ballet Theatre;* James Steichen, "The American Ballet's Caravan," *Dance Research Journal* 47, no. 1 (April 2015): 69–94; and Sally Banes, "Sibling Rivalry: The New York City Ballet and Modern Dance," in *Dance for a City: Fifty Years of the New York City Ballet,* ed. Lynn Garafola et al. (New York: Columbia University Press, 1999), 73–98.
13. Letter, October 17, 1956, Alexander C. Ewing, Ballet Theatre Foundation, to Inness-Brown; Letter, December 11, 1956, Chase to Inness-Brown, NYp, ABT, Folders 3382 and 3383.
14. The New York City Ballet position would later be reversed. For more, see chapter 4. ANTA Dance Panel Meeting Minutes, December 19, 1957, NYp, ABT, Folder 3388.
15. Prevots, *Dance for Export,* 76
16. ANTA Dance Panel Meeting Minutes, October 17, 1957; May 21, 1959; November 19, 1959, NYp, ABT, Folders 3388 and 3396.
17. ANTA Dance Panel Meeting Minutes, October 17, 1957, NYp, ABT, Folder 3388.
18. Ewing, *Bravura!,* 192–203. ANTA Dance Panel Meeting Minutes, August 28, 1958, NYp, ABT, Folder 3393.
19. ANTA Dance Panel Meeting Minutes, September 25, 1958; October 2, 1958; May 21, 1959, NYp, ABT, Folders 3393 and 3396.
20. ANTA Dance Panel Meeting Minutes, October 2, 1958, NYp, ABT, Folder 3393.
21. ANTA Dance Panel Meeting Minutes, May 21, 1959; April 16, 1959; October 22, 1959; November 19, 1959, NYp, ABT, Folder 3396.
22. ANTA Dance Panel Meeting Minutes, February 18, 1960, NYp, ABT, Folder 3402.
23. Maria Tallchief with Larry Kaplan, *Maria Tallchief: America's Prima Ballerina* (New York: Henry Holt, 1997), 256.
24. John Martin, "Dance: Dilemma," *New York Times,* May 15, 1960.
25. Martin, "Dance: Dilemma."

26. Martin, "Dance: Dilemma."
27. Letter, May 18, 1960, Onysko to Chase; Memo, May 20, 1960; Letter, June 14, 1960, Onysko to Chase, NYp, ABT, Folders 3173 and 3169.
28. ANTA Dance Panel Meeting Minutes April 21, 1960; May 11, 1960, NYp, ABT, Folder 3402.
29. Letter, May 13, 1960, Schnitzer to Chase, NYp, ABT, Folder 3400.
30. Letter, May 23, 1960, Chase to Onysko, NYp, ABT, Folder 3400.
31. Letter, January 2, 1960, to Reed from unidentified, Special Assistant to the Ambassador; Letter, January 28, 1960, Reed to Charles (probably Payne); Letter, March 25, 1960, Chase to Thayer, NYp, ABT, Folders 3156 and 3160.
32. Letter, March 25, 1960, Chase to Thayer, NYp, ABT, Folder 3160. Michael Charry, *George Szell: A Life in Music* (Champaign: University of Illinois Press, 2011), 163.
33. Donald Rosenberg, *The Cleveland Orchestra Story: "Second to None"* (Cleveland: Gray and Co., 2000), 286. Anatole Heller Correspondence, New York Philharmonic Digital Archives, Communications/Public Relations, Folder: Bureau Artistique International.
34. Letter, January 2, 1960, to Reed from unidentified, NYp, ABT, Folder 3156.
35. Letter, undated, Onysko to Stevens; Letter, June 21, 1960, Onysko to Chase, NYp, ABT, Folders 3170 and 3174.
36. Letter, July 6, 1960, Payne to Chase, NYp, ABT, Folder 3176.
37. Letter, July 6, 1960, Payne to Chase, NYp, ABT, Folder 3176.
38. Order No. 590 of the Ministry of Culture of the USSR, August 23, 1958, "Ob uporiadochenii gastrol'no-kontsertnoĭ deiatel'nosti," RGALI f. 648 o. 7 d. 269.
39. Letter, July 6, 1960, Payne to Chase, NYp, ABT, Folder 3176.
40. Letter July 29, 1960, Flatow (from Heller Bureau) to Chase, NYp, ABT, Folder 3179.
41. Draft telegram, Chase to Schnitzer; Letter, July 21, 1960, Heller to Chase; Telegram, July 25, 1960; Letter, July 25, 1960, Heller to Chase; July 25, 1960, Chase to Onysko; Letter, July 29, 1960, Flatow to Chase; Letter, August 12, 1960, Onysko to Chase; Telegram, August 12, 1960, Macy to Heller; Telegram from Moscow, Heller to unidentified (presumably Chase). NYp, ABT, Folders 3176, 3177, 3179 and 3181.
42. Letter, June 27, 1960, Heller to Schnitzer, NYp, ABT, Folder 3175.
43. Letter, July 8, 1960, Payne to Chase; Letter, July 11, 1960, Heller to Chase, NYp, ABT, Folder 3177.
44. Telegram, August 17, 1960, Chase to Ballet Theatre, NYp, ABT, Folder 3182.
45. Letter, October 17, 1956, Alexander C. Ewing to Inniss-Brown, NYp, ABT, Folder 3382.
46. Letter, October 15, 1956, Onysko to Schnitzer, NYp, ABT, Folder 3387.
47. Proposed Repertoire for Europe 1960; 1960 Suggested program for Russia; 1960 Suggested Programs for Europe; May 5, 1960, ABT Repertoire for Europe; 1960 Suggested Programs for Russia, July 1, 1960; Suggested Programs for Russia; Programs for Russia, August 7, 1960, NYp, ABT, Folder 2465. Letter, July 8, 1960, Chase to Brady (does not include *Billy the Kid*), NYp, ABT, Folder 3401. Documents Shown to Mr. Hurok, January 24, 1960, NYp, ABT, Folder 3156.
48. Report "The American National Ballet Theatre Goes Abroad," NYp, ABT, Folder 3375.

49. Letter, July 8, 1960, Chase to Brady, NYp, ABT, Folder 3401.
50. ANTA Dance Panel Meeting Minutes, September 17, 1957; December 19, 1957; September 25, 1958, NYp, ABT, Folders 3388, 3393 and 3396.
51. Letter, July 6, 1960, Payne to Chase; Undated letter answering a letter from July 1, 1960, Tuch to Chase, NYp, ABT, Folders 3176 and 3177.
52. Bernstein had programmed *Billy the Kid* in combination with Shostakovich's Seventh Symphony in an attempt to show the similarities between the two styles. Emily Abrams Ansari, *The Sound of a Superpower: Musical Americanism and the Cold War* (Oxford: Oxford University Press, 2018), 190–197.
53. Letter, September 24, 1960, Chase to Onysko; "Report on Tiflis Engagement," enclosed in Letter, October 8, 1960, to Robert Thayer, NYp, ABT, Folders 3184 and 3188.
54. A thorough discussion of the plots typical to socialist realist works is found in Katerina Clark, *The Soviet Novel: History as Ritual* (Chicago: University of Chicago Press, 1981), 162–163, 168–170, 181–182. Chernova, "Ballet 1930–1940kh," 120.
55. Despite the many hesitations toward performing these two works in a Soviet context, Ballet Theatre eventually did perform them on their return trip to the USSR in 1966. Both ballets were received with enthusiasm. Soviet critic Natalia Roslavleva reserved special praise for de Mille's *Fall River Legend*, remarking that "at its core, the ballet is humane and truthful and national." Perhaps by the late 1960s, the spirit of the Thaw was more at work in the American-Soviet exchange, or perhaps following Ballet Theatre's successful 1960 tour the Americans were more confident in their programming choices. Natalia Roslavleva, Draft of "Second Encounter with American Ballet," *Muzykal'naĩa zhizn'*, 1966, RGALI f. 2966 o. 1 d. 29.
56. Nancy Reynolds, "The Red Curtain: Balanchine's Critical Reception in the Soviet Union," *Proceedings of the Society of Dance History Scholars* (Riverside: University of California Riverside, 14–15 February, 1992), 47–57. Homans, *Apollo's Angels*, 376–377.
57. "Report on European Tour," NYp, ABT, Folder 3187. The two pas de deux were somewhat interchangeable in these programs.
58. Catharine Nepomnyashchy, "American Pioneer."
59. "Report on European Tour," NYp, ABT, Folder 3187.
60. Itinerary USSR, NYp, ABT, Folder 3182.
61. Press Clippings, NYp, ABT, Folder 3183.
62. Some accounts of Balanchine's 1962 tour imply that dancing anywhere in Moscow other than the Bolshoi was a subtle insult. Croft, *Dancers as Diplomats*, 60. While New York City Ballet may have regarded the stage in this light, some other Americans believed the Bolshoi's cavernous main stage would make American companies seem small and awkward. ANTA Dance Panel Meeting Minutes, December 19, 1957, NYp, ABT, Folder 3388.
63. Press Clippings from September 13th, NYp, ABT, Folder 3183.
64. Report on European Tour, NYp, ABT, Folder 3187.
65. Telegram, October 12; Telegram, October 22, NYp, ABT, Folders 3186 and 3187. The telegrams guarantee to the company that the performances will be filmed for immediate broadcast, not recorded.

66. List of People on Trip, NYp, ABT, Folder 3154. Michael Colgrass, *American Composer* (Galesville, MD: Meredith Music Publications, 2010), 105.
67. Colgrass, *American Composer*, 111. Colgrass, Interview with Author, June 19, 2014, Toronto.
68. Colgrass, Interview with Author, June 19, 2014, Toronto.
69. ABT Important Notice, NYp, ABT, Folder 3183.
70. Colgrass, Interview with Author, June 19, 2014, Toronto.
71. Tallchief, *Maria Tallchief*, 259–260 and 267. I have not discovered any documents that either confirm or refute the belief that the dancers were under surveillance, but common sense would suggest it was correct. The KGB also sent agents to follow their own dancers in the United States. Memo by Chief of Department of Culture TsK KPSS Polikarpov and Head of Section of Bureau Yarustovsky, March 5, 1959, RGANI f. 5 o. 36 d. 99 l. 19.
72. Colgrass, *American Composer*, 105. This warning included other communist countries that the company visited on the tour, Romania and Bulgaria.
73. Colgrass, Interview with Author, June 19, 2014, Toronto.
74. Letter, September 24, 1960, Chase to Onysko, NYp, ABT, Folder 3184.
75. Letter and Report, October 8, 1960, to Thayer, NYp, ABT, Folder 3188.
76. Letter, October 10, 1960, Chase to Onysko, NYp, ABT, Folder 3186.
77. Tallchief, *Maria Tallchief*, 260 and 265.
78. Colgrass, Interview with Author, June 19, 2014, Toronto.
79. "Pervyĭ spektakl' amerikanskikh artistov," *Zariā Vostoka*, September 21, 1960. "Zakonchilis' gastroli amerikanskikh artistov," *Pravda*, October 24, 1960.
80. Telegram, September 15, 1960, from Chase, NYp, ABT, Folder 3183.
81. Letter, September 24, 1960, Chase to Onysko; Letter and Report, October 8, 1960, Payne to Thayer, NYp, ABT, Bookings, Folders 3184 and 3188.
82. Letter, October 10, 1960, Chase to Onysko, NYp, ABT, Folder 3186.
83. Under the original title *Chopiniana*. V. Gaevskii, "Klassika prikhodit na pomoshch'" *Literaturnaiā gazeta*, RGALI f. 2337 o. 2 d. 202 l. 74.
84. Igor' Smirnov, "Udachi i proschety," *Izvestiiā*, September 17, 1960. RGALI f. 2337 o. 2 d. 202, ABT Scrapbook, 82.
85. V. Gaevskii, "Klassika prikhodit na pomoshch." Other critics were less favorable toward the diverse programming, including the critic for the magazine *Teatr*, who argued that the combination of such different pieces on the same program demonstrated a lack of clear purpose. L.S., "20-let Amerikan balle tietr," *Teatr* (October 1960): 190–192.
86. Mikhail Gabovich, "Amerikanskiĭ balet v Moskve," *Sovetskaiā kul'tura*, RGALI f. 2337 o. 2 d. 202 l. 94.
87. L.S., "20-let Amerikan balle tietr," 190–192.
88. Ėteri Gugushvili, "Sporno, no interesno," *Zariā Vostoka*, September 22, 1960.
89. In Russia, Ballet Theatre also performed one of Balanchine's works, *Theme and Variations*, but unlike New York City Ballet, Ballet Theatre made no effort to present this work as distinctly American. Russian reviews of the tour clearly saw *Rodeo* and *Fancy Free* as a distinct category of ballet.
90. See chapter 1 for a more thorough discussion of the drambalet.

91. Choreographic sources for *Rodeo*: *Rodeo*, performed by American Ballet Theatre, Christine Sarry as Cowgirl, 1973 (posted on YouTube, accessed September 1, 2011). American Ballet Theatre in *Rodeo*, filmed August 1972, produced by Compton Ardolino, NYp, MGZHB 12 1333. *Rodeo*, filmed 1952, American Ballet Theatre, NYp, *MGZHB 12-585. Live performance: *Rodeo*, performed by American Ballet Theatre, City Center, New York City, October 18, 2012. Choreographic sources for *Fancy Free*: *Fancy Free*, performed by Ballet Theatre, Original Cast, Recorded 1944-45, NYp, *MGZIA 4-5120. *Fancy Free*, performed by American Ballet Theatre, Videotaped at John F. Kennedy Center for the Performing Arts, Washington, DC, 1977, NYp, *MGZIDVD 5 1865. *Fancy Free*, performed by New York City Ballet, filmed 1986 (posted on YouTube, accessed February 5, 2015). Live performance: Fancy Free, performed by Boston Ballet, Boston Opera House, Boston, May 12, 2012, and May 17, 2012; *Fancy Free*, performed by Miami City Ballet, Broward Center for the Performing Arts, Ft. Lauderdale, November 8, 2015.
92. As Elizabeth Crist and Barbara Zuck have both discussed, Aaron Copland's involvement in the Popular Front helped inform his compositional style, in particular the incorporation of folk material into many of his works. Bernstein, too, as shown by Carol Oja, was inspired by leftist politics and profoundly affected by Marc Blitzstein's agitprop musical, *The Cradle Will Rock*. Barbara A. Zuck, *A History of Musical Americanism* (Ann Arbor, MI: UMI Research Press, 1980). Elizabeth Bergman Crist, *Music for the Common Man: Aaron Copland during the Depression and War* (Oxford: Oxford University Press, 2005). Oja, *Bernstein Meets Broadway*, 13. Copland also knew the music of Prokofiev and Shostakovich, and it may have been an influence on his compositional style, much as Russian ballet influenced de Mille and Robbins. Howard Pollack, *Aaron Copland: The Life and Work of an Uncommon Man* (Chicago: University of Illinois Press, 2000), 70-72.
93. For more information on Stanislavsky's impact on the drambalet, see chapter 1.
94. Natalia Roslavleva, "Stanislavsky in Ballet," RGALI f. 2966 o. 1 d. 21.
95. Garafola, *Diaghilev's Ballets Russes*, 19-25.
96. Jowitt, *Jerome Robbins*, 14-52.
97. Chamberlain Duerden, *The Choreography of Antony Tudor: Focus on Four Ballets* (London: Fairleigh Dickinson University Press, 2003), 43, 289-290.
98. Letter, October 26, 1967, Roslavleva to De Mille, RGALI f. 2966 o. 1 d. 1181. 7.
99. Chernova, "Balet v 1930-1940kh godov," 113. Harlow Robinson, "The Caucasian Connection: National Identity in the Ballets of Aram Khachaturian," *Nationalities Papers* 35, no. 3 (July 2007): 429-430.
100. Marina Frolova-Walker, *Russian Music and Nationalism from Glinka to Stalin* (New Haven: Yale University Press, 2007), 301-355. Frolova-Walker, "'National in Form, Socialist in Content': Musical Nation-Building in the Soviet Republics," *Journal of the American Musicological Society* 51, no. 2 (Summer 1998): 331-371. For more on nationalities policy and essentializing nationalism, see: Terry Martin, *The Affirmative Action Empire: Nations and Nationalism in the Soviet Union, 1923-1939* (Ithaca, NY, and London: Cornell University Press, 2001).

101. Aaron Copland, *Rodeo: Ballet in One Act* (Boosey and Hawkes, United States, 1946, renewed 1973), Introductory note.
102. Garafola, "Making an American Dance," 121–147.
103. Constance Valis Hill, *Tap Dancing America: A Cultural History* (Oxford: Oxford University Press, 2010), 1–19.
104. Oja, *Bernstein Meets Broadway*, 32–40.
105. L.S. "20-let Amerikan balle tietr," 190–192. Vera Krasovskai͡a, "Na spektakli͡akh amerikanskogo baleta," *Leningradskai͡a Pravda*, October 12, 1960.
106. Gaevskiĭ, "Klassika prikhodit na pomoshch'."
107. Gabovich, "Amerikanskiĭ balet v Moskve."
108. Gleb Tsipursky, "Jazz, Power, and Soviet Youth in the Early Cold War, 1948–1953," *Journal of Musicology* 33, no. 3 (2016): 332–334. Ian MacMillen and Masha Kowell, "Cartoon Jazz: Soviet Animations and the Khrushchev 'Thaw,'" *Film & History* 45, no. 2 (2015): 24–25.
109. Natalia Roslavleva, "Amerikanskiĭ Baletnyĭ Teatr," *Muzykal'nai͡a zhizn'* 19 (1960), RGALI f. 2966 o. 1 d. 15. Gabovich, "Amerikanskiĭ balet v Moskve."
110. Krasovskai͡a, "Na spektakli͡akh amerikanskogo baleta."
111. Doug Fullington and Pacific Northwest Ballet, "After Petipa," Guggenheim Works in Progress, https://www.youtube.com/watch?v=6xpOVN3cfGc, accessed May 28, 2015.
112. Tallchief, *Maria Tallchief*, 263. Tallchief also compares Chabukiani to Rudolf Nureyev, another dancer known for his incredible sex appeal on stage.
113. Choreographic analysis from a 1953 video of *Flames of Paris* starring Chabukiani. Presumably, when he originated the role during the height of his physical prowess in 1932, the jumps were even more impressive. *Flames of Paris* starring Chabukiani, posted on YouTube, https://www.youtube.com/watch?v=L7736Go1uNw, accessed November 5, 2015.
114. Krasovskai͡a, ed., *Sovetskiĭ Baletnyĭ Teatr*, 365, 370. Debra Craine and Judith Mackrell, "Chabukiani, Vakhtang," in *The Oxford Dictionary of Dance* (Oxford: Oxford University Press, 2010).
115. Report and Letter, October 8, 1960, Payne to Thayer; Terms with American Ballet Theatre and Chabukiani Proposed, NYp, ABT, Folders 3188 and 3185. Earlier, Chase had planned on acquiring the Bolshoi version of *Giselle*. Letter, June 9, 1960, Chase to Onysko, NYp, ABT, Folder 3172.
116. Gabovich, "Amerikanskiĭ balet v Moskve." Lifar was one of the last stars of Diaghilev's Ballets Russes. Following Diaghilev's death, he began working for the Paris Opera Ballet, where he choreographed more than 50 works.
117. Gabovich, "Amerikanskiĭ balet v Moskve."
118. Khrushchev and his government decided to retain Stalin's laws criminalizing sodomy, even in the midst of relaxing many other Stalinist laws regarding personal behavior. Dan Healey, *Russian Homophobia from Stalin to Sochi* (London: Bloomsbury Publishing, 2018), 25, 42–43.
119. Oja, *Bernstein Meets Broadway*, 20–27.

120. Gabovich, "Amerikanskiĭ balet v Moskve." V. Gaevskiĭ, "Klassika prikhodit na pomoshch'." Roslavleva Articles 1960–1961, RGALI f. 2966 o. 1 d. 15 l. 2. On the use of these terms: Schmelz, *Such Freedom If Only Musical*, 41.
121. Payne, *American Ballet Theatre*, 144.
122. Both ballets were first staged in Moscow but revised or completely reproduced for St. Petersburg. Roland John Wiley, *Tchaikovsky's Ballets* (Oxford: Clarendon Press, 1985), 242–274. Natalia Roslavleva, *Era of the Russian Ballet*, 95–98, 129–138. For more on the changes in *Swan Lake* and their impact on the Soviet-American exchange, see chapter 3.
123. Ballet Theatre's version of the *Swan Lake* pas de deux had first been staged by English dancer Anton Dolin. Dolin had originally learned the choreography from Nicholas Legat, a Russian dancer and ballet master working in London in the 1920s. Presumably his version was also impacted by the Russian dancers he worked with in the Ballets Russes. The Ballet Theatre version of the *Don Quixote* pas de deux had originally been staged by Russian dancer and teacher Anatole Oboukhoff. Payne, *American Ballet Theatre*, 360, 367. Anton Dolin, *Autobiography* (London: Oldbourne, 1960), 27, 43.
124. Sally Banes, *Dancing Women: Female Bodies on Stage* (London: Routledge, 1998), 57–59.
125. Lynn Garafola, "Russian Ballet in the Age of Petipa," in *Cambridge Companion to Ballet*, ed. Marion Kant (Cambridge: Cambridge University Press, 2007), 151–163.
126. Doug Fullington and Pacific Northwest Ballet, "After Petipa."
127. Tallchief, however, notes in her memoirs that she performed the solo variation in the *Swan Lake* Act III pas de deux that was choreographed for her by Balanchine. Tallchief, *Maria Tallchief*, 257.
128. Tallchief, *Maria Tallchief*, 258.
129. Tallchief, *Maria Tallchief*, 256–262.
130. Krasovskaia, "Na spektakliakh amerikanskogo baleta." Ėteri Gugushvili, "Sporno, no interesno," *Zaria Vostoka*, September 22, 1960. N. Volkov, "Pervoe znakomstvo," *Izvestiia*, September 15, 1960. Igor' Smirnov, "Udachi i proschety," *Izvestiia*, September 17, 1960. Mikhail Gabovich, "Amerikanskiĭ balet v Moskve." L.S., "20-let Amerikan balle tietr." This final author is the only one who had anything negative to say about the pas de deux, claiming that they distorted the choreography and that Maria Tallchief was a disappointment. The author still, however, praised Bruhn.
131. Letter, October 8, 1960, Payne to Thayer; Letter, October 10, 1960, Chase to Onsyko, NYp, ABT, Folders 3186 and 3188.
132. John Gruen, *Erik Bruhn: Danseur Noble* (New York: Viking, 1979), 73–99. List of people filed with Air France Itinerary, NYp, ABT, Folder 3154.
133. Tallchief, *Maria Tallchief*, 266–267.
134. The approach to one Native performer, Tom Two Arrows (Thomas J. Dorsey), gives a sense of the place that the State Department saw for them. Dorsey aimed his program at authentically depicting Native American culture, but foreign audiences often received his work in an exoticist vein inherited from American Western

films. Moreover, multiple officials commented that Dorsey's performances could demonstrate to foreign audiences that the United States treated members of ethnic minority groups well. For more on the treatment of African American artists, see chapter 4. Fosler-Lussier, *Music in America's Cold War Diplomacy*, 152–153.
135. Rebekah J. Kowal, "'Indian Ballerinas Toe Up': Maria Tallchief and Making Ballet 'American' in the Tribal Termination Era," *Dance Research Journal* 46, no. 2 (August 2014): 73–96. Tallchief, *Maria Tallchief*, 197.
136. "Report on European Tour," NYp, ABT, Folder 3187.
137. Tallchief, *Maria Tallchief*, 266. Lucia Chase Personal Diary, Sunday, October 23, NYp, Lucia Chase Collection, *MGZMD 51 Box 3, Item 45.
138. Lucia Chase Personal Diary, 1960, Sunday, October 23, NYp, Lucia Chase Collection, Box 3, Item 45.
139. "Report from 1960," NYp, ABT, Folder 3401.

Chapter 3

1. Advertisement for Bolshoi 1962 Season, RGALI f. 3045 o. 1 d. 326 l. 11. New York Times, "Bolshoi to Give New Works Here," June 5, 1962. "Repertory of Bolshoi Ballet," *Chicago Daily Tribune*, July 15, 1962. David Miller, "A Big Deal in Moscow—By Hurok, of Course," *New York Herald Tribune*, June 10, 1962.
2. Novellino-Mearns, "Ah . . . Spar-tac-ous: Performing in the Bolshoi's Spartacus," *Read What Rosie Wrote*, November 29, 2011, http://readwhatrosiewrote.blogspot.com/2011/11/ahspar-tac-ous.html, accessed July 14, 2014.
3. In order to examine all four tours in this book in detail, two remaining tours from this period have been left out: the Kirov's 1961 tour and the Joffrey Ballet's 1963 tour of the Soviet Union. These tours both merit further study.
4. Powaski, *The Cold War*, 97–166.
5. Zubok and Pleshakov, *Inside the Kremlin's Cold War*, 236–274. Pechatnov, "Soviet-American Relations through the Cold War," 107–123. Powaski, *The Cold War*, 97–166. Don Munton and David A. Welch, *The Cuban Missile Crisis: A Concise History* (Oxford: Oxford University Press, 2012). Aleksandr Fursenko and Timothy Naftali, *"One Hell of a Gamble": Khrushchev, Castro, and Kennedy, 1958–1964* (New York: W. W. Norton and Co., 1997), ix, 246.
6. Jorge I. Dominguez, "The @#$%& Missile Crisis: (Or, What Was 'Cuban' about U.S. Decisions during the Cuban Missile Crisis," *Diplomatic History* 24, no. 2 (Spring 2000): 305–315.
7. Whether or not to call these resulting spheres of influence "empires" is still subject to debate. Odd Arne Westad, *The Global Cold War: Third World Interventions and the Making of Our Time* (Cambridge: Cambridge University Press, 2007), 1–72. Steven Hugh Lee, *Outposts of Empire: Korea, Vietnam, and the Origins of the Cold War in Asia, 1949–1954* (Montreal and Kingston: McGill and Queen's University Press, 1995), 1–28. Heonik Kwon, *The Other Cold War* (New York: Columbia University Press, 2010), 1–11. Justin Hart, *Empire of Ideas: The Origins of Public Diplomacy and the Transformation of U.S. Foreign Policy* (Oxford: Oxford University Press, 2013), 8–9. Tomoff, *Virtuosi Abroad*, 3–4.

8. John F. Kennedy, Letter to the Publisher, *Musical America*, October 1960, 11.
9. Fosler-Lussier, *Music in America's Cold War Diplomacy*, 23–27.
10. Martin, quoted in James Steichen, *Balanchine and Kirstein's American Enterprise* (Oxford: Oxford University Press, 2018), 54.
11. Steichen, *Balanchine and Kirstein's American Enterprise*. Mary Simonson, *Body Knowledge: Performance, Intermediality, and American Entertainment at the Turn of the Twentieth Century* (Oxford: Oxford University Press, 2013), 161–188. Mark Franko, *The Work of Dance: Labor, Movement, and Identity in the 1930s* (Middletown, CT: Wesleyan University Press, 2002), 107–123. Andrea Harris, *Making Ballet American: Modernism before and beyond Balanchine* (Oxford: Oxford University Press, 2017), 134.
12. *Life Magazine*, April 11, 1949, 100–101. Gay Morris, *A Game for Dancers: Performing Modernism in the Postwar Years, 1945–1960* (Middletown, CT: Wesleyan University Press, 2006), 38–63.
13. "Bolshoi Ballet (127 in All) Flies In at Idlewild," *New York Herald Tribune*, September 2, 1962. "Bolshoi Ballet Adds Show Sept. 30 to Met Schedule," *New York Times*, August 20, 1962. "Bolshoi to Give New Works Here," *New York Times*, June 5, 1962. "Bolshoi Ends New York Run; On to Toronto," *New York Herald Tribune*, December 3, 1962.
14. Zarubezhnye gastroli za sezon 1962/1963 god, RGALI f. 648 o. 11 d. 368. Illustrated Programs Bolshoi 1962, RGALI f. 3045 o. 1 d. 326.
15. Harry MacArthur, "The Bolshoi Is Back and Greeted Warmly," *Evening Star*, November 14, 1962.
16. Yuriy Malashev, "The Muses Are Not Silent," *Sovetskaia kul'tura*, November 17, 1962. The article was clipped and stored by the State Department. ABECA, Box 47, Folder 23. Translated by State Department official.
17. David Coleman, ed., *The Presidential Recordings: John F. Kennedy: The Winds of Change, Vol. 5* (New York: W. W. Norton, 2016), 129–408. The substantial literature on the Kennedys and the Cuban Missile Crisis is almost totally silent on the meetings with the Bolshoi. The only one of these incidents that is repeated in political accounts is of Robert Kennedy meeting Maya Plisetskaya at the residence of the Soviet ambassador; the anecdote seems to be valued for the fact that Robert Kennedy flirted a bit with Plisetskaya, rather than for its political implications. Arthur M. Schlesinger Jr., *Robert Kennedy and His Times* (Boston: Houghton Mifflin Company, 1978), 525–527. Michael R. Beschloss, *The Crisis Years: Kennedy and Khrushchev, 1960–1963* (New York: HarperCollins, 1991), 554, 560–561, 594. Most books on Kennedy and the Missile Crisis leave out the Bolshoi Ballet altogether: Peter J. Ling, *John F. Kennedy* (London: Routledge, 2013). Robert Dallek, *An Unfinished Life: John F. Kennedy, 1917–1963* (Boston: Little, Brown and Co., 2003). Richard Reeves, *President Kennedy: Profile of Power* (New York: Simon and Schuster, 1993). Montague Kern, Patricia W. Levering, and Ralph B. Levering, *The Kennedy Crises: The Press, the Presidency, and Foreign Policy* (Chapel Hill: University of North Carolina Press, 1983). Lawrence Freedman, *Kennedy's Wars: Berlin, Cuba, Laos, and Vietnam* (Oxford: Oxford University Press, 2000). Don Munton and David A. Welch, *The Cuban Missile Crisis: A Concise History*, 2nd ed. (Oxford: Oxford University Press, 2012).

18. Betty Beale, "President Goes to Bolshoi Ballet," *Evening Star*, November 14, 1962. "Kennedys at Bolshoi Opening," *Boston Globe*, November 14, 1962. "Kennedy, Wife See Premier of Red Ballet," *Chicago Daily Tribune*, November 14, 1962. "Caroline and Mother Visit Bolshoi Ballet," *Los Angeles Times*, November 14, 1962. Marjorie Hunter, "President Cheers the Bolshoi Ballet," *New York Times*, November 14, 1962. "Mr. Kennedy Meets Members of Bolshoi Ballet," *The Guardian*, November 15, 1962. Jean Battey, "Caroline Sees Ballet Warm Up," *Washington Post, Times Herald*, November 15, 1962. "Bolshoi Dancers Sip Dubonnet with Kennedys at White House," *Boston Globe*, November 16, 1962. "Kennedy Welcome for the Bolshoi," *New York Herald Tribune*, November 16, 1962. "Caroline Watches with Wonder at Bolshoi Ballet Performance," *Hartford Courant*, November 18, 1962.

19. Letter Lavrovsky to Chidson, undated, from Boston, RGALI f. 3045 o. 1 d. 196 l. 42. Otchet gastroliakh kollektiva baleta Bol'shogo teatra v gg. Chikago, Detroĭt, Klivlend, Vashington, Boston, N'iu-Ĭork, RGALI f. 2329 o. 9 d. 292 l. 14. "Russian Dancers Dine with Kennedy's Mother," *Hartford Courant*, November 22, 1962. "2 Kennedys Hosts to Bolshoi," *New York Times*, November 22, 1962.

20. Coleman, *The Presidential Recordings: John F. Kennedy: The Winds of Change, Vol. 5*, 130. Michael Dobbs, *One Minute to Midnight: Kennedy, Khrushchev, and Castro on the Brink of Nuclear War* (London: Hutchinson, 2008), 84.

21. Croft has argued very similar things about the New York City Ballet performers who were concurrently in the Soviet Union. Croft, *Dancers as Diplomats*, 38, 49–53.

22. Letter, Lavrovsky to Chidson, September 7, 1962; Letter, Lavrovsky to Chidson, October 22, 1962; Postcard, Lavrovsky to Chidson, October 26, 1962; Letter Lavrovsky to Chidson, undated, from Boston; Letter, Lavrovsky to Chidson, October 31, 1962; RGALI f. 3045 o. 1 d. 196 ll. 1, 37–38, 41, 43, 50.

23. Letter, Lavrovsky to Chidson, RGALI f. 3045 o. 1 d. 196 l. 2. Report, September 28, 1962, signed Pokarzhevskiĭ, RGALI f. 2329 o. 9 d. 292 l. 33. Thomasina Norford, "Ailey Troupe Overcomes Weather; Bolshoi Visits," *New York Amsterdam News*, September 15, 1962.

24. Otchet gastroliakh kollektiva baleta Bol'shogo teatra v gg. Chikago, Detroĭt, Klivlend, Vashington, Boston, N'iu-Ĭork. "One Must Go to the Attic to Find Modern Russian Art," *Washington Post, Times Herald*, November 19, 1962.

25. Letter, Lavrovsky to Chidson, September 7, 1962, RGALI f. 3045 o. 1 d. 196 l. 1.

26. Pakhomov was director for only a very short time between Orvid and Chulaki. The director of the theater was a separate person from the director of the ballet troupe. Letter, Lavrovsky to Chidson, September 20, 1962, RGALI f. 3045 o. 1 d. 196 l. 18. According to Janice Ross, Yakobson remained with the Bolshoi in the United States, though perhaps she means that he stayed briefly following the *Spartacus* performances, because according to John Martin, whom Ross also quotes, Yakobson met with Balanchine in Leningrad in early November 1962, well before the Bolshoi finished its tour. Ross, *Like a Bomb Going Off*, 290–291. John Martin, "City Ballet Ends Leningrad Stand," *New York Times*, November 9, 1962.

27. Letter, Lavrovsky to Chidson, October 12, 1962, RGALI f. 3045 o. 1 d. 196 l. 26. Report, September 28, 1962, signed Pokarzhevskiĭ, RGALI f. 2329 o. 9 d. 292 l. 36.

28. Julie Kavanagh, *Nureyev: The Life* (New York: Pantheon Books, 2007), 116–150.
29. Report, September 28, 1962, signed Pokarzhevskiĭ, RGALI f. 2329 o. 9 d. 292 l. 35.
30. Plisetskaya, *I, Maya Plisetskaya*, 137–141, 156–158, 179.
31. Report, September 28, 1962, signed Pokarzhevskiĭ, RGALI f. 2329 o. 9 d. 292 l. 35. The representative in question was identified only as "Semenov." This was likely Simon Semenov, a former dancer with the Ballet Russe de Monte Carlo, who worked on the Soviet tours and was friendly with many of the dancers. Maxim Gershunoff and Leon Van Dyke, *It's Not All Song and Dance: A Life behind the Scenes in the Performing Arts* (Pompton Plains, NJ: Limelight Editions, 2005), 105.
32. Albert Eugene Kahn, *Days with Ulanova* (New York: Simon and Schuster, 1962).
33. Letter to Ulanova, May 7, 1962, RGALI f. 2329 o. 8 d. 2314 l. 18.
34. Letter from Ralph Parker to Butrova, August 24, 1962, RGALI f. 2329 o. 8 d. 2314, l. 87.
35. Report, September 28, 1962, signed Pokarzhevskiĭ, RGALI f. 2329 o. 9 d. 292 l. 36. "'Spartacus' Taken Out of Ballet Repertoire," *Los Angeles Times*, September 24, 1962. "Galina Ulanova Will Dance with Bolshoi Company," *Los Angeles Times*, September 29, 1962.
36. Mary Clarke and Clement Crisp, *The Ballet Goer's Guide* (New York: Alfred A. Knopf, 1981), 277. Payne, *American Ballet Theatre*, 58.
37. Debra Hickenlooper Sowell, *The Christensen Brothers: An American Dance Epic* (Amsterdam: Harwood Academic Publishers, 1998), 183–193. ABT has long claimed to have staged the first American full-length *Swan Lake* in 1967. ABT 75th Anniversary Exhibition at Library of Congress, http://www.loc.gov/exhibits/american-ballet-theatre/tradition-and-innovation.html, accessed July 21, 2015.
38. Roland John Wiley and Selma Jeanne Cohen have both documented the extensive changes to the ballet between the 1876 and 1895 stagings. Wiley, *Tchaikovsky's Ballets*, 242–274, 319. Cohen, *Next Week, Swan Lake*, 1–15. Doug Fullington of Pacific Northwest Ballet has recently restaged key pas de deux from Petipa ballets using the Sergeev notations. Though these notations were made between 1901 and 1913, they are the closest existing source to the Petipa choreography. Doug Fullington and Pacific Northwest Ballet, "After Petipa," *Guggenheim Works in Progress Series*, May 13–14, 2012, 2013, https://www.youtube.com/watch?v=6xpOVN3cfGc, accessed March 12.
39. Roslavleva, *Era of the Russian Ballet*, 160–161, 212–213. Morrison, *Swans of the Kremlin*, 233, 343. Illustrated Program, Bolshoi Ballet, October 18, 1962, RGALI f. 3045 o. 1. d. 326 ll. 9.
40. Choreographic analysis of Soviet versions from the 1957 production filmed with Maya Plisetskaya and Nikolai Fadeyechev and a production filmed by the Kirov in 1968 with Elena Evteyeva. *Swan Lake*, performed by the Bolshoi Ballet, directed for film by Z. Tulubyeva, 1957 (VAI International, 2003). *Swan Lake*, performed by Kirov Ballet, directed for film by Appolinariy Dudko and Konstantin Sergeyev (Lenfilm, 1968).
41. Wiley, *Tchaikovsky's Ballets*, 264.
42. Walter Terry, "Bolshoi at Met: A Royal Performance," *New York Herald Tribune*, September 7, 1962. Allen Hughes, "Ballet: Bolshoi Presents 'Swan Lake' at the Met," *New York Times*, September 7, 1962. Allen Hughes, "New Bolshoi Cast Gives 'Swan

Lake,'" September 9, 1962. "The Theater: Swan of the Bolshoi," *Wall Street Journal*, September 10, 1962. P. W. Manchester, "Bolshoi Ballet Revisits U.S.—As Friend," *Christian Science Monitor*, September 15, 1962. Jean Battey, "Contrast in Ballerina Styles Shows in Second Performance," *Washington Post, Times Herald*, November 16, 1962.

43. Alexander Fried, "Moscow's Bolshoi Ballet on the Fox Theater Stage," *San Francisco Examiner*, October 19, 1962.

44. Claudia Cassidy, "On the Aisle: Superb Dancing in Gentle 'Swan Lake' Marks Bolshoi's Chicago Debut," *Chicago Daily Tribune*, October 27, 1962. Allen Hughes, "Ballet: Bolshoi Presents 'Swan Lake' at the Met," *New York Times*, September 7, 1962.

45. Books about the Soviet Union published in the United States during the 1950s and 1960s refer to Leningrad as the more European or Western city. Georges Jorré, *The Soviet Union: The Land and Its People*, translated by E. D. Laborde (New York: John Wiley and Sons, 1961, Original French 1950). David Hooson, *The Soviet Union People and Regions* (Belmont, CA: Wadsworth Publishing Company, 1966). Taper also mentions that Balanchine thought Leningrad and the dancers from the Kirov were more accepting of his ballet because the city was more cosmopolitan. Bernard Taper, *Balanchine: A Biography* (Berkeley and Los Angeles: University of California Press), 276.

46. Diaghilev's Ballets Russes had been largely, though not entirely, composed of dancers from the Mariinsky Theater, and many of those dancers settled permanently in the West following the Russian Revolution. Garafola, *Diaghilev's Ballets Russes*, 4–6, 189–193. During the Cold War, the Kirov continued to be the most prominent source of ballet defections, Nureyev being the most famous example in 1961. Caute, *The Dancer Defects*, 493–501.

47. Kenneth Rexroth, "Bolshoi vs. Kirov," *San Francisco Examiner*, October 24, 1962. Rexroth ingeniously anticipated my critique of his writing, claiming, "The Bolshoi is a hard outfit to pan, because then all your intellectual friends who know nothing about dancing will say you're just a hireling of the capitalist press and making cold war propaganda. Sorry—hold on to your little red shirts, kids, cause here goes."

48. Kenneth Rexroth, "Bolshoi vs. Kirov," *San Francisco Examiner*, October 24, 1962.

49. Pierre Bourdieu, *Distinction: A Social Critique of the Judgement of Taste* (Cambridge, MA: Harvard University Press, 1984), 1–2.

50. Rosalyn Krokover, "At 'Met' in Park," *New York Times*, September 2, 1962. "Bolshoi Ballet Bows to Full House," *Chicago Daily Tribune*, September 7, 1962. Alan Rich, "Met Is Planning Longest Season and Higher Prices for 1962–63," *New York Times*, January 5, 1962. The 2019 equivalents of top face-value ticket prices are $302 and $504. Monetary conversions calculated using the income value calculator from *Measuring Worth*, accessed April 24, 2020.

51. Advertisement, *New York Herald Tribune*, April 6, 1959. During the 1959 tour it was difficult to get tickets if one was not on this list. For 1962, Hurok had the Met box office open for six days in June, two months in advance of the performances. Lines started three hours before the box office opened, so even purchasing tickets through

this more open method required a substantial investment of time and effort. "Bolshoi Draws Crowd 2 Months in Advance," *New York Times*, June 26, 1962.
52. Dorothy Townsend, "Both Shrine Crowd and Cast Glitter at Bolshoi Benefit," *Los Angeles Times*, October 6, 1962. Albert Goldberg, "Showy Bolshoi Ballet Matched by Audience," *Los Angeles Times*, October 7, 1962. "Bolshoi Ballet Bows to Full House," *Chicago Daily Tribune*, September 7, 1962. "'Giselle' Replaces 'Spartacus' as English Union Benefit," *New York Herald Tribune*, September 19, 1962. Jean Battey, "'Ballet School' Seeks Locals," *Washington Post, Times Herald*, November 7, 1962.
53. Prevots, *Dance for Export*, 71.
54. Prevots, *Dance for Export*, 71–74. Anthony Shay, *Choreographic Politics: State Folk Dance Companies, Representation, and Power* (Middletown, CT: Wesleyan University Press, 2002), 68–69.
55. Victoria Anne Hallinan, "Cold War Cultural Exchange and the Moiseyev Dance Company: American Perception of Soviet Peoples" (PhD diss., Northeastern University, 2013), 132.
56. Kristin Roth Ey, *Moscow Prime Time: How the Soviet Union Built the Media Empire That Lost the Cold War* (Ithaca, NY: Cornell University Press, 2011), 2–5. Pauline Fairclough, *Classics for the Masses: Shaping Soviet Musical Identity under Lenin and Stalin* (New Haven: Yale University Press, 2016).
57. Anne Searcy, "The Recomposition of Aram Khachaturian's *Spartacus* at the Bolshoi Theater, 1958–1968," *Journal of Musicology* 33, no. 3 (2016).
58. Ezrahi, *Swans of the Kremlin*. Christina Ezrahi, "The Thaw in Soviet Culture and the Return of Symphonic Dance," *International Symposium of Russian Ballet* (Columbia University, October 12–13, 2007).
59. For more on other choreographic symphonists, see chapters 1 and 4. Choreographic analysis of Yakobson's version of *Spartacus* comes from two sources; the first is a nine-minute film of highlights from the Bolshoi's 1962 production held at the New York Public Library for the Performing Arts and the second is a viewing of the reconstructed version at the Mariinsky Theater. "Spartacus: Excerpts (Motion Picture)," NYPL *MGZHB 4-871. *Spartacus*, revived by Vyacheslav Khomyakov, performed by Mariinsky Theater (St. Petersburg, July 19, 2010).
60. Janice Ross, *Like a Bomb Going Off: Leonid Yakobson and Ballet as Resistance in Soviet Russia* (New Haven: Yale University Press, 2015), 12–17, 78–82.
61. Leonid Iakobson, *Pis'ma Noverru* (Tenafly, NJ: Hermitage Publications, 2001).
62. Searcy, "The Recomposition of Aram Khachaturian's *Spartacus* at the Bolshoi Theater."
63. Jon Solomon, *The Ancient World in Cinema* (New Haven and London: Yale University Press, 1978, revised and enlarged 2001), 1–36.
64. Joanna Paul, *Film and the Classical Epic Tradition* (Oxford: Oxford University Press, 2013), 228–229.
65. "Bolshoi to Give New Works Here," *New York Times*, June 5, 1962.
66. David Miller, "A Big Deal in Moscow—by Hurok, of Course," *New York Herald Tribune*, June 10, 1962.

67. Stephen C. Meyer, *Epic Sound: Music in Postwar Hollywood Biblical Films* (Bloomington and Indianapolis: Indiana University Press), 13–14.
68. The similarities were partially due to the fact that some Hollywood composers used Soviet film scores, particularly Prokofiev's *Alexander Nevsky*, as models for composing for epic movies. Kevin Bartig, *Composing for the Red Screen: Prokofiev and Soviet Film* (Oxford: Oxford University Press, 2013), 146.
69. Ross, *Like a Bomb Going Off*, 249–250.
70. Meyer, *Epic Sound*, 10.
71. Maria Wyke, *Projecting the Past: Ancient Rome, Cinema, and History* (London: Routledge, 1997), 14–15. Classicist Adeline Johns-Putra similarly argues that the postwar Hollywood epics were designed to soothe American audiences in the face of postwar anxieties. In her words, the 1950s Hollywood epic films display "a completely nostalgic embrace of an utterly coherent past," a type of comfort to a people dismayed by the toll of the world wars. Adeline Johns-Putra, *The History of the Epic* (London: Palgrave Macmillan, 2006), 191.
72. Film scholar Geraldine Murphy, for example, has argued that in *Spartacus* (1960) and *Ben-Hur* (1959), Americans are represented on two different levels, both as imperial rulers and as revolutionaries. On the one hand, the heroic central groups rebelling against the Roman empire could be read by mid-century audiences as Christian Americans fighting against an oppressive Soviet state. Simultaneously, however, the Americans could seem themselves reflected in the more charismatic, heroic Roman roles, such as Julius Caesar in *Spartacus*. Geraldine Murphy, "Americans in Togas," *Journal of Film and Video* 56, no. 3 (Fall 2004): 3–19.
73. *Ben-Hur: A Tale of the Christ*, directed by William Wyler (Burbank, CA: Metro-Goldwyn-Mayer, 1959).
74. Searcy, "The Recomposition of Aram Khachaturian's *Spartacus* at the Bolshoi Theater."
75. Aram Khachaturiȃn, "Balet: Spartak," *Sovetskoe iskusstvo*, January 9, 1951; quoted in G. Tigranov, *Balety Arama Khachaturiȃna* (Moscow: Sovetskiĭ kompozitor, 1960), 95.
76. Stenogramma khoreograficheskoĭ kompozitsii 'Spartaka' baletmeĭster L. V. Iakobson, January 9, 1962, Museum of GABT, Spartacus Collection, 18.
77. Both Aleksandr Solzhenitsyn's *Day in the Life of Ivan Denisovich* and Dmitri Shostakovich's *Satires*, for instance, challenged the strict morality of the Stalinist era, and both were subjects of debate in broader Soviet culture. Miriam Dobson, "Contesting the Paradigms of De-Stalinization: Readers' Responses to *One Day in the Life of Ivan Denisovich*," *Slavic Review* 64, no. 3 (Autumn 2005): 588–592. Vladimir Orlov, "Shostakovich and the Soviet Eros," in *Contemplating Shostakovich: Life, Music, and Film*, ed. Alexander Ivashkin et al. (Burlington, VT: Ashgate, 2012), 204–205.
78. Stenogramma obsuzhdeniia spektaklia 'Spartak' posle prosmotra general'noĭ repetitsii, April 2, 1962, Museum of GABT, Spartacus Collection.
79. Stenogramma obsuzhdenii baleta: 'Spartak,' March 16, 1962, RGALI f. 648 o. 11 d. 22 l. 7.

80. Wendy Perron, "My Spartacus," *Wendy Perron*, July 6, 2014, http://wendyperron.com/my-spartacus/, accessed July 14, 2014. Novellino-Mearns, "Ah... Spar-tac-ous." Audiences may have been more accepting on later nights. In Terry's second review of *Spartacus*, the critic noted that "the gathering on this occasion seemed much more enthusiastic" than the previous night's crowd. Walter Terry, "For the Bolshoi: 2d 'Spartacus,' Warmer Crowd," *New York Herald Tribune*, September 14, 1962.
81. Allen Hughes, "Ballet: Bolshoi Stages U.S. Premiere of 'Spartacus,'" *New York Times*, September 13, 1962.
82. "Bolshoi, in Shift, Cancels 3 'Spartacus' Showings," *New York Times*, September 18, 1962.
83. Plisetskaya, *I, Maya Plisetskaya*, 233.
84. Perron, "My Spartacus." Novellino-Mearns, "Ah . . . Spar-tac-ous." Walter Terry, "DeMille Out-DeMilled," *New York Herald Tribune*, September 16, 1962. John Chapman, "Ballet: Big Business with a Soviet Beat," *Los Angeles Times*, September 30, 1962.
85. This is the argument that Janice Ross makes in her biography of Yakobson. Ross, *Like a Bomb Going Off*, 282–289.
86. Allen Hughes, "About 'Spartacus': Can It Be Understood Though Disliked?" *New York Times*, September 23, 1962. Seymour Topping, "Bolshoi Dancers Give 'Spartacus,'" *New York Times*, April 6, 1962.
87. Hughes, "Ballet: Bolshoi Stages U.S. Premiere of 'Spartacus.'"
88. Paul, *Film and the Classical Epic Tradition*, 229. Babington and Evans, *Biblical Epics*, 1–3. Meyer, *Epic Sounds*, 1–2.
89. Thomas R. Dash, "New York Is Conquered! But Only by Bolshoi's Art," *Women's Wear Daily*, April 17, 1959.
90. Meyer, *Epic Sound*, 19.
91. Terry, "DeMille Out-DeMilled." Jean Battey, "Bolshoi Offers Modern Slant," *Washington Post, Times Herald*, November 17, 1962. Rosalyn Krokover, "At 'Met' in Park," *New York Times*, September 2, 1962.
92. Manchester, "Bolshoi Ballet Revisits U.S.—As Friend."
93. Jean Battey, "Bolshoi Schedules the Tried and True," *Washington Post, Times Herald*, September 30, 1962. Hughes, "Ballet: Bolshoi Stages U.S. Premiere of 'Spartacus.'" Terry, "For the Bolshoi: 2d 'Spartacus,' Warmer Crowd."
94. Perron, "My Spartacus."
95. Terry, "DeMille Out-DeMilled."
96. Chapman, "Ballet: Big Business with a Soviet Beat."
97. Chapman, "Ballet: Big Business with a Soviet Beat."
98. "Repertory of Bolshoi Ballet," *Chicago Daily Tribune*, July 15, 1962. John Chapman, "Bolshoi Skill Is Shown in New 'Ballet School,'" *Chicago Daily Tribune*, September 19, 1962. Albert Goldberg, "'School' Hit of Bolshoi Ballet Bill," *Los Angeles Times*, October 11, 1962. Walter Terry, "The Bolshoi Ballet's Glamorous Maverick," *New York Herald Tribune*, September 2, 1962. Illustrated Program, Bolshoi Ballet, Cleveland, November 1962, RGALI f. 3045 o. 1 d. 326 l. 35.

99. Battey, "'Ballet School' Seeks Locals." "Ballet School—Trying Out for the Bolshoi," *Washington Post, Times Herald*, November 13, 1962. Allen Hughes, "Ballet: Bolshoi and American Children," *New York Times*, September 18, 1962. Claudia Cassidy, "On the Aisle: Bolshoi's 'Ballet School' Bravura Showpiece for Russian Virtuosi," *Chicago Daily Tribune*, October 31, 1962. Chapman, "Bolshoi Skill Is Shown in New 'Ballet School.'" P. W. Manchester, "Bravura at the Bolshoi," *Christian Science Monitor*, September 29, 1962. Choreographic analysis has been taken from archival footage of *Ballet School,* recorded without sound on 8mm film by Michael Truppin. Michael Truppin, "Ballet School [excerpts]," NYp, *MGZIC 9-5013. It has also been supplemented with additional silent film recorded by Truppin at a 1963 performance of the ballet by the Stars of the Bolshoi. Michael Truppin, "Stars of the Bolshoi Ballet [video recording]," NYp *MGZIC 9-5025. I have also consulted an archival copy of a 1965 performance of "Klass Kontsert" in Moscow, posted to YouTube. "Asaf Messerer. 'Klass-Kontsert', 1965," posted by Triatsetat TV, https://www.youtube.com/watch?v=ZouKlBqsmlc, accessed September 26, 2019. In addition, particularly to study the music-choreographic connections, I have consulted the recent restaging of the ballet via a 2011 broadcast and via YouTube footage. "1/3 Bolshoi Ballet Class Concert.2011," "2/3 Bolshoi Ballet Class Concert.2012," "3/3 Bolshoi Ballet Class Concert," all posted by lapinneuf on YouTube, https://www.youtube.com/watch?v=DTrt15q7RLk&t=3s, accessed June 7, 2018. "Alexander Tseitlin: Bolshoi Theater Ballet 'Class Concert' Zakharova Matvienko Vasiliev Osipova" posted by Michael Tseitlin on YouTube, https://www.youtube.com/watch?v=PLbTCaFp9_I, accessed July 3, 2018.

100. "Seek Ballet Students for Bolshoi," *Chicago Daily Tribune*, October 13, 1962. Battey, "'Ballet School' Seeks Locals." "Ballet School—Trying Out for the Bolshoi."

101. Clarke and Crisp, *The Ballet Goer's Guide,* 116.

102. In an interview with Mikhail Messerer, Asaf Messerer's nephew, for *Ballet Magazine,* Charlotte Kasner claims that Lander's work was the inspiration for *Ballet School.* Charlotte Kasner, "Mikhail Messerer and the Bolshoi Ballet and Class Concert," *Ballet Magazine,* September 2007, http://www.ballet.co.uk/magazines/yr_07/sep07/interview_mikhail_messerer.htm, accessed July 8, 2014.

103. John Martin, "Dance: Audit II," *New York Times*, June 3, 1962. Jean Battey, "Soviets, Too, Captured by the Storyless Ballet," *Washington Post, Times Herald*, October 14, 1962.

104. Clarke and Crisp, *The Ballet Goer's Guide,* 116.

105. Illustrated Program, Bolshoi, 1962, San Francisco, RGALI f. 3045 o. 1 d. 326 l. 14.

106. Michael Truppin, "Ballet School [excerpts]." "1/3 Bolshoi Ballet Class Concert.2011."

107. Manchester, "Bravura at the Bolshoi."

108. Michael Truppin, "Ballet school [excerpts]."

109. George H. Jackson, "Bolshoi's Wealth of Talent Put on Display," *Los Angeles Herald and Express*, May 22, 1959. John Martin, "Bolshoi Dancers in 2d 'Highlights,'" *New York Times*, May 1, 1959. John Martin, "Ballet: Ulanova's 'Giselle,'" *New York Times*, May 2, 1959.

110. Julie Gilmour and Barbara Evans Clements, "'If You Want to Be Like Me, Train!': The Contradictions of Soviet Masculinity," in *Russian Masculinities in History and Culture*, ed. B. E. Clements, R. Friedman, and D. Healey (Chippenham, Wiltshire: Palgrave: 2002), 210–221.
111. GABT Order no. 705, November 11, 1966, RGALI f. 648 o. 12 d. 6 l. 183.
112. Walter Terry, "New Spectacle: Simple Beauty," *New York Herald Tribune*, September 23, 1962.
113. Chapman, "Ballet: Big Business with a Soviet Beat."
114. Hughes, "Ballet: Bolshoi and American Children."
115. Alexander Fried, "Bay Area Youngsters Dance with the Bolshoi," *San Francisco Examiner*, October 21, 1962.
116. "Messerer Chooses 18 U.S. Children for Bolshoi Ballet," *New York Times*, September 6, 1962. Battey, "'Ballet School' Seeks Locals." "Ballet School—Trying Out for the Bolshoi." "Aspiring Ballerinas Audition for the 'Bolshoi,'" *Christian Science Monitor*, November 24, 1962.
117. As Fosler-Lussier argues, cultural détente led the way toward more peaceful political relations between the Soviet Union and the United States in the early 1960s. Fosler-Lussier, *Music in America's Cold War Diplomacy*, 200–203.

Chapter 4

1. Reynolds does use translations of Soviet reviews, but the narrative drawn from them echoes the other American-centered accounts. Nancy Reynolds, "The Red Curtain: Balanchine's Critical Reception in the Soviet Union," *Proceedings of the Society of Dance History Scholars* (Riverside: University of California Riverside, 14–15 February, 1992), 47–57. Prevots, *Dance for Export*, 81–87. Homans, *Apollo's Angels*, 376–379. Caute, *The Dancer Defects*, 490–493. Yale Richmond, *Cultural Exchange and the Cold War: Raising the Iron Curtain* (University Park: Pennsylvania State University Press, 2003), 125. Taper, *Balanchine*, 273–289.
2. Croft, *Dancers as Diplomats*, 35–65, 75–83.
3. Nancy Condee, "Cultural Codes of the Thaw," in *Nikita Khrushchev*, ed. William Taubman et al. (New Haven: Yale University Press, 2000), 160–176. For more on this stylistic shift, see chapters 1 and 3.
4. Elizabeth Kendall, *Balanchine and the Lost Muse* (Oxford: Oxford University Press, 2013), 42–56, 186, 229–231. Taper, *Balanchine*, 25, 37–51, 53–55, 394.
5. Steichen, *Balanchine and Kirstein's American Enterprise*. James Steichen, "The American Ballet's Caravan," *Dance Research Journal* 47, no. 1 (April 2015): 69–94. Taper, *Balanchine*, 207, 227–228.
6. Lynn Garafola, "Lincoln Kirstein, Modern Dance, and the Left: The Genesis of an American Ballet," *Dance Research: The Journal of the Society for Dance Research* 23, no. 1 (Summer 2005): 18–35.
7. Prevots, *Dance for Export*, 147–149.

8. ANTA Dance Panel Meeting Minutes, March 21, 1957, ABECA Box 101. ANTA Dance Panel Meeting Minutes, January 13, 1955; October 2, 1958; December 18, 1958; February 19, 1959; October 22, 1959, NYp, ABT, Folders 3384, 3393, 3396.
9. ANTA Dance Panel Meeting Minutes, October 17, 1957, NYp, ABT, Folder 3388.
10. Letter, Balanchine to C. Douglas Dillon, Under Secretary of State, August 21, 1959; Letter, Dillon to Balanchine, September 3, 1959; Letter, H. Franklin Irwin to Balanchine, February 3, 1960; Letter, Het Amsterdams Ballet to Douglas Dillon, February 2, 1960; Letter, Mary Stewart French to Betty Cage, June 12, 1964, CAh, Thr 411, Balanchine Collection, Folder 1943. John Martin, "The Dance: Export," *New York Times*, November 8, 1959.
11. Letter, October 13, 1959, from Balanchine to Thayer, CAh, Thr 411, Balanchine Collection, Folder 1943.
12. Steichen, *Balanchine and Kirstein's American Enterprise*, 222–223. Jennifer Dunning, "Balanchine's All-American Dedication," *New York Times*, November 20, 2001.
13. ANTA Dance Panel Meeting Minutes, December 19, 1957, NYp, ABT, Folder 3388.
14. ANTA Dance Panel Meeting Minutes, October 2, 1958, NYp, ABT, Folder 3393.
15. ANTA Dance Panel Meeting Minutes, January 26, 1961, and March 16, 1961, ABECA, Box 101, Folder 17.
16. Letter, October 27, 1961, Hurok to Max Eisenberg, ABECA, Box 50, Folder 75.
17. Memo, March 8, 1962, to Isenburgh from Coriden through Boerner, ABECA Box 50, Folder 75.
18. ANTA Dance Panel Meeting Minutes, April 17, 1962, ABECA, Box 101, Folder 17.
19. ANTA Dance Panel Meeting Minutes, April 17, 1962, ABECA, Box 101, Folder 17. Balanchine's claims about the food in the USSR were based on accurate reports from the ABT dancers in 1960 (see chapter 2). It is possible that Balanchine's impression of touring as a hardship activity was at least partially related to the tragic circumstances of NYCB's 1956 European tour, on which Balanchine's wife, ballerina Tanaquil LeClercq, contracted polio and was paralyzed for life. ANTA Dance Panel Meeting Minutes, November 15, 1956, NYp, ABT, Folder 3384.
20. ANTA Dance Panel Meeting Minutes, April 17, 1962; June 19, 1962, ABECA, Box 101, Folder 17.
21. Any proceeds from the tour would be returned to ANTA. 1962 Agreement between ICES of ANTA and New York City Ballet, ABECA, Box 73, Folder 77.
22. Garafola, *Diaghilev's Ballets Russes*, 16, 39–43. Elizabeth Souritz, "Fedor Lopukhov: A Soviet Choreographer in the 1920s," trans. by Lynn Visson, trans. revised and with intro by Sally Banes, *Dance Research Journal* 17, no. 1, 2–18 (Autumn 1985–Spring 1986): 3–20. Chantal Frankenbach, "Dancing to Beethoven in Wilhelmine Germany: Isadora Duncan and Her Critics," *Journal of Musicology* 34, no. 1 (January 2017): 71–114.
23. Ezrahi, *Swans of the Kremlin*, 41–66, 248–249.
24. Souritz, "Fedor Lopukhov," 6. On Lopukhov's birthday, Balanchine sent him a telegram thanking him for his support during his early days as a choreographer, claiming, "my young dancers know you were the first one to show that symphonies could be used for dance." Telegram, from Balanchine to Lopukhov, CAh, Thr 411, Folder 1091.

25. Steichen, *Balanchine and Kirstein's American Enterprise*, 57–60. Stephanie Jordan, *Moving Music: Dialogues with Music in Twentieth-Century Ballet* (London: Dance Books, Ltd., 2000), 50–56.
26. *Choreography by Balanchine: A Catalogue of Works* (New York: Viking Penguin, 1983), 148–150, 178–179, 198–199.
27. "Absolute music" was actually a negative term used by composer Richard Wagner, and Hanslick avoided it. Nevertheless, this is the term used even by scholars of Hanslick, and thus I continue to use it here. Mark Evan Bonds, *Absolute Music: The History of an Idea* (Oxford: Oxford University Press, 2014), 141–209, 297–301. Chantal Frankenbach, "Disdain for Dance, Disdain for France" (PhD diss., University of California at Davis, 2012), 106, 113.
28. Edwin Denby, "Forms in Motion and in Thought" (1965), in Denby, *Dance Writings*, ed. Robert Cornfield (New Haven: Yale University Press, 1998), 303. Denby was also influenced by the philosophy around abstract expressionism in the visual arts, which similarly promoted abstraction as a way out of political systems. Andrea Harris, *Making Ballet American: Modernism before and beyond Balanchine* (Oxford: Oxford University Press, 2017), 103–144.
29. Under socialist realist aesthetics, form was to be molded to fit content perfectly. Schmelz, *Such Freedom If Only Musical*, 6–13. Jan Plamper, "Abolishing Ambiguity: Soviet Censorship Practices in the 1930s," *Russian Review* 60 (October 2001), 526–544.
30. Krasovskaia, "V seredine veka," in *Sovetskiĭ baletnyĭ teatr*, V. M. Krasovskaia (Moscow: Iskusstvo, 1976), 218–290, especially 268–276. A. A. Sokolov-Kaminskiĭ, *Sovetskiĭ balet segodnia* (Moskva: Zdanie, 1984), 81. Iuriĭ Grigorovich, "Traditsii i novatorstvo," in *Muzyka i khoreografiia sovremennogo baleta*, ed. I. V. Golubovskiĭ (Leningrad: Muzyka, 1974), 7–9. A. P. Petrov, "Kompozitor i baletmeĭster," in *Muzyka i khoreografiia sovremennogo baleta*, 53–54. Schmelz, *Such Freedom If Only Musical*, 220–221. Christina Ezrahi, "The Thaw in Soviet Culture and the Return of Symphonic Dance" (International Symposium of Russian Ballet, Harrison Institute, 2007). Stenogramma vsesoiuznogo soveshchaniia deiateleĭ khoreografii, June 1963, RGALI f. 2329 o. 3 d. 1928. Reynolds has also noted the importance of "content" in the 1962 Balanchine reviews. Reynolds, "The Red Curtain."
31. Choreographic analysis of *Symphony in C* comes from a recording of the New York City Ballet as well as live viewing of Boston Ballet. *Symphony in C*, on *New York City Ballet in Paris* (Bel Air Classiques, 2017). George Balanchine, *Symphony in C*, performed by Boston Ballet, May 2013.
32. Choreographic analysis uses recordings of the Mariinsky Theater's revival. "Leningrad Symphony," https://www.youtube.com/watch?v=ycnWh_yjLBk, accessed July 22, 2015. For the date of choreography: Ezrahi, *Swans of the Kremlin*, 242.
33. Kirov Leningrad Ballet, program, 1961, CAh, Thr 411, Folder 2744. A number of Balanchine's abstract ballets had originally been given imaginative names, only to be renamed in later stagings according to their scores. For example, the ballet *Le Palais de Cristal*, with music by Bizet, premiered in 1947, only to be renamed *Symphony in C* in 1948 when it was restaged for Ballet Society. Some Balanchine ballets were still going

under their more elaborate titles (for example, *Ballet Imperial* would not be renamed *Piano Concerto No. 2* until 1974), but the Soviets would have been aware of the *Palais de Cristal* change to *Symphony in C. Choreography by Balanchine*, 148–149, 178.

34. Choreographic analysis comes from a variety of sources. *Serenade* performed by New York City Ballet, 1957 (VAI, 2014). *Serenade,* performed by New York City Ballet, 1969, NYp, *MGZHB 12-639. *Serenade,* performed by New York City Ballet, New York, May 1, 2012; May 2, 2012; and January 16, 2013. *Serenade,* performed by Boston Ballet, Boston, May 11, 2013.
35. In the third iteration of the motto theme, at the end of the "Tema Russe" movement, the women are arranged in parallel and perpendicular lines, as if the diamonds have been broken apart and rotated. In addition, the female soloist is in front joined by a man.
36. For more on the relationship between choreography and music in *Serenade,* see: Gretchen G. Horlacher, "Stepping Out: Hearing Balanchine," *Music Theory Online* 21, no. 8 (March 2018).
37. Jordan, *Moving Music,* 128–129.
38. Letter, Sol Hurok to Max Eisenberg, October 27, 1961, ABECA, Box 50, Folder 75.
39. Dance Panel Meeting Minutes, June 19, 1962; February 20, 1962, ABECA, Box 101, ANTA.
40. Otchet P. F. Abolimov i M. N. Anastas'eva o poezdke v SShA Dzhazorkestr p.r.b. Gudmana, N'iu-Iork siti balet, oznakomlenie s teatral'no—kontsertnoï zhizn'iu N'iu Iorka, RGALI f. 2329 o. 8 d. 2320 l. 53.
41. Otchet P. F. Abolimov i M. N. Anastas'eva o poezdke v SShA Dzhazorkestr p.r.b. Gudmana.
42. Quoted in Clare Croft, *Dancers as Diplomats,* 61.
43. "Rasskazyvaet Dzh. Balanchin," *Sovetskiï artist,* October 19, 1962, RGALI f. 2337 o. 2 d. 204 l. 77.
44. "Rasskazyvaet Dzh. Balanchin." This was a favorite metaphor of Balanchine's, often deployed in interviews to ridicule audience members who sought meaning in dance gesture. Arlene Croce, "Balanchine Said," *New Yorker,* January 26, 2009.
45. "Vstrecha s moskichami raduet," RGALI f. 2337 o. 2 d. 204 l. 60.
46. Reynolds, "The Red Curtain," 49.
47. It was common for American embassy staff to produce this type of material for local audiences. Fosler-Lussier, *Music in America's Cold War Diplomacy,* 42–43.
48. "Novosti Amerikanskoï Kul'tury," RGALI f. 2337 o. 2 d. 204 l. 150; RGALI f. 2966 o. 1 d. 454 l. 47.
49. See chapters 1 and 2.
50. "Novosti amerikanskoï kul'tury," RGALI f. 2337 o. 2 d. 204 l. 150.
51. Program notes, RGALI f. 2337 o. 2 d. 204 l. 23.
52. Program notes, RGALI f. 2337 o. 2 d. 204 l. 23.
53. Theodore Shabad, "New York Ballet Lands in Moscow," *New York Times,* October 7, 1962. John Martin, "Ballet: Visit to Bolshoi," *New York Times,* October 10, 1962.
54. Croft, *Dancers as Diplomats,* 37. ANTA Dance Panel Meeting Minutes, December 20, 1962, ABECA, Box 101, Folder 17. As Ezrahi discusses, the Kremlin Palace of

Congresses functioned as a secondary stage for the Bolshoi. Ezrahi, *Swans of the Kremlin*, 214.
55. Allen Hughes, "Americans in Moscow," *New York Times*, October 7, 1962.
56. John Martin, "Ballet: New York City Troupe in Tiflis," *New York Times*, November 22, 1962. "Russians Cheer New York Ballet," *Washington Post, Times Herald*, October 10, 1962. Croft, *Dancers as Diplomats*, 37.
57. Croft, *Dancers as Diplomats*, 38.
58. Milton Bracker, "City Ballet Back from Soviet Trip," *New York Times*, December 3, 1962. "Balanchine Meets Brother in Russia," *The Sun*, October 7, 1962.
59. Taper, *Balanchine*, 278–279, 288.
60. Croft, *Dancers as Diplomats*, 48–51.
61. Croft, *Dancers as Diplomats*, 51. Memo, March 16, 1962, Heath Bowman to Alfred Boerner, ABECA, Box 73, Folder 28.
62. Condee, "Cultural Codes of the Thaw," 166–169, 173.
63. Leonid Lavrovsky, "O putiakh razvitiia sovetskogo baleta," RGALI f. 3045 o. 1 d. 159, especially l. 27.
64. Ezrahi, *Swans of the Kremlin*, 245.
65. Choreographic analysis based on film of *Paganini* from 1974 starring Marina Kondratieva and Yaroslav Sekh. "Paganini," https://www.youtube.com/watch?v=_K_2M0_oyBU, accessed July 22, 2015. "Paganini Libretto," 1960, RGALI f. 3045 o. 1 d. 127.
66. A. Lapauri, "Razdum′ia posle spektaklei gostei," RGALI f. 2337 o. 2 d. 204 l. 123.
67. Reynolds, "The Red Curtain."
68. Sherry, "Better Something Than Nothing," 731–758.
69. Alexei Yurchak, *Everything Was Forever, until It Was No More* (Princeton: Princeton University Press, 2006), 14–29.
70. Elizabeth Souritz, "Balanchine in Russia," *Ballet Review* 39, no. 1 (2011): 53–55.
71. Souritz, "Balanchine in Russia," 54.
72. Alexei Yurchak, *Everything Was Forever*, 8.
73. Aram Khachaturian, "Vstrecha s Amerikanskim Baletom," October 10, 1962, RGALI f. 2337 o. 2 d. 204 l. 52. Iu. Gerber argued that Balanchine was a "very interesting ballet master, possessing a great fantasy in the creation of dance combinations." Iu. Gerber, "Pervoe znakomstvo," RGALI f. 2337 o. 2 d. 204.
74. M. Sabnina, "Iskaniia . . . vo imia chego? Gastroli N′iu–Iorkskoi Baletnoi Truppy," RGALI f. 2337 o. 2 d. 204 l. 115.
75. Brenda Dixon Gottschild, *Digging the Africanist Presence in American Performance: Dance and Other Contexts* (Westport, CT: Praeger, 1996), 59–79. Sally Banes, "Balanchine and Black Dance," in *Writing Dancing in the Age of Postmodernism* (Middleton: Wesleyan University Press, 2011), 53–69.
76. V. Bogdanov-Berezovsky, *Ulanova and the Development of the Soviet Ballet*, trans. Stephen Garry and Joan Lawson (London: Macgibbon and Kee, 1952). V. Bogdanov-Berezovskii, *Galina Sergeevna Ulanova*, 2nd ed. (Moscow: Iskusstvo, 1961), 70–71.
77. Khachaturian, "Vstrecha s Amerikanskim Baletom"; Rostislav Zakharov, "Pervyi spektakl′ gostei," October 11, 1962, RGALI f. 2337 o. 2 d. 204 ll. 52, 55.

78. Gerber, "Pervoe znakomstvo."
79. A. Ilupina, "Balet Balanchina," *Komsomol'skaia Pravda,* October 12, 1962. RGALI f. 2337 o. 2 d. 204 l. 68.
80. "Eugenie Ouroussow, Director of City Ballet's School, Dead," *New York Times,* January 8, 1975. Jack Anderson, "Felia Doubrovska Dies at 85; Ballerina and Noted Teacher," *New York Times,* September 21, 1981.
81. "N'iu-Iork Siti Balet v Moskve," RGALI f. 2337 o. 2 d. 204 l. 40. New York City Ballet Program, RGALI f. 2337 o. 2 d. 204 l. 23.
82. Khachaturian, "Vstrecha s Amerikanskim Baletom." Mikhail Gabovich, "Moskovskiĭ debiut," *Sovetskaia kul'tura,* October 13, 1962, RGALI f. 2337 o. 2 d. 204 l. 72. Natalia Roslavleva, "Ėtogo nikogda ne budet," *Teatr zhizni,* RGALI f. 2337 o. 2 d. 204 l. 124.
83. Sabnina, "Iskaniia... vo imia chego?"
84. Croft, *Dancers as Diplomats,* 61–63.
85. Stenogramma vsesoiuznogo soveshchaniia deiateleĭ khoreografii, June 1963, RGALI f. 2329 o. 3 d. 1928.
86. Zakharov, "Pervyĭ spektakl' gosteĭ."
87. Gerber, "Pervoe znakomstvo."
88. Boris L'vov-Anokhin, "Askety Tantsa," *Nedelia,* October 14–20, 1962, f. 2337 o. 2 d. 204 l. 86.
89. Roslavleva, "Ėtogo nikogda ne budet."
90. Lepeshinskaya commented on New York City Ballet in a film made by Katanian. V. Katanian, *Amerikanskiĭ balet v Moskve* (Tsentral'naia Ordena Krasnogo Znameni Studiia Dokumental'nykh Fil'mov Moskva, 1962), located in Personal Collection of Wenshuo Zhang. Sabnina, "Iskaniia... vo imia chego?"
91. Sabnina, "Iskaniia... vo imia chego?"
92. Mikhail Gabovich, "Panorama tantsev," RGALI f. 2337 o. 2 d. 204 l. 119.
93. A. Lapauri, "Razdum'ia posle spektakleĭ gosteĭ"; Sabnina, "Iskaniia... vo imia chego?" Gabovich, "Panorama tantsev." Katanian, *Amerikanskiĭ balet v Moskve.*
94. Quoted in Schwarz, *Music and Musical Life in Soviet Russia,* enlarged ed. (Bloomington: Indiana University Press, 1983), 225. For more on the shake-up: Kiril Tomoff, *Creative Union: The Professional Organization of Soviet Composers, 1939–1953* (Ithaca, NY: Cornell University Press, 2006), 122–151.
95. Schmelz, *Such Freedom If Only Musical,* 39–54.
96. Kevin Bartig, "Commentary and Observations on *Le sacre* in Russia: An Overview," in *The Rite of Spring at 100,* ed. Severine Neff et al. (Bloomington: Indiana University Press, 2017), 182–183.
97. L'vov-Anokhin, "Askety tantsa." Similarly, Zakharov claimed the ballet was "closer to mathematics than to art." Zakharov, "Pervyĭ spektakl' gosteĭ."
98. Gabovich, "Moskovskiĭ debiut."
99. Gabovich, "Moskovskiĭ debiut."
100. Some researchers, such as Don McDonagh, have suggested that the grouping and regrouping of twelve dancers may have had symbolic connections to Stravinsky's use

of serial techniques in the ballet score, although as Irene Alm points out, Balanchine and Stravinsky devised the dance's structure long before Stravinsky decided to compose in a serialist style. Irene Alm, "Stravinsky, Balanchine, and Agon: An Analysis Based on the Collaborative Process," *The Journal of Musicology* 7, no. 2 (Spring 1989), 254–269. Don McDonagh, *George Balanchine* (Boston: Twayne, 1983), 119. For more on the choreographic-musical analysis of *Agon*, see: Stephanie Jordan, "Music Puts a Time Corset on the Dance," *Dance Chronicle: Studies in Dance and the Related Arts* 16, no. 3 (January 1, 1993): 295–321.

101. Sabnina, "Iskaniĭa . . . vo imĭa chego?"
102. Roslavleva, "Ėtogo nikogda ne budet."
103. Choreographic analysis based on *Agon*, performed by New York City Ballet (New York: Lincoln Center, June 12, 2011). *Balanchine: New York City Ballet in Montreal*, volume 2 (Vai, 2014). Katanĭan, *Amerikanskiĭ balet v Moskve*. *Agon*, performed by New York City Ballet with Darcey Bussell (New York, 1993), posted to YouTube by ear8002, https://www.youtube.com/watch?v=Ud8zVcHPnuM, accessed October 25, 2019.
104. L'vov-Anokhin, "Askety tantsa."
105. Sabnina, "Iskaniĭa . . . vo imĭa chego?"
106. Zakharov, "Pervyĭ spektakl' gosteĭ." Similarly, in the film of the NYCB performances, Lepeshinskaya claims that *Agon* is "cold" but that she liked the performances by Arthur Mitchell and Allegra Kent. Katanĭan, *Amerikanskiĭ balet v Moskve*.
107. Croft, *Dancers as Diplomats*, 75–83. Fosler-Lussier and Penny von Eschen have pointed out that the State Department used many black performers for similar ends. Von Eschen, *Satchmo Blows Up the World*. Fosler-Lussier, *Music in America's Cold War Diplomacy*, 101–122.
108. Sabnina, "Iskaniĭa . . . vo imĭa chego?" Gabovich, "Panorama tantsev." Roslavleva, "Ėtogo nikogda ne budet."
109. Katanĭan, *Amerikanskiĭ balet v Moskve*.
110. John Martin, "New York City Ballet Is Success in Soviet Union," *New York Times*, October 22, 1962.
111. John Martin, "Ballet: Adieu to Moscow," *New York Times*, October 31, 1962.
112. Walter Terry, "A Revelation for Russians," *New York Herald Tribune*, November 25, 1962.
113. Terry, "A Revelation for Russians."
114. Arlene Croce, "Balanchine Said," *New Yorker*, January 18, 2009.
115. Mikhail Gabovich, "Panorama tantsev." The phrase is even closer to Balanchine's than this translation conveys, as the Russian language does not have definite articles. Therefore, while I have translated Gabovich's as closely as possible, and in so doing have not inserted unnecessary definite articles, it would be perfectly possible for a bilingual person to read the Gabovich as "he truly sees the music and hears the dance." Terry included this quotation in his truncated version of Gabovich's article, so it is likely that Wescott saw the phrase there.
116. Translation from Balanchine's personal files. CAh, Thr 411, Balanchine, Folder 2239.

Epilogue

1. *Colbert Report*, December 7, 2011, http://thecolbertreport.cc.com/videos/pueyvf/david-hallberg, accessed July 10, 2015. Hallberg was hired at an unusually friendly period for Russian-American relations, following the Obama-Medvedev reset and before Vladimir Putin made the decision to run for a third term as president. It is also worth noting that Colbert used an invented persona for this television show, so the remarks almost certainly do not reflect the comedian's actual opinions.
2. Alastair Macauley and Daniel J. Wakin, "American Is to Join the Bolshoi Ballet," *New York Times*, September 20, 2011.
3. David Hallberg, *A Body of Work: Dancing to the Edge and Back* (New York: Touchstone, 2017).
4. Kathy Lally, "Moscow's Bolshoi Prepares to Reopen," *Washington Post*, October 12, 2011. Miriam Elder, "Tsar Quality: Bolshoi Theatre Reopens after Six-Year Overhaul," *The Guardian*, October 27, 2011.
5. Sergei L. Loiko, "David Hallberg, Bolshoi Newcomer, Greeted with Praise, Criticism," *Los Angeles Times*, November 19, 2011.
6. "Balet 182," http://forum.balletfriends.ru/viewtopic.php?t=3950&postdays=0&postorder=asc&start=150, "Balet 183," http://forum.balletfriends.ru/viewtopic.php?t=3993&postdays=0&postorder=asc&start=105, *Balet i opera*, both accessed June 11, 2018.
7. Robert Greskovic, "Don't Blame the Dancers," *Wall Street Journal*, July 22, 2014. The critic from the *Washington Post* was more favorable about the company. Sarah Kaufman, "Bolshoi Ballet's Uncommonly Intimate *Giselle*," *Washington Post*, May 21, 2014.
8. Alastair Macaulay, "The Lake Is Frozen in Time," *New York Times*, July 16, 2014. See also: Alastair Macaulay, "Planting Their Feet in a Soviet Past, from Tone to Style to Repertory," *New York Times*, June 28, 2014.
9. Joan Acocella, "Man of the People," *New Yorker*, July 20, 2014.
10. The complaint was that the bottoms of the pointe shoes looked gray or black. There was speculation that this "dirty" look was possibly a result of the fact that Russian dancers generally wear longer-lasting Gaynor Minden pointe shoes and can thus pick up more grime from the floor. The criticism was reminiscent of the American reporting on the 2014 Olympic Games in Sochi, which emphasized the dilapidated state of the facilities. "Summer 2014 NYC Saratoga Tour," http://balletalert.invisionzone.com/index.php?/topic/38497-summer-2014-nyc-saratoga-tour/page-7, accessed November 4, 2015. On the Sochi coverage: Angela E. Stent, *The Limits of Partnership: U.S.–Russian Relations in the Twenty-first Century* (Princeton: Princeton University Press, 2014), 283. Julia Ioffe, "The Russians Think We're Engaging in Olympic Schadenfreude. They're Right," *New Republic*, February 6, 2014, http://www.newrepublic.com/article/116507/russians-hit-back-west-cool-it-olympic-schadenfreude, accessed November 2, 2015.
11. "Gastroli Bol'shogo v SShA—2014," *Balet i opera*, http://forum.balletfriends.ru/viewtopic.php?t=6534, accessed November 3, 2015.

12. *Don Quixote,* performed by the Bolshoi Ballet at Lincoln Center, July 23, 2014. *Spartacus,* performed by the Bolshoi Ballet at Lincoln Center, July 26, 2014.
13. Hallberg, *A Body of Work,* 153–164, 291.
14. "Alexei Ratmansky," *ABT,* https://www.abt.org/people/alexei-ratmansky/, accessed November 12, 2018.
15. Anne Searcy, "Alexei Ratmansky's Abstract-Narrative Ballet," in *The Oxford Handbook of Contemporary Ballet,* ed. Jill Nunes Jensen and Kathrina Farrugia-Kriel (Oxford: Oxford University Press, forthcoming).

Index

Figures are indicated by *f* following the page number

For the benefit of digital users, indexed terms that span two pages (e.g., 52–53) may, on occasion, appear on only one of those pages.

abstraction, 119, 123, 167n28
   and Balanchine, 100, 103–4, 109–10, 167–68n33
   Soviet government relationship with, 55, 109, 115
   State Department downplaying, 110–12
   in US reception of Soviet ballet, 9, 34, 94–95
Adams, Diana, 110–11, 111*f*
African American dance, 116
African American performers, 67, 123
Afternoon of a Faun (Robbins), 88, 109
Agon (Balanchine), 110–12, 122*f*, 126–27, 170–71n100
   Soviet reception of, 119, 120–23
All-Union Choreographic Conference (1963), 117
Alonso, Alicia, 49
Alvin Ailey American Dance Theater, 77
American Ballet Theatre, 54, 92–93, 131
   1960 Metropolitan Opera House Season of, 50–51
   1960 tour schedule of, 56–57
   1966 Soviet tour of, 139n41, 151n55
   history of, 47–49, 65
   and negotiations for the 1960 tour, 49–50, 51–53
   orchestra for, 58
   personnel of, 49, 50
   programming of, 53–56, 57*f*, 88
   Soviet reception of, 59–60, 64, 66–67, 68, 117, 152n85, 155n130
   and *Swan Lake*, 159n37
   tour experience of, 58–59, 68–69

American National Theatre and Academy (ANTA), 4, 5, 136n11
   reports to, 58, 69
Anisimova, Nina, 75
ANTA Dance Advisory Panel, 4, 51–52, 123, 136n11, 137n22, 158n21
   and American Ballet Theatre, 48–51, 53, 54
   and New York City Ballet, 99–101, 109
Asafiev, Boris, 63
audiences, 10
   composition of, 22, 57, 83, 112
   and the experience of seeing ballet, 8
   reactions of Soviet, 58, 59, 97, 112, 123, 124–25
   reactions of US, 1–2, 17, 21–22, 71, 88–89, 131, 163n80

Balanchine, George, 99, 112
   artistic influences on, 102–3, 139n37, 166n24
   and Gabovich, 125–27
   and plans for the 1962 Soviet tour, 100–1, 166n19
   sayings of, 125–26, 168n44, 171n115
   vs. Soviet choreographers, 34, 40–41, 94–95, 124, 147n116
   Soviet interviews with, 109–10, 119
   and Soviet officials, 109
   Soviet reception of, 114–19, 120–24, 129–30, 160n45, 169n73
   and the US State Department, 99–100
   and *Swan Lake*, 155n127
   use of musical form by, 9, 103, 103*f*, 104–5, 108
   and Yakobson, 158n26

Balanchivadze, Andrei, 112
ballet
  as American art form, 47, 48, 49, 53, 67, 149n12
  and class hierarchy, 74–75, 89–91, 95
  as Russian art form, 48–49, 59, 115, 116–17
  training for, 91, 92–94, 95
  as universal language, 6–7, 8–9
  use in cultural diplomacy of, 4, 12, 74, 136n11, 139n41
Ballet School (Messerer), 11–12, 75, 91–95, 92*f*, 129–30
Ballet Theatre. *See* American Ballet Theatre
Ballets Russes, 99, 155n123, 160n46
Ballets U.S.A., 50, 100–1
La Bayadère (Petipa), 63, 75
Bass, Milton, 42–43
Battey, Jean, 90
Bazhev, Pavel, 36
Belsky, Igor, 84–85, 105–6, 119
Ben-Hur, 85, 86–87, 91
Bernstein, Leonard, 55, 60, 62, 153n92
  and New York Philharmonic tour, 54–55, 151n52
Beryozka State Folk Dance Troupe, 4
Bessmertnova, Natalia, 104*f*
Biancolli, Louis, 34
Billy the Kid (Loring), 9, 48, 53–55, 88
  music of, 56
Bizet, Georges, 120–21
  Symphony No. 1 in C Major, 102–3, 104–5
Bluebeard (Fokine), 55, 56, 59–60
blues, 62
Bolshoi Ballet, 6, 12, 18–19, 101, 139n41
  1956 London tour by, 23, 26, 36, 145–46n99
  1962 US tour schedule of, 75
  2014 US tour by, 130–31
  and Hallberg, 129
  and Hurok, 5, 20, 21, 23–24, 43, 78–79, 159n31
  and Kennedy family, 76–77
  vs. Kirov, 18–19, 80–83
  vs. Moiseyev, 83

US critical reception of, 33–35, 40–43, 81–83, 88–91, 94–95, 123–24, 130–31
US popular reception of, 1, 17, 19–20, 21–22, 71, 130–31
Bolshoi Choreographic Academy, 131
Bolshoi Theater, 112
  artistic committee of, 87–72
  stage size of, 21, 86, 151n62
  supplying musicians, 58
Boorstin, Daniel, 10–11
Boston, 76–78
Bourdieu, Pierre, 82–83
Broadway, 20, 99, 116
Bruhn, Erik
  citizenship of, 45, 49, 67
  and classical pas de deux, 66–67, 155n130

The Cage (Robbins), 88, 109
Canada, 21, 75
Cassidy, Claudia, 81, 147n116
censorship, 10, 114–16
Chabukiani, Vakhtang, 63–64, 140n4
Chapman, John, 35, 90–91, 94–95
character dance, 85
Chase, Lucia, 48, 58, 68
  and Anatole Heller, 51–52
  and campaign for Soviet tour, 49–50, 53
  and Chabukiani, 63
  as member of ANTA dance advisory panel, 48–49
  and John Martin, 51
  repertory selection by, 53–54, 59
Chausson, Ernest, 56
Chichinadze, Alexei, 52–53
Chopin, Frédéric, 55
Chopiniana. See *Les Sylphides*
choreographic symphonism
  aesthetic theory of, 104*f*, 104, 138–39n36
  development of, 9, 102
  vs. drambalet, 113–14
  impact of on Ratmansky, 131–32
  vs. neoclassical ballet, 105–6, 108, 117–19, 120–21, 129–30
  Stone Flower as example of, 37–40
Christensen, Willam, 79–80
Chulaki, Mikhail, 142n43, 158n26

Cinderella (Zakharov), 25–26, 36, 84
Class Concert. See *Ballet School*
Colbert, Stephen, 129, 172n1
Colgrass, Michael, 58–59
The Combat (Dollar), 56, 62
comedy, 56, 58, 59–60, 65
Condee, Nancy, 113
conductors, 1, 20, 51, 58, 78
conservatism, 34–36, 41, 90, 110, 130–31, 145n98
contemporaneity. See modernism
Copland, Aaron, 53–54, 55, 60, 61–62, 153n92
Craft, Robert, 120
Croft, Clare, 6–7, 97–98, 112–13, 117, 123
Cuban Missile Crisis, 73–74, 75–77, 112–13, 157n17
Cullberg, Birgit, 56
cultural diplomacy
　funding of, 5–6, 50, 99–100, 101, 137n22, 166n21
　and reception, 7, 10–12
　Soviet, 3, 4–5, 26
　United States, 3–5
Czerny, Carl, 93

dancer vs. choreographer, 41–44, 123–24
Dash, Thomas, 35
Daughters of the American Revolution, 20
de Banfield, Raffaello, 56
de Mille, Agnes
　and American Ballet Theatre, 48, 51, 52–55
　and ANTA, 48–49
　choreographic style of, 60–61, 62
　Soviet reception of, 61–62, 151n55
de-Stalinization. See the Thaw
Dean, Robert D., 42
defection, 78
Denby, Edwin, 103, 167n28
Desyatnikov, Leonid, 131–32
Diner, Akiva, 110
Dobrynin, Anatoly, 76–77
Dollar, William, 56
Don Quixote (Petipa), 130, 131
　pas de deux from, 55, 65, 66–67, 155n123
Donizetti Variations (Balanchine), 112

Dorsey, Thomas J., 155–56n134
drambalet, 143n65
　aesthetics of, 9, 26–28, 103–4, 104f
　vs. American populist ballet, 56, 60–61, 62
　vs. Balanchine's style, 100, 109–11, 116, 117, 119
　vs. choreographic symphonism, 37, 38–40, 102, 113–14
　and gender, 63–64
　Romeo and Juliet as example of, 28, 29, 30–33
Drigo, Riccardo, 80
Duncan, Isadora, 102, 139n37

empire, 73–74, 86–87, 88–89, 138n34, 149n7, 162n72
Episodes (Balanchine), 119, 121
Études (Lander), 92–95
experience of touring, 20, 21, 58–59, 77–79, 112–13, 158n19

Faier, Yuri, 20, 43, 78
Fall River Legend (de Mille), 9, 48, 52–55, 151n55
Fancy Free (Robbins), 9, 48, 52–53, 55, 56
　audience reactions to, 58
　as example of populist ballet, 60–61, 62
　and masculinity, 63–64
　music of, 58, 60, 62
　Soviet reception of, 59–60, 64
femininity, 42–43
film. See Hollywood
Flames of Paris (Vainonen), 27–28, 63, 84
Fokine, Michel, 39–40
　and American Ballet Theatre, 47–48, 55, 59
　connections to Stanislavsky of, 27, 60–61
　use of music by, 102, 118
　and Yakobson, 85
folk dance
　in ballet, 38, 39–40, 41, 61–62
　use in cultural diplomacy of, 4, 83, 136n11
folk music, 39, 53–54, 61–62, 110–11, 153n92
formalism, 25–26, 33, 103–4

Fosler-Lussier, Danielle, 5, 10–11, 74, 139n40, 165n117, 171n107
Fountain of the Bakhchisarai (Zakharov), 36, 84
Fried, Alexander, 81, 95

Gabovich, Mikhail, 39–40, 59, 62, 64, 118–19, 120–21
"Dance Panorama," 125–27, 171n115
Gaevsky, Vadim, 59, 62
Gayane (Anisimova), 75
gender, 42–44, 63–64, 147n124
Genauer, Emily, 34, 35
Gerber, Iu., 118, 169n73
Giselle (Coralli, Perrot), 126
and American Ballet Theatre, 54, 63
and Bolshoi, 24–25, 36, 75, 130
film of, 22
Glazunov, Alexander, 93–94
Good Neighbor Policy, 3, 99–100, 138n34
Gorsky, Aleksander, 27, 80–81
Gould, Morton, 53–54
Gounod, Charles, 75
Goskontsert, 3, 5
and American Ballet Theatre, 52–53
vs. Hurok, 5–6
and repertory selection, 55, 88, 109
Govrin, Gloria, 123
Graduation Ball (Lichine), 52–53, 55, 56
Graham, Martha, 4, 100–1
Grigorovich, Yuri, 84–85, 123–24
as artistic director of Bolshoi Ballet, 113–14, 146n111
and *Stone Flower*, 37–38, 39–40
Grosz, Elizabeth, 42
Gugushvili, Eteri, 59–60

Hallberg, David, 129, 131, 132, 172n1
Hanslick, Eduard, 103, 105, 167n27
Harrison, Jay, 41
Hayden, Melissa, 123
Heller, Anatole, 51–52
historicism, 26–27, 31–33, 86
Hollywood, 74–75, 99, 162n68
celebrities, 21
celebrity culture, 22–24
epics, 85–91, 162n71, 162n72

homophobia, 64, 154n118
Hughes, Allen, 81, 88–90, 95
Hurok, Sol, 5–6, 76*f*
and American Ballet Theatre, 47–48, 51–52, 149n7
and *Ballet School*, 91, 92–93
and Bolshoi Ballet, 20, 21, 23–24, 43, 78–79, 159n31
and distribution of tickets, 19–20, 83, 160–61n51
and NYCB, 101, 109, 166n21
and *Spartacus*, 71, 85–86, 88–89

Ilupina, Anna, 116–17
Interplay (Robbins), 53, 108
Ivanov, Lev, 79–81
Ivesiana (Balanchine), 109

Jardin aux Lilas (Tudor), 56
jazz, 53–54, 58, 62
Joffrey Ballet, 12, 148n3

Kahn, Albert Eugene, 78–79
Kastendieck, Miles, 24, 34, 41–42
Kaye, Nora, 49, 51
Keldysh, Iurii, 120
Kennedy, Jacqueline, 76–77, 76*f*
Kennedy, John F., 73, 74, 76–77, 76*f*, 157n17
Kennedy, Robert, 157n17
Kent, Allegra, 122*f*, 122–23
KGB, 21, 78, 142n47, 152n71
Khachaturian, Aram, 79, 84, 86, 87–88, 89–90, 116
Khrennikov, Tikhon, 120
Khrushchev, Nikita, 18–19
and American Ballet Theatre, 56–57, 67, 68
and the Cuban Missile Crisis, 73, 77
and homophobia, 64, 154n118
and the Thaw, 37, 88
Kiev, 57, 112
Kirov Ballet
1961 US tour of, 12, 79–80, 105–6, 148n3
vs. Bolshoi, 18–19, 80–83, 160n45
cultural diplomacy tours of, 3, 139n41

dancers defecting from, 78,
    81–82, 160n46
and Petipa, 65, 80
Spartacus premiere at, 84
Kirov Theater, 29–30
Kirstein, Lincoln, 99–101
Kondratieva, Marina, 20, 22,
    41–42, 140n18
Krasnapolsky, Urey, 58
Krasovskaya, Vera, 62, 66–67
Kremlin Palace of Congresses, 112,
    168–69n54

Lacy-Zarubin agreement, 4, 5, 6–7,
    18–19, 49
Lady from the Sea (Cullberg), 56
Lander, Harald, 92–95
Lapauri, Alexander, 1–2, 114, 119
Lavrovsky, Leonid, 32–33
    and drambalet, 26–27, 60, 113–14
    impressions of the United States of,
        20, 21, 78
    and *Paganini*, 75, 86
    and *Romeo and Juliet*, 29–33, 31*f*
    and *Stone Flower*, 36–37
    US reception of, 34, 41–42,
        123–24, 145n92
Lavrovsky, Mikhail, 31*f*, 91
leitmotif, 29, 30–31, 31*f*, 37, 38, 144n74
Lenin Palace of Sports, 68
Lenin Prize, 26
Leningrad, 25–26, 99
    audiences in, 58, 59, 66–67
    critics in, 62
    as destination for cultural diplomacy
        tours, 6, 57, 112
    vs. Moscow, 18–19, 81–82, 160n45
Leningrad Choreographic Academy, 22,
    99, 116–17
Leningrad Symphony, 105–6
Lenoe, Matthew E., 33–34
Lepeshinskaya, Olga, 118–19, 142n44
Levine, Irving R., 35
Liadov, Anatoly, 93–94
Liapunov, Sergei, 93–94
Lichine, David, 55
Liepa, Maris, 78
Lifar, Serge, 64, 139n37

Límon, José, 4
Lloyd, Margaret, 40
Lopukhov, Fyodor, 102–3, 118,
    139n37, 166n24
Loring, Eugene, 48, 53–54
Los Angeles, 21, 90–91
Lvov-Anokhin, Boris, 118, 119,
    120–21, 122

MacArthur, Harry, 75–76
Macaulay, Alastair, 130–31
Madison Square Garden, 1–2, 20, 22
Magallanes, Nicholas, 110–11, 111*f*
Magnificence of the Universe
    (Lopukhov), 102
Manchester, P.W., 90, 94
Mariinsky Theater. *See* Kirov Theater
Martin, John
    on American Ballet Theatre, 51
    on Bolshoi, 19, 34, 40–41
    and NYCB tour, 124–25, 158n26
masculinity, 42, 63–64
Massine, Leonid, 102–3, 139n37
Maximova, Ekaterina, 91
Mazzo, Kay, 113
Messerer, Asaf
    and *Ballet School*, 75, 91–92, 92*f*,
        94, 129–30
    and Plisetskaya, 23
    Swan Lake production of, 80–81
Metropolitan Opera House, 140n14
    performances at, 21, 71
    stage of, 20, 140n19
    tickets for, 83, 160–61n51
Midsummer Night's Dream
    (Balanchine), 110–11
Mills, Fred, 58
mind-body dualism, 42–43
Ministry of Culture, 3, 5, 50, 109, 142–43n54
Minkus, Ludwig, 55, 65
Miss Julie (Tudor), 52–53
Mitchell, Arthur, 122*f*, 122–23
modern dance, 4, 74–75, 136n11
modernism, 103, 110–11
    vs. contemporaneity, 64, 145n92
    and Soviet government, 103–4, 109, 120
    in US reviews of Soviet ballet, 34, 40–41,
        147n116

modernization theory, 33–35, 82, 110
Moiseyev State Folk Dance Troupe, 4, 83
Mordkin, Mikhail, 47–48, 60–61
Moscow
   as destination for cultural diplomacy tours, 6, 56–57, 59, 68, 109–10, 112
   vs. Leningrad, 18–19, 81–82, 160n45
   stages in, 151n62
Moscow Choreographic Academy, 91
Mukhina, Vera, 30–31, 31*f*
music
   absolute, 103, 167n27
   as foundation for ballet, 9, 37, 100, 102–3, 104–8
   meaning of, 103–4, 103*f*, 104*f*, 118–19
   relation to dance of, 10, 41, 66, 84–85
   as universal language, 6–7
musicians, 1, 20, 43, 58
My Fair Lady tour, 52

narrative ballet, 9
   Balanchine's works as, 107–8, 109
   populist ballet as, 53–54, 60–61
   theorization of in Soviet aesthetics, 37, 103–4, 105–6, 113–14, 119
nationalism, 9, 61–62, 85, 110–12, 151n55
Native American performers, 67, 155–56n134
negotiations, 5–6, 19, 52–53, 100–1
   in Cuban Missile Crisis, 73–74, 76–77
Nemirovich-Danchenko, Vladimir, 27
neoclassicism, 40–41, 64, 95, 97, 131–32
   vs. choreographic symphonism, 102, 108, 119
Nepomnyashchy, Catharine, 56
Nestyev, Izrail, 120
New Soviet Man, 56, 63, 64, 94
New York City, 6, 75, 77–78
   Soviet impressions of, 20, 21
New York City Ballet, 8, 12, 99, 131–32
   1956 European tour of, 158n19
   1962 tour schedule of, 109–10, 112
   1972 Soviet tour of, 139n41
   vs. American Ballet Theatre, 49
   vs. Bolshoi, 34, 35, 40–41
   negotiations for 1962 tour of, 100–1
   repertory of, 55, 88, 108–9
   Soviet reception of, 115–19, 120–24, 125–27, 129–30
   and State Department, 99–100
   US press coverage of, 124–25
Novellino-Mearns, Rosie, 89, 90–91
Noverre, Jean-Georges, 85
Nureyev, Rudolf, 78
Nye, Joseph, 11–12

O'Brien, Shawn, 113
Oboukhoff, Anatole, 155n123
Offenbach, Jacques, 55, 59
Orpheus (Balanchine), 34, 74–75, 109
Owen, Irving, 58

Paganini (Lavrovsky), 75, 113–14
Pakhomov, Vasily, 78, 158n26
Palace of Culture, 57
pantomime
   in choreographic symphonism, 37–38, 39–40, 41
   in drambalet, 26–27, 30–31
   in populist American ballet, 60
   in *Spartacus*, 85
pas de deux, 65–66
   in *Agon*, 121–23
   in American Ballet Theatre repertory, 52–53, 55, 56, 65, 66–67, 155n130
   in *Romeo and Juliet*, 28–29, 30–31
Pavlova, Anna, 5, 47–48
Payne, Charles, 51–52, 65
Pearson, Drew, 43
Perron, Wendy, 89, 90–91
Petipa, Marius, 45, 55, 65–66, 79–81
Plisetskaya, Maya, 142n47
   in *Ballet School*, 91
   and Kennedy family, 76–77, 157n17
   and Rudolf Nureyev, 78
   and *Spartacus*, 88–89, 91
   in *Swan Lake*, 79
   touring for Soviet Union, 141–42n42, 142n43
   vs. Ulanova, 78–79
   US reception of, 22, 23–24, 25*f*, 41–42, 81
   watching American Ballet Theatre, 56–57, 66

populist ballet, 9, 53, 56, 60–64, 152n89
press, 20, 113
  coverage of Bolshoi, 19, 22–24, 42–44, 75–76, 83, 92, 95
  interviews with Balanchine, 109–10
  on NYCB 1962 tour, 124–25
programs, 26, 111–12, 143n63
Prokofiev, Sergei, 25–27
  and Balanchine, 118–19, 120–21
  and *Romeo and Juliet*, 28–30, 32–33, 34, 60
  and *Stone Flower*, 36, 37, 39–40
  Symphony No. 5, 25–26
  US reception of, 34, 41
Prokofieva, Mira, 36
pseudo-event, 10–11
purges, 23

race, 87
  and choreography, 61–62
  in US cultural diplomacy program, 67, 123, 171n107
Rachmaninoff, Sergei, 75, 113–14
Ratmansky, Alexei, 131–32
Ravel, Maurice, 102–3, 118–19
realism, 26–27, 38, 60–61, 85, 109
reception history, 7–8, 9–12, 138n34
reciprocity, 5–7, 137n21
Reisinger, Julius, 80
repertory selection, 11
  by Ballet Theatre, 52–56, 59, 88, 152n85
  by New York City Ballet, 88
  by Soviet companies, 24–25, 36, 40, 75, 85, 142–43n54
Rexroth, Kenneth, 81–83, 160n47
Reynolds, Nancy, 110, 114
Riisager, Knudåge, 56, 93
Rimsky-Korsakov, Nikolai, 102
Robb, Inez, 44
Robbins, Jerome
  and Ballets U.S.A., 50, 100–1
  and *Fancy Free*, 48, 53, 55, 60, 62
  and *Interplay*, 108
  Soviet reception of, 123–24
  and Stanislavsky, 60–61
Robeson, Paul, 40

Rodeo (de Mille), 51, 55, 56
  masculinity in, 63–64
  music in, 58, 60, 61–62
  as populist ballet, 9, 48, 53, 60–62
  Soviet reception of, 54–55, 59–60, 64, 110–11
Romanoff, Dimitri, 52–53
Romeo and Juliet (Lavrovsky), 32f, 109–11
  choreography of, 29–33
  as drambalet, 26–28, 29, 30–33
  film of, 22
  London reception of, 36
  music of, 28–29, 31f, 32–33, 60, 144n72
  programming of in US, 25–26
  suites of, 26, 34
  and Ulanova, 22–23
  US reception of, 24–25, 33–35, 41–42, 71, 90
Roslavleva, Natalia, 62, 110, 118, 119, 121
  and de Mille, 60–61, 151n55
Royal Ballet, 35
Russian Seasons (Ratmansky), 131–32

Sabnina, Maria, 116, 117, 118–19, 122–23
San Francisco Ballet, 79–80
Sargeant, Winthrop, 24
Scheherazade (Fokine), 102
Schermerhorn, Kenneth, 58
Schmelz, Peter, 120
School of American Ballet, 99, 116–17
Scotch Symphony (Balanchine), 111–12
Serenade (Balanchine), 106–8, 106f, 108f, 118, 126–27, 168n35
serialism, 110–12, 119, 120–21, 126–27, 170–71n100
Serrano, Lupe, 45, 66–67
sexuality
  in *Agon*, 121–22
  in *Ben-Hur*, 87
  debates in Soviet Union about, 162n77
  and the Soviet government, 55, 62, 109
  in *Spartacus*, 87–89
  See also homophobia
Shchedrin, Rodion, 23–24, 142n44
Sherry, Samantha, 114
Shostakovich, Dmitri, 40, 93–94, 147n113, 162n77
  Symphony No. 7, 105–6, 151n52

Shrine Auditorium, 21
Smith, Oliver, 48, 50, 62
socialist realism, 26–27, 37, 55, 56, 84, 144n70, 167n29
soft power, 11–12, 139n40
Solzhenitsyn, Aleksandr, 162n77
La Sonnambula (Balanchine), 111–12
Sorell, Walter, 41
Souritz, Elizabeth, 115
Sousa, John Philip, 100
Soviet-American cultural exchange, 5, 9–10, 12, 37
  approval of, 75–76
  condemnation of, 20
  reasons for, 4–5, 129
  and transliteration, 8–9, 129–30, 132
Spandorf, Lily, 79f
Spartacus, 75, 79, 84
  1968 production of, 38, 84, 130–31
  vs. Hollywood epic films, 85–88, 89–90
  music for, 79, 84, 86, 87–88, 89–90, 91
  US premiere of, 71
  US reception of, 88–91
  Yakobson production of, 78, 84–85, 86, 87–89, 91
Stalin, Joseph, 4, 9, 33–34, 37, 82
Stalin Prize, 25–26, 32–33
Stanislavsky and Nemirovich-Danchenko Academic Musical Theater, 45, 52–53, 57, 81, 151n62
Stanislavsky, Konstantin, 27–28, 31–32, 60–61
Stars and Stripes (Balanchine), 100
State Committee for Cultural Ties (GKKS), 3, 23–24
State Department (US)
  and American Ballet Theatre, 48–49, 50, 51, 58
  and cultural diplomacy funding, 5–6, 50, 137n22
  and gender, 42
  and Lacy-Zarubin agreement, 5
  and NYCB, 99–101, 109, 110–11, 113
  and race, 67, 123, 171n107
  and US cultural diplomacy program, 3–4, 12, 74
Stone Flower, 36–40
  as cultural diplomacy tool, 24–26
  and Plisetskaya, 24
  US reception of, 40–41
Strauss, Johann, II, 55
Stravinsky, Igor, 118–22, 170–71n100
Struchkova, Raissa, 1–2
subversion, 46–47, 68, 136–37n20
Swan Lake
  and 2014 Bolshoi tour, 130
  and Chabukiani, 63
  and Cuban Missile Crisis, 76–77, 76f
  different versions of, 79–81, 155n123, 159n37, 159n38
  music of, 55, 65, 80
  pas de deux from, 55, 65–66
  and Plisetskaya, 24
  as Soviet cultural diplomacy tool, 24–25, 26, 36, 75, 79
  as standard for ballet performance, 54
  US reception of, 79f, 81
Les Sylphides (Fokine), 47–48
  and American Ballet Theatre, 52–53, 55, 56, 59, 65
  and Bolshoi, 75
  vs. *Serenade*, 118
Symphony in C (Balanchine), 104–5, 129–30, 167–68n33

tablework, 27–28, 31–32
Tallchief, Maria
  and American Ballet Theatre personnel, 49, 50, 51
  on Chabukiani, 63
  Native American heritage of, 67
  and Soviet audiences, 58–59
  and *Swan Lake*, 66–67, 155n127, 155n130
tap dance, 61–62
Taper, Bernard, 112
taste, 82–84, 90, 95, 130–31, 147n118, 172n10
Tbilisi, 63
  American impressions of, 58
  audiences in, 59
  as cultural diplomacy tour destination, 57, 68, 112
  Opera House of, 57
  performance of *Billy the Kid* in, 54–55
Tchaikovsky, Pyotr, 55
  and Balanchine, 118–19, 120–21

Piano Concerto No. 2, 102–3
Serenade for Strings, 106–8
Suite No. 1 for Orchestra, 45, 55, 56
and *Swan Lake*, 65, 80
Terry, Walter
and Gabovich, 125, 126
reviews of Bolshoi by, 21, 24, 34, 41–42, 90–91, 94–95
the Thaw
and censorship, 114
and choreographic symphonism, 9, 37, 102, 104, 113–14
and debate, 98, 114, 127
and Soviet-American exchange, 4
and Soviet morality, 88, 162n77
and *Spartacus*, 84–85
Theater of the Cultural Cooperative Center, 57
theaters, 5–6, 21, 151n62
Theme and Variations (Balanchine), 45, 55, 56, 152n89
tickets, 5–6, 19–20, 83, 137n26, 160n50, 160–61n51
Timasheff, Nicholas, 33–34
Tomasov, Jan, 58
transliteration
effects on ballet of, 14–15, 129–32
impact on cultural diplomacy of, 68
and Soviet critics, 62, 113, 125, 126–27
theorization of, 6–12
and US critics, 40–41, 94–95, 96
Tsiskaridze, Nikolai, 129
Tuch, Hans, 113
Tudor, Antony, 52–53, 56, 60–61
twelve-tone composition. *See* serialism

U.S. Embassy in Moscow, 110–11, 113
Ulanova, Galina
on 1962 tour, 78–79
and American Ballet Theatre, 56–57
and drambalet, 26–27
and *Romeo and Juliet*, 32–33
and Tallchief, 66, 67
and US audiences, 21
and US press, 20, 22–23, 41–42, 43

Union of Soviet Friendship Societies (SSOD), 3

Vainonen, Vasily, 26–27, 63
La Valse (Balanchine), 108
Vasiliev, Vladimir, 91
Vecheslova, Tatiana, 140n4
Verdy, Violette, 49
Viliams, Pëtr, 31–32, 32f
Villella, Edward, 112, 123
Vinogradova, Maria, 131
Virsaladze, Simon, 38, 40–41
virtuosity
in *Ballet School*, 91, 92–93, 94
as marker of male style, 63–64
and Moiseyev Company, 83
and NYCB, 116, 123, 125
pas de deux as measurer of, 65–67
and reception of Soviet dancing, 43, 82, 124
Volkov, Nikolai, 84

Walpurgis Night (Lavrovsky), 24, 75
Washington, DC, 6, 21, 76–78
Webern, Anton, 119
Wescott, Glenway, 125–26
Westad, Odd Arne, 73–74
Western Symphony (Balanchine), 108, 110–12, 111f, 123
West Side Story, 20
Williams, Kimberly A., 43–44
World War II, 3, 100, 103, 105–6
Wyke, Maria, 86–87

Yakobson, Leonid, 79
on 1962 tour, 78, 158n26
and *Spartacus*, 84–85, 86, 87–89, 91
Youskevitch, Igor, 45, 49
Yurchak, Alexei, 114–15

Zakharov, Rostislav, 26–28, 31–32, 60, 117, 122–23
Zayugina, Susanna, 43
Zhukov, Georgi, 23–24, 142n44